AESTHETIC DIMENSIONS OF
RELIGIOUS EDUCATION

Aesthetic Dimensions of Religious Education

Edited by
Gloria Durka
and
Joanmarie Smith

PAULIST PRESS
New York/Ramsey/Toronto

Library of Congress
Catalog Card Number: 78-65903

ISBN: 0-8091-2164-6

Published by Paulist Press
Editorial Office: 1865 Broadway, New York, N.Y. 10023
Business Office: 545 Island Road, Ramsey, N.J. 07446

Printed and bound in the
United States of America

Contents

Acknowledgements

We would like to thank both Professor Margaret Jennings of St. Joseph's College, Brooklyn, New York and Professor Bonnie Stevens of William Paterson College, New Jersey for their editorial assistance. This is the third book for which we have sought the suggestions of Professor Stevens.

Finally, we must express our affection and gratitude to Paul Bumbar the husband of one of us (Gloria Durka) and a friend to both of us, who has consistently and kindly critiqued our work, and whose ideas have undoubtedly passed into ours without their being specifically and properly acknowledged.

TO OUR MENTORS

Lee A. Belford
of
New York University
and
Robert O. Johann
of
Fordham University

who helped us to see the other side.

Introduction

In 1969 Andrew Greeley surveying the subject of many of the most outstanding religious books published that year predicted that the seventies would usher in a period of concentration on the aesthetic dimension of experience. Harvey Cox's work was most symbolic of the movement. His *Secular City* had seemed to set the tone of the theological discussion in the mid-sixties. Then he published *Feast of Fools* in which he acknowledged that he was turning somewhat to "the other side." Peter Berger also turned momentarily from his exploration of the sociology of knowledge and religion to detail *A Rumor of Angels*. Sam Keen burst on the scene with his *Apology for Wonder* at the same time that Robert E. Neale was publishing *In Praise of Play*, and just shortly before David Miller's *God and Games* made the scene. The brilliantly colored and brilliantly executed work of Sister Corita seemed to capture the sensation that we were on the brink of a new era of attention to the aesthetic.

By 1973 however, those professional interpreters of contemporary religious thinking, Martin Marty and Dean Peerman, were remarking that thinking reflected a "sense of exhaustion."

The theological world sometimes resembles the postradical, political world of the 1970's: *anomie* afflicts many. There is a kind of joyless, directionless continuation of courses upon which one has embarked. Enthusiasm is left to the enthusiasts who cover up the emptiness of their lives by premature closure, who participate in pep rallies devoted to Jesus as the "one way."[1]

The world of the religious educators sometimes appears to be similarly permeated by *anomie*. Having embraced a much more flexible approach to their ministry in the latter half of the sixties, a frustration, even a backlash seems to be occurring. Although the aesthetic dimension of religious education, indeed, of all education, had been highlighted during that period, there does at present seem to be an attitude of, "Just how many pictures can you draw and how many balloons can you release—and to what end?"

It often appears that attention to the aesthetic was a fad and not a conviction; that it was viewed as a means to an end, viz., the learning of doctrine, and not as an expression of communion with that which doctrine explores. This book has been assembled in the belief that the aesthetic is not something we may or may not use in the process of educating depending upon how comfortable we are with it. It is our contention, and we think the point is at least implicit in the work of all contributors, that unless the process is aesthetic it is not education and it is certainly not religious.

The point has received renewed emphasis from (of all people!) neurologists. An increased interest in the possibly distinct powers of each hemisphere of the brain has led to a general conclusion that the right side of the brain (that side which seems to direct our intuitive, holistic or aesthetic engagement to reality) is underutilized or even almost atrophied in some of us. Yet, surely, the Divine is more appropriately probed from a right lobe perspective.

While those contributors who specially address themselves to the phenomenon of right lobe/left lobe brain research caution us to be tentative in our generalizations, we think the findings have been significant enough to act as a catalyst for renewed study of the aesthetic dimension. *Aesthetic Dimensions of Religious Education* addresses itself to those issues in religious education that would appear to be the specific province of the right lobe. There is something incongruous about discursive analyses of the aesthetic dimension in education. We consider ourselves privileged, however, to have persuaded both outstanding professional artists and educators who artfully educate to submit previously unpublished articles which address these issues.

The collection begins with lived aesthetic experience and concludes with complementary theories of that experience. In aesthetics, unlike the technological aspect of science, theory follows, or better, is distilled from practice. We have attempted to trace that pattern in arranging the essays. The first section addresses the aesthetic quality of contemporary spirituality. In the second section the arts are treated more specifically. The next section is devoted to worship and educating the aesthetic sensibility. Finally, there are those articles which deal with aesthetic theory as such.

Gloria Durka
Fordham University
Bronx, New York

Joanmarie Smith
St. Joseph's College
Brooklyn, New York

1. Martin Marty and Dean Peerman, *New Theology 10* (New York: Macmillan Co., 1973), pp. xi, xii.

I
THE AESTHETIC DIMENSION
OF CONTEMPORARY SPIRITUALITY

1.
Aesthetic Experience and Redemptive Grace

Anthony Padovano

Conceiving of religion as essentially an aesthetic phenomenon, Anthony Padovano, a well-known theologian and author of many works on the spiritual life, identifies the similarities in artistic and religious experience.

Aesthetic experience preserves spirituality from the temptation of becoming ethereal. It disengages us from a world of ideas and abstract forms, from a Platonic universe which centers reality in an event beyond the fabric of our everyday lives. Aesthetic experience seeks the spirit in the depths of matter. By so doing, it emphasizes the sacramentality of the world.

Aesthetic experience and sacramental experience deal with the physical world directly but beneath the surface appearance. They transform the vision we have of the world which engages us. The artist reveals the glory within an otherwise unexceptional experience. We encounter the familiar as charged with mystery. A sacramental world view likewise reveals a world straining to become more than it is. The common-place actions of washing or breaking bread or anointing give us a sense of presence and life.

There is no way to learn cognitively how to appreciate good art just as there is no way logically to believe in a sacramental universe. Life becomes for us what we allow it to become. People react in the same manner. Good art is recognized by those who bear grace in their hearts, a sensitivity to presence or mystery which allows them to see what is there and to submit to it. God is encountered in bread or water, in human needs and hopes when the heart of a believer is graced with the capacity to respond to the fullness of life in a concrete situation. Art and sacraments both bring and evoke grace. They enable us to see beneath the surface and to encounter the heart of the matter.

Aesthetic experience and religious experience are closely allied. Both are concerned with the creation and discovery of beauty, with the communication of deeper meanings, with the transformation of the vision in which we behold the world. The artist is oriented to beauty. When the grotesque is artistically rendered, it is presented so that evil may be named and known, detected beneath its surface and effectively exorcised. Religious experience deals with sin or Satan, death or the devil in the same manner. The artist is able to portray a nightmare because beauty is affirmed as the normative human condition. A believer is conscious of hell only when heaven has already been considered. No genuine art rejoices in darkness; no historic faith celebrates damnation. Art and faith confront the void and engender approaches to life which seek to save us from it.

AESTHETIC AND RELIGIOUS AUTHORITY

Both art and faith exercise authority over those who participate in the experience. Each requires submission to a reality larger than self, a reality whose influence can be felt only intuitively. The authority of the artist does not reside in the artist but in the vision of reality the art unfolds. One is captivated by beauty, submits to truth, surrenders to the whole. The artist is the agent, the minister, the priest, if you will, through whom another presence is made manifest. Artists, like lovers or mystics, allow others to exist through them.

Faith functions in the same manner. The authority of a religion does not abide in the official representatives of the structure but in the message they declare or the meaning they announce. Conversion is the result of an insight into the ultimate, a sense of comprehensive love or truth which exceeds all understanding. The agent who introduces a believer to this more significant experience is a minister, a priest, an artist, if you will. Adult believers in the traditional religions are aware that they are more drawn by the vision of life than by those who serve as catalysts or agents for the experience. Adults proceed more often in terms of their experience of life, by their own revelation, than by guidelines offered by religious leaders. Only when religious leaders witness to a reality already perceived by the believer to be both real and compelling are they heard.

But how do we know if the faith we affirm gives us a vision of reality which is real rather than feigned? How are we protected from the religious charlatan? We cannot be sure rationally or logically.

Since the reality to which we are alluding is responsible for life or at least for summoning life to a more human expression, we have a sense that we are not self-deceived by the way we care for the lives of others. The artist and the believer become guardians of the human spirit because of the vision they have experienced.

AESTHETICS AND GRACE

There have been frequent attempts in human history to make art a religion or to render religion more artistic. The latter presents little problem. Religion seeks the artistic as naturally as sight seeks color. Religion is sensitive to its vocation to make life beautiful, aware of its mission to encounter and make manifest the beauty and meaning beneath the surface of life. Art is a symbol of the effort, a means to its accomplishment, an appeal to the total person that religion cannot make without aesthetics. Aesthetic experience seeks immortality as religion does, either through absorption of artists into the undying vision to which they give themselves or by the affirmation of their own deathless wonder of reality. Neither artist nor believer deals with the transitory.

The effort to make art a religion is more complicated. When the artist deals with an ultimate or universal problem and does this with commitment and sacrifice, the artist engages in religious experience. Paul Tillich's principles are valid, it would seem, in this instance. A vocation to a personal concern with the most ultimate and universal experience one can possibly affirm is a vocation from God enacted in the atmosphere of grace.

Concern with the ultimate requires the grace of sensitivity to it. The grace of self-forgetfulness or of self-transcendence makes the ultimate worthwhile to the person who seeks it. Howsoever our definitions of God may differ, they converge in this: God is the most ultimate and universal experience imaginable. Howsoever our theologies of grace may be defined, they share this in common: grace is an experience of the ultimate and universal in one's personal life. Art becomes a religious experience when it seeks and affirms, communicates and celebrates, makes possible and indeed inescapable the experiences we are describing. Art and religion fail if they do not bring beauty into life. Grace is the experience which compels the artist to reject a world of no meaning, a world in which the human spirit is distorted. Grace is the summons which makes the believer seek a world of purpose in which the human spirit enshrines the holiness of life.

The testimony of art and religion differ only in this: artists are faithful to their mission if they render palpable the mystery which guides them, even if their personal lives do not embody this vision; believers, however, are expected to incarnationalize and live out the vision which guides them.

The vision we have of the world is the reason why we act as we do. There is no sound or permanent modification of human behavior without a previous transformation of vision. We act in a certain manner because we view the world in a particular perspective. Examples of this can be given from secular or religious life. Hiroshima becomes a target for nuclear destruction because people believed that unconditional surrender was the only way to terminate the Second World War. Correlatively, many of the issues which seem necessary to Christianity today, alternatives which are deemed unviable, derive from the vision one has of the Church.

VISION AND CONVERSION

How do we change the vision of people? It is love that art and religion have most in common. The artist convinces us of the truth by dealing with us wholistically. Artists try to make us feel the truth. Good art gets the truth inside us on a level deeper than the surface of our minds. On this level, truth is most irresistible. The mind may not only resist the truth but may even accept it and keep it at a personal distance. Logical convictions are not necessarily existential imperatives. The artist makes us nostalgic for the beauty we have missed, the life we have forfeited, the meaning which somehow eluded our grasp. Art haunts us with the spectre of a lost humanity and bids us return to paradise. There is something prelapsarian about genuine art.

Religion likewise makes us sensitive to levels of our lives, indeed a different future and a new world which at first seemed nonexistent or perhaps so impossible of attainment that it held no genuine interest for us. Religion by-passes the mind and demands conversion of heart. It does not dismiss the mind but it seeks much more than intellectual understanding. Religion, like art, does not debate or delay; it is urgent, imperative, totally personal. True religion may be accepted or rejected but it offers no compromise and it dies in dilution. It announces the true even if not the obvious and those who hear its voice have no choice but to follow. For, religion speaks of meaning and love, of the whole and the holy. We cannot turn from such realities without having our humanity diminished. It is impossible to distance ourselves from such realities because they are already present within us. They are the grace given us at birth, the human inheritance woven into the fabric of our spirits, channeled into the core of the heart. Religion too is a process of nostalgia, an animation of a collective memory which reaches from the dawn of history to the hidden recesses of a heart now illumined and enlightened.

Art and religion do their work most effectively when they insert themselves into the experiences of our lives and become vital for our self-definition. They accomplish this most persuasively and humanly when they reveal to us the beauty of life. It is, then, not reform and conversion we choose primarily. It is a need not to let beauty pass from our lives, slip through our hands.

CREATIVITY AND TOTALITARIANISM

One cannot force true art or genuine religion on anyone. Proselytism is the work of a personal tyrant or at least of one whose ideology of religion is tyrannical. Official art is a prerogative of civil or ecclesiastical dictators.

Real religion and art do not operate with hidden or overt agenda. They are tolerant with dissent and rejection. They present beauty and become ministers of its power and its glory. Each does its work in revealing, not in conversion. Conversion is the achievement of the vision, not of the artist or the believer. Conversion without revelation of the beautiful makes the artist a purveyor of propaganda and the believer an ideologue or fanatic. The strength of religion and art derives from the fact that the human spirit is always there to receive beauty when it is present. They endure because a subtle sense of celebration and a yearning for beauty permeate every age. We are endlessly converted to a more profound appreciation of the human because this is what we wish. We look to religion and art to aid us in this task and we are never wholly disappointed.

Both art and religion seek mystic experience. Each is the result of an immersion in life. The artist and the believer go into the wilderness of the unexplored life and bring from it the fruit of their encounter. Each is a hermit, an anchorite. Each makes an inner journey to the center of the self where one's true nature, communality with others, and the power of transcendent presence converge. The journey is well advanced before the artist creates. Otherwise, there would be nothing to express. The pilgrimage of faith has taken the believer far from the first steps into the unknowing. Otherwise, belief would have nothing significant to declare. It is necessary to add that art and religion do not seek the exotic. The road which is travelled is long and arduous but it is the near and the ordinary which is ultimately discovered. It is not the new which enchants but the "un-covering", the "dis-covering" of the familiar. Art and religion rejoice in showing us all the things we have seen before, the events we have looked at many times but never noticed until this moment.

TRUTH AND IMAGINATION

Truth is in the whole person because beauty cannot be grasped by the mind. Truth and beauty are interchangeable terms. There is no cognitive truth, only cognitive data or facts. Truth is always in the imagination. This is the way truth is encountered in the physical sciences, art, and theology. The contemporaries of Albert Einstein had the same data available to them as he did but less imagination. Creative work in physics or poetry or theology demands the same imaginative approach to the truth.

The modern age has made a romance of factual knowledge and found the experience disappointing. We are beginning to affirm the truth of that which we once called fiction. Fiction is based on a vision of life. Facts deal with things as they are. Facts do not require a human perceiver; fiction can only be accomplished by us. We make of one another's lives, we make of our own life, a fictional account rather than a factual rendition. We choose some facts, reject others, emphasize certain data, ignore others as we define ourselves and achieve our identity.

The account given by ourselves or by others of who we are is never an account of the data available on us or the facts that may be garnered about us. An appreciation of this phenomenon has led us to utilize myth, story-telling, symbol in contemporary theological work. These three instruments are the work of the human aesthetic imagination. Life comes from submitting to the truth; death, in submitting the truth to ourselves. Truth abides in the whole person. It resides therein by means of the beauty which internalizes it and makes it irresistible.

The knowlege which drives the human family forward in an endless quest is not the gathering of data but a need to assimilate the truth. The endeavor to uncover the mystery of the universe does not rest on a need to know it as it is but to gain from it an understanding as to how we might give ourselves to its mystery. Truth is always an experience of unity. Sacrifice and commitment are related to truth because both are necessary to achieve one-ness. It is a terrible thing as well as a joyous event to know the truth. For truth must lead to sacrifice or commitment or else it turns to illusion, the illusion of supposing that with knowledge we can control the universe or life, the illusion of thinking we can keep truth at a distance with data and go on with our lives as though little had happened. No one sees the truth and walks away from it. This can no more be done than to perceive beauty and remain unaffected by it. To walk away one must turn the truth into error, render it partial, and handle the resulting information as though one owned it and therefore could deal with it at one's pleasure rather than at truth's demand.

The deepest dimensions of religious life, like the highest forms of art, are those which are non-cognitive. It is not in doctrine but in liturgy, celebration, or mystic experience that believers encounter God. The purpose of doctrine is to deepen the mystery, not to control it or clarify it. Heresy is the effort to possess the mystery, to render it so intelligible that one can deal with God on one's own terms. Doctrine leads to liturgy or else it becomes sterile and illusory.

Religions sound least convincing when they struggle to be most convincing. They appear artificial, constrained, narrow when they define themselves doctrinally. The expansiveness of religion is made manifest in its non-cognitive life. Artists, likewise, are least artistic when they comment on their own art and attempt to convey it cognitively. The philosophy or doctrine behind a work of art is not impressive when abstracted from it. The meaning of art is embedded in the very form in which it is presented. The same principle operates with religious truth. The orthodoxy of a believer resides in the believer's life style. It is possible to deny cognitively that which one loves existentially or to reject existentially that which one cognitively possesses. This is why the charism of love rather than the character of a creed defines faith more accurately.

AESTHETICS AND TRADITION

Religion and art present a vision, a way of looking at the world. When they present the world in its wholeness, people preserve the vision, pass on the meaning, and weave the experience into the fabric of tradition. Religion and art act in the hope, never fully disappointed, that every age is gifted with people to see and hear what must be seen and heard. Each generation is peopled with those who realize the truth is not obvious and who respond to the intrinsic beauty of life. Life goes on because so few miss the point entirely.

As a theologian, I am impressed with the fact that those who differ on doctrinal or theological issues experience their greatest unity with one another in liturgy, celebration and mystic yearning. The most profound of all truths are those which bring the human family unity and peace.

This century has marked the beginning of our emergence from a technological age in which the key questions concerning function are being converted into questions concerning beauty. Technology leads easily to manipulation and mechanization even though it achieves results we appreciate. Religious and aesthetic experience, however, are too elusive to utilize in a manipulative manner. Totalitarian institutions try to eliminate or manufacture both experiences because those who govern such institutions are aware of the dangers of free religious and aesthetic expression. Totalitarian civil institutions create national churches and official art. Totalitarian religious institutions regulate liturgy excessively, condemn creative theology, and relegate to unimportance those whose vocation is mystic and contemplative. Such institutions prefer politics to poetry, law to the Gospel, dogma to theology, monarchical administration to conciliar consensus, mystification to mystery, documents to dialogue. Totalitarianism is always the achievement of an excessively cognitive and rational approach to life. Totalitarianism asks of the nation and the church the same question technology asks: does it work? Truth and beauty are less important to dictators than efficient functioning.

Cognitive knowledge and reason feed the illusion of control. Such approaches, therefore, must always be carefully balanced with aesthetics and intuition. Genuine religion and art summon us to surrender rather than control.

Freedom and creativity go hand in hand. An unfree church dies every day the death of dullness. An unfree nation keeps its citizens on schedule perhaps but stifles the human spirit. Freedom and commitment also go hand in hand. When people are free, they seek to give themselves away as gift or donation; the unfree seek only a means to survive. In a totalitarian nation or church, accommodation becomes more important than passion.

Artists, like contemplatives, are not persuaders; their goal is immediacy of contact. Indeed, the artist has no obligation to promote ethical lessons any more than political or economic lessons. The creative artist does not deal in propaganda or proselytism. It is beauty that is made, not policy.

Believers do not wish to subject others to their control. When faith is profound, the believer is not even eager to guide others with an ethical system. If a person sees what is there, respect for it follows in due course. A believer is never a magisterial propagandist or a denominational proselytyzer but the disciple of a vision so compelling that it becomes the pearl of great price.

The totalitarian imperative derives from the conviction that there can be one idea or system to solve all problems, one situation to assure happiness for everyone, one culture for the world, one church for the entire range of human history. Religious and aesthetic experience is always plural in its form though strangely homogeneous in its final statement. The plurality of religious experiences and historic faiths terminates in a vision of unity which brings peace in much the same manner to all believers. The variety of religious experience witnesses to the unity of reality precisely because plurality does not lead to fundamental diversity. Schism derives from a partial vision of the whole and from a fear of pluralism. On the deepest levels of life, there are no divisions.

The plurality of aesthetic experiences, likewise, terminates in a perception of beauty which transcends all boundaries and witnesses in its own way to the unity of life and the joy that such a unity engenders. Aesthetic plurality does not divide the human family; indeed, an effort to control art and restrain its pluralism is the beginning of divisiveness.

AESTHETICS AND REDEMPTION

Genuine aesthetic experience is also a redemptive act. It encompasses the complex intermingling of sin and grace in our hearts and assures us that no one of us is all that different from the other. There is no one without sin in our midst or without grace. Genuine religious experience redeems us not by cancelling sin irremediably out of our lives; somehow sin always returns. It redeems us by keeping sin from becoming a complacent experience and by maintaining a tension with sin through grace.

Complacency is the adversary of religious experience more pointedly than evil. The sinner is capable of conversion but not the self-satisfied. The constant vision of beauty is the grace religious experience offers to the person who accepts evil helplessly. Conversion allows grace and beauty to abide in the heart and to do their work.

Genuine aesthetic experience is also a redemptive act. It portrays the admixture of baseness and nobility in our experience and allows us to sense both in ourselves. We all live with compromise and purity. Genuine aesthetic experience humanizes us not by making us suppose we shall no longer be weak but by allowing us to sense the grace within us. It convinces us that our eyes can still behold beauty and our heart can still retain youth. We sense our humanity in the fact that life never takes from us the capacity of enchantment and wonder, for joy and inner freedom. Aesthetic experience reaches into the recesses of our spirit and severs the bonds of age and fear. It makes us free, not forever free nor irrevocably free but free for a moment. This is sufficient for us to know that bondage and blindness are not ultimately tolerable for us or for others.

There has been a vast literature in this century dealing with the triumph of the technocrat and the totalitarian. There have been depictions of brave new worlds and dire predictions about 1984. But the technocrat and the totalitarian never ultimately succeed. It is true that the artist and the believer do not achieve permanent victories. But if they are true artists and genuine believers they do not require total success. They differ from the technocrat and the totalitarian because they never seek control and because they never expect perfect order. Just a little tension.

2.
Contemporary Spirituality: Revelation, Myth and Ritual

John H. Westerhoff

John Westerhoff contends that the spiritual life necessitates the development and unification of both our intuition and intellectual modes of consciousness. A renewed concern for revelation, ritual, and myth can provide us with a means for regaining balance and unity.

It was during the early 1950's that Joseph Kamiya and other researchers at San Francisco's Langley Porter Clinic began working with laboratory animals and human beings in whom the large nerve that connects the two hemispheres of the brain, the corpus callosum, had been severed. Their work took shape in a hypothesis that each lobe of the brain functioned independently of the other. Further, they hypothesized that during the early years the two hemispheres of the brain began to differentiate in function. In our culture, they concluded, the left hemisphere of the brain connected to the right side of the body assumed the functions of speech, logic, cognitive reasoning, analysis, and linear activities, while the right hemisphere of the brain connected to the left side of the body assumed the functions of visual, artistic, imaginative, associative, and relational activities. The left lobe made possible those intellectual modes of consciousness which are signative, conceptual, analytical, and informational; the right lobe made possible those intuitional modes of consciousness which are symbolic, mythical, imaginative, and emotive.

Just a few years ago (1972) Roger Ornstein popularized this research in *The Psychology of Consciousness*. More recently Julian Jaynes, a psychologist at Princeton University, published a massive work, *The Origin of Consciousness and the Breakdown of the Bicameral*

Mind, which applied the split brain thesis to the history of mankind. Only a year before, Henry Mintzberg wrote in the *Harvard Business Review* (July-August 1976) an article entitled "Planning on the Left Side and Managing on the Right" which suggested that good managers operate out of the right side of their brain and planners out of the left. While popularity for the split-brain hypothesis grows and a host of folk rush in to build on its preliminary findings (witness this book), numerous researchers and scholars reveal contradictory evidence, while others draw alternative conclusions. Whether or not the two-lobe hypothesis is correct, I leave open to further investigation. What is important, from my point of view, is the commonly agreed upon awareness that since the enlightenment the intuitional mode of consciousness has been increasingly devalued.

Surely no one will question that reality as understood can assume either a symbolic or a signative, mythic or conceptual, imaginative or analytical, emotive or informational character. No one can deny that signative, conceptual, analytical reality is more highly favored by our culture's educated leaders. All of this, therefore, might be simply an academic exercise in cognitive description, if it were not for the current enthusiasm for the interior life, self-awareness, anti-intellectual enlightenment, pseudomysticism, exotic forms of meditation, glossalalia, spiritual euphoria, and personal ecstasy. It seems that in spite of our secular, scientific, historicist age a host of people are in search of God, an experience of the divine, a sense of the transcendent, or depth in their lives. At the same time mainline liberal Protestant and Roman Catholic churches recede from popularity and influence in the culture. It appears as if these churches, through the years, have attempted to emphasize the intellectual mode of consciousness while increasingly people are realizing that the intellect is not of sole importance for meaning and purpose. In any case, my radical contention is this: the *overemphasis* on theological formulation (doctrine), political and economic social actions,and the literary, historical, critical approach to the Scriptures has made contemporary Christian spirituality difficult. To counter this unfortunate situation, I will suggest a number of radical alternatives, namely a renewed emphasis on revelation, ritual, and myth. But first a few words about my understanding of the spiritual life.

THE SPIRITUAL LIFE

The twentieth century will never be named the age of spirituality. More reasonably, it may be known as the era of retarded consciousness. We have lost or forgotten the experience of God which lies at the heart of Christian faith. Still, we long and search for some sense of the Divine. Just witness the renewed interest in the occult, Eastern religion, meditation and personal religious experience. It is as if we humans knew we were more than intellect and that truth was more than reason could prove. Even we modern humans are, I suggest, *homo religiousus*. Prayer is still the most basic expression of our humanness.

Aquinas wrote, "Prayer is the peculiar proof of religion"; faith in Luther's judgment was "prayer, nothing but prayer"; Baron von Hugel concluded that "prayer is the essential element of all life"; and Schleiermacher observed "to be religious and to pray are really the same thing." But even the word "prayer" lacks clarity in our day. Some think of prayer as the distressed cries to the heavens, others a formality before meals and meetings, an experience in mountaintops, a ritual in a church. Prayer for some is a spontaneous emotional discharge and for others a fixed rational formula to be recited. However, prayer, as I am using the word, is a generic term to describe every aspect of our conscious relationship with God. Prayer represents what I mean by the spiritual life—daily existence lived in relationship with God—or piety (spirituality), the daily activity of living in the presence of God through adoration, confession, praise, thanksgiving and petition/intercession.

To live in adoration is to focus our life upon the nature and qualities of God. It is the life of the lover, of God, the dreamer, and visionary which makes possible viewing every aspect of life as a miracle. Confession is life lived under the judgment and grace of God. It is the life of those striving to bring their individual, interior, experience and belief into harmony with their social, exterior, practice and action. The life of praise is a life alive with the memory of the mighty acts of God. It is life lived dancing, singing, and praising God even in evil days. Thanksgiving is our celebrative awareness of God's continuing actions in our historical midst. It is the life that can still spy burning bushes, hear the voice of God, and grasp the presence of Christ in contemporary culture. Petition/intercession is the continuous striving to bring our wills in line with God's will. It is the moral life lived in conscious loyalty to the conviction that Jesus is Lord, passing moral judgments on what is the means to be faithful.

The spiritual life then is an historical life lived with a conscious awareness of God's presence; it is life so lived that our minds, hearts, and wills and God's are united in common historical reflective action. Surely, this understanding rules out prayer in which the world or the self is depreciated or denied, in which the human personality is dissolved or absorbed into a unity with an otherwordly reality. Prayer is not a negative process moving us out of our normal state or condition, a passive resigned contemplation of otherness, nor a striving after emotional ecstasy through the extinction of thought or volition. Prayer is ultimately an ethical activity. History is the peculiar province of God's revelation and fellowship. Blessedness of life with God is life in this world; it is in our daily lives that we meet and have communion with God.

For such an understanding of prayer to prevail we need to recover the proper place of religious experience. The popularity of the charismatic and Jesus movements are evidence of our neglect of experience, but that does not mean that we ought to turn uncritically to speaking in tongues, pseudo-mysticism, exotic forms of meditation, or uncontrolled emotion. The switch from doctrine and dogma to silence or glossalalia is no solution nor is the switch from formal institutional and ritual life to simplistic emotional commitment to Jesus. Spiritual euphoria without social action may be religious, but it is not Christian. Personal ecstasy is no substitute for social justice. "Thy kingdom come" is an essential petition of Jesus' prayer: *Maranatha*, "Come Lord Jesus", the central petition of the early church. Both call us to live in a conscious relationship to God's kingdom. Prayer or true religious experience, for the Christian, is living in communion with God in the midst of personal and social history making.

However, a warning! I'm concerned—frightened might be a more accurate word—that our current enthusiasm for the split brain hypothesis could result in a neglect for the unity of the brain and an affirmation of *both* the intellectual and intuitional modes of consciousness, or worse, that religion and spirituality will be isolated in one hemisphere, the right lobe. Right lobe religion is no more healthy than left. Dissatisfied with intellectual, verbal, and analytical life, some are seeking self-knowledge, self-awareness, and self-development through anti-intellectual escapist mechanisms. Disenchanted with society dominated by one mode of consciousness, others are seeking unity with the transcendent reality through exercises aimed at transporting the self into another state of existence. The spiritual life of the Christian, however, must focus upon the spirit of God in us and in the world. Its quest is for an active unity with the God of history through thought, feeling, and will. The climax of Christian life is not enlightenment but unification with the will and activity of God. Christian spiritual life assumes both an historical awareness and the integration of the intuitional *and* intellectual modes of consciousness in political, social, and economic activity.

The current bankruptcy in our spiritual lives is not primarily or only the result of a misplaced, singular concern for the intellectual mode of consciousness, but rather it is in an actual denial of the intuitional mode. It is simply that we have attempted to foster intellectual development at the expense of the intuition. (I say attempted, because, in point of fact, we are, as a people, as anti-intellectual as anti-intuitional.) It is the artificial separation of these two modes of consciousness, the depreciation of the signative, conceptual, and analytical aspects of life and the benign neglect of the symbolic, mythical, imaginative and emotive aspects of our human life which have limited our spiritual development and crippled us as a people. A whole person, living the spiritual life, has developed fully both modes of consciousness. A new awareness of the visual, artistic, imaginative, associative, and relational activities of the brain cannot be permitted to dull or limit our concern for speech, logic, cognitive reasoning, analysis, and linear activities. I cannot make this warning too strong, for in the next pages I will be emphasizing only one mode of consciousness and I worry that someone may conclude that I believe the spiritual life can be reduced to intuition. It can not. The religious life of activity and the interior life of experience must be united. Christian spirituality has a symbolic-signative, mythic-conceptual, imaginative-analytical, informational-emotive character. Inherent in every individual, intense, interior, religious experience is the passionate need to express creatively, socially, through word and deed, the wholeness of life. Correspondingly every verbal expression or behavioral act shared in community has a passionate need to secure itself in the world of depthful, transcendent experience, ritual and myth. We humans are created in the image of God. We are, therefore, historical actors. Our wills, to be Christian, need to unite intellect and intuition into ethical activity in our personal and social history. That is what it means to live the spiritual life.

We humans are spiritual beings. Our human spirituality has not dried up. Dimensions of our spirituality have been suppressed but not destroyed. Eventually they will emerge and seek to express themselves, for the human spiritual quest is the natural drive of persons to become human in the fullest sense. Nevertheless, in the introduction, I made the bold statement that our overemphasis on theology as rational discourse about God in the form of doctrine and dogma on social, political, economic action as concrete external works, and on the literary historical-critical approach to the Scriptures, have made the spiritual life difficult. This contention is not based on the assumption that any of these concerns are unimportant to the Christian life, but because, like the intellectual mode of consciousness in which each of these participate, they represent only half of reality. (Correspondingly, we could also make a case that in the typical congregation theology, social action and the critical approach to the Scriptures have also been ignored.) Revelation as a relational experience, ritual as symbolic action, and myth as symbolic narrative—each of which has its foundations in the intuitional mode of consciousness—provide a necessary balance, but have been ignored with even greater severity. Without then denying the significance of theology, social action, and a critical understanding of the Scriptures, I would like to emphasize the contemporary importance and significance of revelation, myth and ritual.

REVELATION

Revelation and faith belong together, just as theology and religion do. To speak of religion is to speak of institutions, documents, artifacts, customs, ceremonials, creedal statements and codes of conduct. Faith on the other hand is deeply personal and dynamic. Faith is a centered act of the total personality. Faith is not a result of a purely rational process. It is affectional, a relationship with God which embraces the whole person and about which it is difficult to be objective. To be sure, faith always expresses itself in religion and as such religion provides us with the means by which we grow in faith. Religion is a witness to and stimulant of faith. But religion is never an end, only a means; faith is an end. For example, Bach wrote his "B Minor Mass" as an expression of his faith. Whenever I sing or hear the "B Minor Mass" I am moved to faith, but to know all about the "B Minor Mass" is of little significance for faith. The Nicean Creed, Augustine's theology, and the Heidelberg Catechism are all expressions of faith. My faith is aided by these doctrinal statements, but they are examples of religion and to make them the focus of our attention is to ignore the issue of faith. Surely, there is a difference between learning about the Heidelberg Catechism and being a faithful disciple of Jesus Christ; there is a difference between learning about the doctrine of salvation and being saved; there is a difference between understanding justification by faith and being justified by it; there is a difference between understanding religion and religious experience and having an experience of God's presence. Faith is not knowledge about or even intellectual assent to truth or ideas. It is a response to a person.

Revelation refers to those actions of God to which we respond in faith. For too long theology, as an intellectual body of doctrine to be conserved and transmitted, has been emphasized, though never fully accepted. Revelation is a different matter. God does not reveal truths about God's self. God reveals God's self. Through God's actions God communicates and relates. Revelation affects our consciousness and re-creates us. It transforms our relationships to self, neighbor and world. Revelation is best understood as a personal encounter with a living, acting God. Revelation, therefore, is essentially a relationship with God, not a set of doctrines, ideas about the world or new knowledge.

Theology is doctrine. It is a natural consequence of revelation, just as religion is a natural consequence of faith. Revelation, however, is always prior and, therefore, foundational to the spiritual life. For example, the message of eternal life is not essentially information about another world, but first and foremost the Word of God's presence in creating life out of death. Our lives can be shattered by sickness, failure, or accident. We are all vulnerable to forces beyond our control. Still the good news is that in every experience of death God is present transforming it into life. For those who have experienced this revelation there is reason to reflect and express it theologically. Being aware of the resulting doctrinal formulations can even aid us to understand better our experience. But revelation, as a relational experience of God, is of primary importance. Never was this truth made clearer than in a story told by a colleague. It seems that one of his academic friends was critically ill, paralyzed, incontinent, bowel and bladder, and unable to speak. There he was helpless in a hospital bed, wanting to communicate but unable to do so. My friend, an Episcopal priest, went to see him. The man's wife sat helpless at his side. The priest stood by him, held his hand, and said, "I know you want to speak and can't. I also know that you are a believer in Jesus Christ and would want in such a time the ministrations of a priest and so I have come to sign you with the cross." As he put his thumb to his forehead, the bowel and bladder of the helpless man emptied themselves. The odor filled the air and his wife, in despair, with tears in her eyes, exclaimed, "Oh why did he have to do that now!" And my colleague responded, "What better time to acknowledge that you have no control over your life, even in the presence of your dearest friend, than when you are being signed with the cross?" Revelation! The presence of God bringing life out of death—not ideas about God confined to the intellect, but a relationship involving the world of intuition.

We need to revolt against the objective consciousness so that we might regain our mystical sensibilities. Ultimately the only authority for faith is the Word of God, the activity of God, the revelation of God, the Word made flesh in Jesus Christ. The Bible as the story of the relationship between God and God's people is an approximate authority. The tradition, as the interpretations and understandings of the story by the community of faith through the ages, is an approximate authority. So, importantly, is contemporary personal experience. Scripture and experience must judge the tradition; scripture and the tradition judge experience; tradition and experience judge the Scriptures; while all are judged by the final authority upon which the community of faith rests: God's action in Jesus Christ. Theology, at its best, is a process of thinking, of reflecting on revelation—the relationship that God initiates with God's people in every age—which can and needs to be experienced again in our own. However, neither Scripture, tradition, or experience can become revelation—God's Word—without the operation of the intuitional mode of consciousness. That is, we only experience this relationship with God metaphorically. We do not have direct experiences of God; no one has seen God. But neither do we know God essentially through ideas. A metaphorical, poetic, symbolic, mythical relationship to God is always prior to any signative, conceptual, analytical explanation. Our ideas about God are important. Indeed they can influence the sort of experiences of God we have and do not have. In one sense then, our revelation of God is made possible through the ideas of God which are passed on through the tradition. But that is only half the truth. Our experiences also form our ideas. People in the first century experienced the crucified and resurrected Christ and his presence at the breaking of the bread. Their idea about God and God's coming community were framed by that relational experience which, metaphorically, we communicate each time we celebrate the Lord's Supper. To become aware of God's continuing revelation is to nurture the intuitional mode of consciousness.

For too long we have been living in the prosaic world of surface reality. We need to affirm the poetic truth of metaphor and myth by questioning the basic premise of the naturalistic universe and social science's search for clear explanations. Perhaps the true explanations of life are beyond concepts, to be reached only through the intuition. Human intellect may never comprehend the full set of causes preceding any experience, thought, or feeling. We need to repeal the fundamental law of cause and effect which has been an unquestioned statute since the Enlightenment. It is important for the spiritual life that we replace the sole rule of linear, logical, rationalistic thinking and return to the earlier age of mystery, which held sway before the advent of Newtonian physics, Cartesian logic and behavioral psychology.

One of the early representations of Christ in Christian art depicts a crucified human figure with the head of an ass. The debate on its meaning continues, but I am convinced that these catacomb Christians had a deep sense of the comic absurdity of their position. A wretched band of slaves, derelicts and square pegs, they must have sensed how ludicrous their claims appeared. The revelation they announced, lived and died for was irrational and illogical. Christ for them must have seemed something of a holy fool and they knew that they were fools for Christ. More important, they had faith and hope in the eternal foolishness of God. To have faith in the revelation of God in Jesus Christ is to live in the ludicrous world of imagination, poetry, and metaphor. As Herbert Marcuse put it, "We need to break the power of facts over the world and speak a language which is not the language of those who establish, enforce, and benefit from the facts." To live in and for the Gospel is to be a Godly fool, a laughing stock for the Word of God. Revelation and intuition are closely connected, just as theology and intellect are synonymous. Both are necessary. An overemphasis on theology has distorted our spiritual life. A new emphasis on revelation can provide the necessary balance and stimulate spirituality. However, if intellectual reflection and theological thinking are neglected, spirituality will once again be denied.

MYTH

Two and a half centuries ago a struggle emerged within the faculty of Saint Thomas' School in Leipzig, an unresolved struggle which still marks a schism in the soul of the church. It was a conflict between the intellectual and intuitional modes of consciousness, the struggle between the school's cantor, Johann Sebastian Bach, and its rector, Johann August Ernesti. Ernesti, a pioneer in the literary, historical, critical study of the Scriptures, believed the students should study more and sing less; Bach thought faith and its musical expressions more important. As Jan Chiapusso put it, "Here we see the tragic conflict between the last and most mighty musical respresentative of the age of faith and the younger protagonist of the age of reason and science." Two epics, two cultures, two understandings were at stake. Ernesti wished to make the study of religion the sole purpose of the school. Bach tried to defend the position that the Biblical text was designed to release within the reader an intense sort of spiritual activity: faith. Ernesti chose religion—a rationalistic, analytical, intellectual perspective. Bach chose faith—an intuitional experiential perspective. Since those days, the rationalists, with their emphasis on theological reflection and their interest in the literary, historical, critical method of Biblical study, have dominated the church's intellectual life. While these scholars never won the people's hearts or had any great success in training the masses in their methods, they did influence our understandings and ways. However, it is not that their understanding and ways are unimportant; it is just that their emphasis on the intellectual mode of consciousness has contributed to the demise of intuition and the sickness of the spiritual life. One way to return the intuitional dimension of life to its proper place is to remind ourselves of the centrality of myth. Myths provide the foundations for our rituals and the means for expressing God's revelation. More important, they point to and participate in the spiritual dimension of life. Unfortunately myth has been erroneously understood as distinct from reality, possessing only a pretense at historical reliability. Regretfully, this understanding of myth has caused Christians whose faith is based upon God's historical actions to consider myth to be irrelevant. The faith of the church rests upon the Biblical record of God's history-making, especially upon a particular historical person, Jesus Christ, and his actual passion and resurrection. Some contend that while the Gospel is not myth, it had to be set forth in the form of myth so it would reach the depths of human consciousness in the first century. Therefore, they conclude, it is necessary to demythologize the Bible in order to discover its true significance and/or to make it speak to modern, secular, urban humans who cannot understand or appreciate its mythical form. I simply want to go on record as not accepting either of these latter contentions. Myth can be understoood by moderns. More importantly, it is essential to the spiritual life of the Christian. The attempt to demythologize the Scriptures may not be as important as we once thought. Myths have their life in the symbolic and are, therefore, best understood through the intuitional mode of consciousness.

The Pawnee, an American Indian tribe, differentiated between true and false stories. True stories were about the sacred; false stories about the profane. True stories are myths: they are stories because they recount events that did take place. That is, they are not fiction or fable but history; however, their truth lies in the recounting of sacred history. Profane stories only explain historical events. Sacred stories—myths—point beyond their historical roots to the dimension of depth, of the Transcendent, in history. They are true not in the sense of logic or intellectual analysis, but in terms of mystery and intuition. Myth unites history with the sacred giving it particular symbolic significance in the lives of people. The story of the life, death and resurrection of Jesus is on the one hand a profane, historical account but it is also much more. It is a sacred story—myth—because it points beyond its historicity to the cosmic action of God in the salvation of the world. To demythologize the story is to lose its dimension of depth and significance.

Myths are never told for their own sake nor as a means of expressing intellectual doctrines. They are a mode of expression which as symbolic narrative transmits the truths only the intuition can grasp and understand. There are various sorts of knowledge; each has its own significance and character. Scientific, rational knowledge is only one kind. The Scripture contains the sacred myths of the Christian community. They ought not be reduced to rational discourse. The Bible is poetry plus, not science minus. Our myths communicate the revelation of God and sustain the understandings and ways of the faithful. For too long we have attempted to understand reality solely through reason and have forgotten the importance of symbolic narrative, metaphor, and sacred story. Christianity is a historical, but also a metaphorical, religion. In our culture, we have lost our intuitional power to grasp the truth of myth because we have canonized historic and scientific positivism. Nevertheless, we no more live in a post-mythical age than we live in a post-intuitional age, except in the sense that our intuitional mode of consciousness has atrophied. Our myths have been so rationally explained, through critical study, that they have lost some of their ability to speak to the depths of our existence and thereby to integrate us with ourselves and our universe. Just as intuition can be nourished once again, so myth can be reborn in the lives of us moderns. The challenge before us is to do just that, for our spiritual health is dependent upon our ability to do so.

RITUAL

Liberal Protestants, in particular, but also some Roman Catholic liberals, have tended to put more emphasis on political and economic social action than on corporate symbolic action—ritual—forgetting that ritual is necessary to support, inspire, and sustain significant social action over time. And perhaps even more important, it is our rituals themselves which either encourage or discourage political and social action. The result has been disastrous. While the church, in general nurtured by otherworldly, individualistic rituals, has denied the importance of political, economic, social action, those most committed to a this-worldly, social understanding of the faith have typically left the church or at least stopped participating in its rituals. In our quest for historical relevance and faithfulness, we have forgotten that ritual is at the heart of all social change.

It is not so much in rational planning as in the imagination that the world is changed. We live by our images and dreams, our visions and hopes. That is why ritual is so important (and often must be reformed). As Karl Marx rightly observed, religion can either be an opiate of the masses or a prophetic protest against injustice and in support of change. Whether it will be an opiate or a prophetic protest will be determined by the people's rituals. Ritual is at its core political; prayer is a political act. As Amos Wilder once wrote, "It is in the area of liturgies—the idiom and metaphors of prayer and witness— that the main impasse lies today for the Christian.

Without ritual (symbolic actions) to support it, there is no meaningful personal life or political social action. Liturgy, the activity of the community, unites symbolic action. Each needs and supports the other. To deny either one is to deny the whole. Liturgy, the life of the community, includes discipleship within the community expressed through ritual and apostleship in the world expressed through personal and social service and action. Insofar as we have neglected ritual we have starved and discouraged social action. By emphasizing social action we have lost our roots and inspiration. If we are to maintain a healthy spiritual life, ritual must once again become an essential focus of our concern.

Ritual, revelation, and myth share much in common. Ritual too is about relationships: who we are, whose we are, and who are we to become? Through our rituals, undergirded by our myths, we recapture a memory of our origins and are captured by a vision of our destinies. Like revelation and myth, ritual emerges from intuitional experience; similarly, our rituals nurture our intuition and make possible new experiences.

Ritual is a social drama which embodies the experiences of a community. It is through the repetition of these symbolic actions that we evoke the feeling of the primordial event, which initially called the community into being, with such power that it effects a contemporary presence at that event. In other words, through the intuitional mode of consciousness, ritual re-presents revelation. An example would be the Christian ritual of baptism or the Lord's Supper, both of which re-present the event of Jesus' death and resurrection.

This truth took on significance one night, a number of years ago, when I was in Paraguay. A political prisoner had escaped from prison and told me about his celebration of Easter two days before. It appears as if the prisoners had been forbidden to worship, but while the non-Christians kept the guards busy, the Christians huddled together. The pastor, also a prisoner, began, "This meal in which we are part, reminds us of the prison, the torture, the death, and the final victory and resurrection of Jesus Christ. He asked us to remember him by repeating this action in the spirit of fellowship. The bread which we do not have today, but which is present in the spirit of Jesus Christ, is the body which he gave for humanity. The fact that we have none represents very well the lack of bread and the hunger of so many millions of human beings. When Christ distributed it among his disciples and when he fed the people he revealed the will of God that we should all have bread. The wine which we do not have today is his blood present in the light of our faith. Christ poured it out for us to move us toward freedom, in the long march of justice. God made all persons of one blood: The blood of Christ represents our dream of a unified humanity, of a just society without difference of race or class."

The pastor told us of a man, about sixty, whose daughter had died fighting with the guerrillas, who commented, "I think this communion means that our dead are alive, that they have given their bodies and blood making Christ's sacrifice their own. I believe in the resurrection of the dead and feel their presence among us." There was silence and the pastor continued, "This communion is not only a communion between us here, but a communion with all our brothers and sisters in the church or outside, not only those who are alive, but those who have already died. But still more it is a communion with those who will come after us and who will be faithful to Jesus Christ." He then told us how he held out his empty hands to each person placing his hand over theirs as they together boldly exclaimed, "Take, eat, this is my body which is given for you; do this in remembrance of me. Take, drink, this is the blood of Christ which was shed to seal the new covenant of God with humanity. Let us give thanks, sure that Christ is here with us, strengthening us." Then they raised their hands to their mouths and received the body and blood of Christ and after sharing the kiss of peace returned to their life in prison with new hope.

Through the power of symbolic actions we order our experience; through the use of symbolic narrative we explain our lives. Ritual operates on those levels of existential reality that undergird the conceptual. Importantly, ritual points to and participates in that primordial truth which is located at the expanding edge of our horizon of knowing, in the affections and the intuition, not common sense or reason. Just as it is the language of myth which at the most fundamental level enables us to perceive reality in its depth, so it is in our symbolic actions—our rituals, our social dramas—that we experience the ultimate meanings and purposes of life and our lives. Without ritual life becomes mundane and profane, for it is through ritual expressive of the symbolic and founded in the intuitive mode of consciousness that the sacramental and the sacred are best known and expressed.

When we participate in a ritual, we experience community, we reconcile and identify ourselves with our foreparents from whom the ritual has descended and we re-establish continuity with the past and attain a vision for the future.

Ritual is drama; it is life in the world of intuition. When our intuition atrophies, our rituals lose their power. Correspondingly, meaningful ritual can enhance and enliven our intuitional mode of consciousness. Unless, therefore, ritual is raised to its proper significance our spiritual lives will remain impotent.

CONCLUSION

To summarize, our contentions in this essay have been that the spiritual life necessitates the development and unification of both our intuition and intellectual modes of consciousness. In our culture we have estranged these two modes, neglected the intellect and permitted the intuition to atrophy. Our emphasis and the people's rejection of theological formulation, social action, and a critical approach to the Scriptures have encouraged and supported this tragedy. A renewed concern for revelation, ritual, and myth can provide us with a means for regaining balance and unity. Healthy Christian spirituality is dependent upon such efforts. Obviously I advocate that those responsible for catechesis take the lead in these efforts.

Suggested Reading

Baum, Gregory. *Man Becoming*. New York: Herder and Herder, 1970.
Dulles, Avery. *Revelation and the Quest for Unity*. Washington: Corpus Books, 1968.
Eliade, Mircea. *Images and Symbols*. New York: Sheed and Ward, 1961.

Gibbs, Lee, and Stevenson, Taylor. *Myth and the Crisis of Historical Consciousness*. American Academy of Religion Section Papers, 1975. Missoula, Mt.: Scholars Press, 1975.

Halbfas, Hubert. *Theory of Catechetics: Language and Experience in Religious Education*. New York: Seabury, 1971.

Holmes, Urban T. *Ministry and Imagination*. New York: Seabury Press, 1976.

Jaynes, Julian. *The Origin of Consciousness in the Breakdown of Bicameral Mind*. Boston: Houghton Mifflin, 1977.

Polanyi, Michael. *Personal Knowledge: Towards a Post-Critical Philosophy*. Chicago: University of Chicago Press, 1958.

Turner, Victor. *Dramas, Fields and Metaphors; Symbolic Action in Human Society*. Ithaca, N. Y.: Cornell University Press, 1974.

Westerhoff, John H. *Will Our Children Have Faith?* New York: Seabury, 1976.

TeSelle, Sallie. *Speaking in Parables: A Study in Metaphor and Theology*. Philadelphia: Fortress, 1975.

Wilder, Amos N. *Theopoetic: Theology and the Religious Imagination*. Philadelphia: Fortress Press, 1976.

II
THE ARTS
AND
RELIGIOUS EXPERIENCE

3.
Art and the Religious Experience

Norma H. Thompson

Referring to specific works of art, Norma Thompson illustrates her thesis that art is at once a lure into the religious dimension as well as an interpreter of religious experience.

Religion from its earliest forms has been closely related to art, and thus to aesthetic experience. The liturgies, myths, symbols, and sacred places of religion have been clothed in the forms of art, and throughout much of the history of humankind the aesthetic and the rational have been so interrelated in the total religious experience that little effort was made to analyze the aesthetic as distinct from the rational. It appears primarily as an accompaniment to the development of the scientific mind and the movement of art out of the churches in the Western world that these elements were divorced from one another. The rational has tended to become the heart of the religious expression and the aesthetic has been relegated to an inferior status in religious circles. The attitude of separating these two aspects of religion and giving primacy to one or the other is found in a statement made a few years ago by a professor of biology in speaking about his own involvement with his church as a member of the vestry. He did not find a meaningful belief system in the church, nor were the sermons delivered by the clergyman intellectually stimulating. Yet he stated: "I am involved in the church because I find the worship service aesthetically satisfying."

In contemporary times the aesthetic dimension in religious experience is receiving new attention, sometimes almost negating the intellectual aspects. The reaction of young people and many sensitive, older people to rational religion, as exhibited by fascination with meditation, drug-induced "trips," the occult, witchcraft, and other forms of religious experience centering on the emotions—a movement which began in the sixties and continues today—gives support to the aesthetic in human experience. But any religious experience must, if it shall remain satisfying to human beings, include in balance both the cognitive and affective aspects.

Realizing the difficulty of speaking rationally about the non-rational, the present discussion will deal with the aesthetic aspect of religious experience; but the very fact that one chooses an intellectual framework within which to discuss the aesthetic testifies to the importance of the ideas which undergird the emotional life. In particular, the discussion here will focus upon art and its relation to religious experience.

The aesthetic side of religious experience encompasses the same large expanse of ritual, myth, symbol, involvement with the arts, psychological interpretations, and sensitivities to human relations which the intellectual side involves. It is doubtful if one engages in pure feeling or pure thought. In fact, when one experiences what appears to be pure feeling, "feelings felt rather than pondered," this experience is almost always interpreted as abnormal. Pruyser points this out in speaking of the sensation of pure feeling recounted by Jane Hillyer in *Reluctantly Told*. She wrote:

> Lying there I came as close, I think, as I ever have to a state of emotion unaccompanied by thought. I simply *felt*. Again, I have never learned words to describe sensations so far removed from what is called normal. General misery, physical discomfort, degradation not born of intellectual concept, but a deep, bodily and inner mental state; a feeling of being lost, lost utterly with no sense of place or time, no idea as to whom voices belonged, no clear realization of my own identity, lost in mind and body and soul, lost to light and form and color; a distinct, acid nausea of self-revulsion—all these were in the feeling that swept over me. But they do not describe it any more than a list of ingredients describes any assembled whole.[1]

Using the categories of psychology, Pruyser sees the religious experience as involving perceptual processes, intellectual processes, thought organization, linguistic functions, emotional processes, the motor system, and relations to persons, things, ideas, and self. The complexity of the religious experience can be seen from the aspects of perception alone—vision, audition, tactual sense, kinesthesis, pain, taste, smell, and other sensory experiences, including the sense of vibration and of temperature, as well as pathological perceptions such as hallucinations. Vision, for example, is used in religion to denote not only those experiences involving sight (stained glass windows, altars, symbolic gestures, crosses, ikons, etc.), but it is used also to describe experiences in which there is no visual process (mystic "vision," apparitions).[2]

Religious experiences are rich in sound, both the actual sounds of prayers, chants, incantations, hymns, musical instruments, and spoken words, and the metaphysical sounds used to describe the activities of the gods.

> Gods allegedly make noise, and their worshippers listen and make noises in turn. The gods roar in thunderstorms, howl in whirlwinds, rustle in the leaves of sacred oaks, sing in the zephyr, gurgle in brooks, whisper in the leaves that drop in the fall. They are capable of an astounding array of formless or organized sounds. Sometimes they raise their voices and speak words. They say "Hark" or "Stop and listen" or "Hear my word." When that happens, certain men attune their ears and forget everything else around them. Indeed, they may so identify themselves with the divine voice they hear that they in turn start to speak, presumably in God's voice. They say things like "Hear, O Israel" and "Thus says the Lord." Or they utter nonsense syllables and sputter and gargle strange noises in states of frenzy.[3]

These illustrations from vision and sound demonstrate the variety and intensity of the sensations in the religious experience. They also intimate the rich contribution which the arts make to that experience, since architecture, painting, sculpture, poetry, music, dance, procession, and drama form the great bulk of the stimuli for visual and auditory sensations in experiences which human beings call religious.

RELIGIOUS ART

Although the common view tends to differentiate religious art from secular art, using the term "religious art" to denote those works which contain subject matter religious in nature, some theologians and artists have gone so far as to state that all art is religious. Tillich's famous statement that "An apple of Cézanne has more presence of ultimate reality than a picture of Jesus by Hoffman"[4] suggests that every work of art interprets the meaning of life; it is concerned with the ultimate. But is also suggests that some works of art are more capable than others of drawing persons deeper into ultimate reality, and those works may or may not contain subject matter usually termed "religious." Picasso's "Guernica" was called by Tillich "the great Protestant painting of our time," though it has no overt religious content. It assumes that human beings ought to love each other; that war and destruction should cease; that swords should be beaten into plowshares; and that peace and brotherhood should prevail. It is a protest against the present violence and inhumanity; it cries out in the name of the highest, in the name of the Ultimate.

According to Reimer, "the subject matter of an art-work has nothing whatever to do with its being religious, but . . . every great work of art, by its nature *as a work of art*, is religious art."[5] He notes that the human organism is able to create symbols of the basic stuff of life and that these symbols are art-works. "This is precisely what art-works do. They symbolize life itself, and allow us to participate very immediately and deeply in the basic stuff and process of all life . . . The deepest meaning in all art is basically the same meaning— the sense of life itself."[6] Works of art do this by using different materials to set up a system of interrelationships. It is this system of interrelationships which symbolizes the condition of life, not the particular subject matter. As life consists of "stresses and releases, of actions and reactions, of anticipations and resolutions, so every art-work is a system of stresses and releases, of actions and reactions, of anticipations and resolutions."[7] The way in which an art work speaks of reality is seen in a sculpture formed by welding piano wires in such a fashion that tension is suggested in every aspect. One feels that if one wire is clipped, the whole "piece" will collapse. Clark Fitzgerald's "Fabric of Human Involvement" has much of the same quality. It consists of steel human figures welded together in four tiers, with all persons in the upper tiers standing on the shoulders of the persons below, with some persons touching others, holding hands, carrying others, and with various other indications of mutual interdependence. Again, the viewer has the sense that removing one human figure would seriously affect the whole structure, or at least would affect radically one segment of the human population. The Jewish Museum in New York City several years ago exhibited enormous paintings in its main hall. When one walked into this hall, the effect was of a huge room, dimly lit, with small benches in the center of the hall, surrounded by wall expanses on which the paintings were hung. Each painting was predominantly one color, but smaller rectangles, triangles, or stripes of other colors gave life to the paintings. The museum had created a system of relationships, including forms, light, colors, which spoke of the immensity of the Ultimate, the simplicity and profundity of life, and the quiet of solitude.

Subject matter may complicate the symbolization process, actually diverting attention from the system of interrelationships and obscuring the meaning of the art work as a symbol of life. This complication presents a danger for any medium; thus, the words of hymns, the Biblical content of paintings, the story portrayed through dance or drama may focus attention upon themselves and prevent the deeper sense of the Ultimate from being experienced. Whether the art work presents religious or so-called "secular" subject matter, or no subject matter at all (as in many modern works), and regardless of medium, a great art work brings to the sensitive mind insights into the human condition and into the nature of reality. When an art work provides this depth experience in which one knows and feels the meaning of life it can truly be called "religious art." When it raises, consciously or subconsciously, such questions as "Who am I?" "Why am I here?" and "Where am I going?" it is asking the religious questions. "Art mirrors something of the prevailing interpretations of man and his condition and shapes that of future generations," according to Harned.[8] Is the human being just another machine, as suggested in paintings by the French artist, Léger? In his paintings men and women resemble a collection of nuts, bolts, and pipes welded together (see his "Woman Holding a Vase," 1927, for example), giving an impression of machines.

Since artists live within their own cultures, their works reflect their views of that culture. Some of the most sensitive artists seem ahead of the culture, since they create art works which comment upon the values and problems of their time, intensively challenging a society to see itself as it really is. Often it seems it is the younger generation which responds to these creative artists and experiences the sense of frustration, of brokenness, and of alienation in contemporary culture. It is the youth who are asking the essentially religious questions and who may find in contemporary art experiences of the spirit which cannot be expressed in words.

FUNCTIONS OF ART IN RELATION TO THE RELIGIOUS DIMENSION

Martin suggests that the arts may perform two functions in relation to the religious dimension.[9] They may lure persons into participation in the religious dimension, and they may interpret that dimension. Other writers corroborate these two functions, though they use various terms to denote them. These functions cannot be separated in experience, forming what Martin sees as a particular kind of aesthetic experience, that is, the "participative experience." In this experience "self-consciousness is lost," one becomes "absorbed in empirical grounds," and one finds direct access to "a further reality."[10] If such an experience of participation is deeply felt, one senses the "awe-full-ness" of that further reality, and one desires even deeper participation and feels a sense of reverence, awe, and concern for the ultimate. The human being is drawn into Being.

ART AS A LURE INTO THE RELIGIOUS DIMENSION

Art attempts to establish a world of its own and to invite the participant into that world. But, paradoxically, art also leads out toward the world beyond. As Hazelton points out, " . . . art that deserves to be called great possesses a strange capacity to lead us beyond its presented surface toward quickened awareness, perhaps even rediscover, of the common surrounding world that is both wider and deeper than art's own."[11] He illustrates this paradox by Arthur Miller's play, "After the Fall," noting that Miller had asserted that "the play was not *about* something, but hopefully *was* something." Miller then went on to remark that the play was *about* "the terrifying fact of human choice." The point here is that regardless of the integrity of the world of art, great art does have this potential for leading the human being into dimensions outside that world. The religious dimension is one of those worlds.

From the moment a child is born, this new person is exposed to the symbols and rituals of ultimate reality which are meaningful to its parents, its religious community, and its primary personages. Though many of these symbols and rituals could not be called great art, they have the potential for luring the child into the sense of the mysterious, the holy, the sacred. They provide the clues to reality which become the means by which the child satisfies his/her needs and develops a sense of the goodness or badness of the universe, the rightness and wrongness of life, and the ups and downs of existence. Formal operational thinking about these symbols and rituals may not come until early adolescence, as Piaget, Goldman, Peatling, and others have demonstrated, but feelings and responses, as well as some verbalization, begin immediately. The stories, or myths, are accepted as true; pictures of God creating Adam may bring a sense of security in the power and concern of God for his creatures, but pictures of Noah and his family being rescued by God whereas all the rest of the human population were drowned may strike terror into the heart of the child; use of the terms "God is love" or "God is like a father" may bring children to react with warmth and love to the idea of God, or it may bring them to fear and withdraw, depending upon their own experiences with fathers, mothers, and other persons in the environment. The argument here is that children are brought into a participative experience with the ultimate through the art forms which are found in their primary group experiences. So, too, with youth and adults. They may be able to engage in abstract thinking about religious ideas to a greater extent than the child, but they are lured into participation with the ultimate through the symbols, myths, and rituals to which they are exposed. From time to time some art work—a painting, a hymn, music, a word symbol, a sacred place—will for some reason touch them more deeply and they experience the "awe-full awareness" of further reality.

Art may be interwoven into a total religious experience, or it may relate to a single work of art which provides a depth dimension and drawing in to the meaning of life. The biology professor mentioned above experienced a setting in which the artistry of the processional combined with the movement through the liturgy and the architecture, sculpture, and decorations of the sanctuary to provide a total experience. The focus was not upon one piece of art which gave life and meaning to all the rest, but rather all forms of art coalesced into a total experience which he called "aesthetic." The awe, reverence, sense of the "holy," inspired by the religious setting, is akin to the sense of mystery which Einstein felt in confrontation with the universe when he said that a "spirit tremendously superior to the human spirit manifests itself in the law-abidingness of the world, before whom we, with our simple powers, must humbly stand back."[12] Whether the sources are natural, as in the universe, or formed through human creativity, as in words—such art, the sense of the mysterious, the awe-full, evokes feelings which are never put into words, such feelings as fear, love, pain, joy, peace, as well as mystery and awe. The totality of the worshipping environment, then, may provide the occasion for aesthetic experience within the religious dimension.

Lest one think only of the towering spires of Gothic Cathedrals, the plain meeting houses of the New England Puritans, or other sanctuaries of the western world, or lest one focus only upon Gregorian chant, hymns, and prayers from the various prayer books, attention is called to the fact that Buddhists experience similar aesthetic-religious experiences in temples ornate with the Rama story; Southern Africans find the deepest sense of beauty and faith in rhythmic music and lively song and dance. As Durka and Smith remind us, the model is "generated by our training and/or by our environment."[13] They state that "Models are the organizational and interpretive schemes which inform our perceptions and therefore our experience."[14] In a sense, then, human minds put together all the perceptions of the situation—crosses and crucifixes, statues and walls, mosaics and ikons, hymns, dances, music, sermons, anthems, and a myriad of other forms, shapes, colors, and sounds—and combine them with their own training and experience. They respond to this total environment, and sometimes they respond aesthetically; that is, they interpret it as an experience of harmony and beauty, and they may couple it with some sense of the Beyond, with a spirit superior to the human spirit, or a sense of the ultimate. When this occurs, the aesthetic experience is also a religious experience.

An individual work of art, such as one of Nevelson's constructions in scrap wood, may lure one into participation in the religious dimension. For her contemporary sculptures she uses old and discarded wood crates, stair railings, knobs, balls, chair rungs, and pieces of scrap wood tossed aside by workmen. She arranges these into various shapes and sizes, and paints them all one color—black, gold, or white. Some works she calls "walls." A "wall" resembles the reredos of a church, or a three-dimensional triptych. Speaking of Nevelson's works, Williams has called them "beauty from rubbish," and she describes a possible participative experience in relation to the Christian faith. "Christ is found in the everyday objects and in the common things of life—even in that which the world has discarded or despised."[15] These sculptures remind one that Christ is present in the slums and rubbish heaps and with the persons who work there and who must live there. "The central doctrine of Christianity, the Incarnation, means that God is with us in the person of Jesus Christ, who was born in the dirt of the stable and executed as a common criminal and rose again from a borrowed tomb."[16]

ART AS AN INTERPRETER OF RELIGIOUS EXPERIENCE

A second function which the arts may perform is to interpret religious experience, as they interpret other experience. Theologians writing on the arts have developed "theologies of art" in which they have interpreted the work of art in the context of God, the human, and the meaning of life, usually within a Christian context. Harned notes that such a theologian of art seeks "to develop a systematic perspective on what artists are doing, why they are doing it, and what it means."[17] Such theologians are able to do this because they possess "myths and symbols which, to the eyes of faith, illuminate the human situation."[18] The Scriptures, holy books, and liturgies of the faith provide resources for the interpretation of the present experience of human beings, but it is in the arts that particular images emerge as helpful in interpreting experience.

Contemporary theologies of art focus on one of three great themes of the Christian message. These three themes include faith in the Creator, the message of the cross, and hope for the consummation. For each theologian, and for each layman, one of these three themes is most important for the Christian faith. One motif is dominant.

Should the artist's venture be understood primarily in context of man's origin or his end, his creation or his redemption, with reference to the Creator or to the fulfillment of all things in the Kingdom of God? Where can principles of discrimination or standards of criticism be found, in Genesis or in the gospel?[19]

A theology of art has been developed by some Christian theologians using each of these images as foundational. For example, Tillich views the arts in the light of the message of the cross; Berdyaev interprets them in view of the eschatological significance; and Maritain interprets the artist's work as a response to what the Creator has done.[20]

Theologians, however, do not have special privileges in interpreting poetry, music, or sculpture, privileges not enjoyed by ordinary persons. Although theologians may have greater stores of myths and symbols for use in interpretation, every person interprets artworks through his own unique situation, utilizing whatever myths, symbols, and models of Ultimate Reality he has acquired. Some see Death as an Avenging Angel, or the Grim Gray Reaper, the terror-evoking Rider on the Pale Horse. But some see Death as a sheltering, protective woman invoking no sense of the horrible in those she touches, as in the sculpture of Daniel Chester French. Käthe Kollwitz' "Woman Welcoming Death" (1934) seems to portray woman as the Universal Mother who welcomes death as a release from the suffering of the world. Her post-World War I lithographs and woodcuts "make us realize the truth that human misery is itself an unforgettable sign of human dignity."[21]

The symbol of the Crucifixion is portrayed variously in art works, helping persons experiencing the work to sort out their own feelings and thoughts and to find interpretations which fit their own situations. For many persons the crucifixion is tied unalterably to the

Christian faith, and it speaks to the question of Christ's humanity or divinity. The cover of the Carolingian Lindau Gospels (about 870 A.D.), for example, protrays a crucified Christ who shows no hint of pain or death. Christ appears to stand rather than to hang from the cross. There are no signs of suffering humanity in the Divine Figure. Such a suffering human being was unthinkable. But the Gero Crucifix (an Ottonian work about 975-1000 A.D.) depicts an image of the crucified Saviour showing the agony and strain of the cross. The heavy body bulges forward; the face is filled with agony; the arms and shoulders show strain. Here the crucified Saviour suffers as human beings suffer. These two views of the Crucifixion can be traced through the Byzantine mosaic in the Monastery Church at Daphne (11th c.) in which the figure and facial expression of Christ are devoid of pathos and the Saviour's divine wisdom and power are stressed, to Cimabue's Crucifixion (13th c. Arezzo, San Domenico) with its obvious sagging abdomen, agony of face, and grieving figures; and on to Grunewald's portrayal of the crucifixion on the Isenheim Altarpiece (c. 1510-15) with its twisted limbs, many lacerations, and streams of blood, yet on a heroic scale that denotes the more than human, bringing together in one work the two natures of Christ. The divine and human natures of Christ are further shown in the grieving figures. The three figures on the left of Christ mourn his death as a human, while on the right side John the Baptist points calmly to Christ as the Divine Savior.

More recent artists portray the crucifixion as speaking to the human condition. Roualt's Crucifixion from the Miserere Series (1922-27) with its heavy black lines giving a leaded effect, its massiveness of form, its flashes of light, and its absence of the trivial, seems to show not tragedy, but hope. One does not pity Jesus but one feels concern yet hopefulness in the face of the troubled life of humanity. Finally, in Chagall the crucified figure seems to symbolize every person's crucifixion, reminiscent of Tillich's view of the universality of the cross as a symbol. Speaking of Tillich's view, Harned comments:

> The story of the crucifixion offers a symbol through which the ontological awareness presupposed by every religious faith can become concrete without any distortion or loss of purity at all.[22]

Artists are concerned with the real, as are other human beings. They may see reality as subjective and specific; or they may see reality as objective and universal. Leamon has pointed out that Klee sees reality as the "inner essence of creation."[23] He used every possible phenomenon and experience as subject matter, interpreting the inner reality by his independent constructions of color, line, and form. Klee wrote that "Art does not reproduce what we see. It makes us see."[24] Leamon uses Klee's "Child Consecrated to Suffering" to illustrate how Klee evokes "the inner feeling, the inner reality, of a suffering child and his inwardness, patience, and pain." But he also shows how Braque's " Man With a Guitar" suggests that reality is the "mind's knowledge of nature." Whereas Klee's work is intuitive, irrational, and filled with feeling, Braque's work is logical, rational, objective. The guitarist is seen "as the artist's brain knows him, as an object—from many different viewpoints (above, below, behind, from all around)." The Dadists seem to interpret reality as "Man's folly and absurdity," as seen in Max Ernst's "The Gramineous Bicycle Garnished with Bells the Dopples Fire Damps and the Enchinoderms Bending the Spine to Caresses"; in the "Guernica" Picasso sees reality as "Man's inhumanity to man"; Edwardo Paolozzi's "St. Sebastian, No.2," a sculpture whose "visage reminds us of rubber factories, the backbone of war, ravaged by bombs," in which we see "hints of the dehumanized time-clock punching, assembly line consumer," speaks that reality is "the industrial technology in which man survives."[25]

Thus art provides both cognitive and affective models for the interpretation of experience.

RELIGIOUS EDUCATION AND THE FULFILLMENT OF THE PARTICIPATIVE EXPERIENCE

How shall religious education relate to these two functions of the participative experience? Realizing that the models of reality which various pupils bring to educational activities provide the framework within which they experience worship, study, social action, and communal activities, and realizing that the myths, symbols, rituals, and artifacts of religion provide a rich panorama of art works which are already entering into the experiences of the students and which have already, consciously or sub-consciously, been integrated into the way they view and respond to the Ultimate, how shall the religious educator relate art to religious development? Three obvious approaches present themselves immediately: (1) Experiences of enrichment which involve sight, sound, and tactile sensations can be promoted, including the creation of one's own art. (2) Experiences with works of art which are especially dynamic and helpful in luring one into the participative experience can be planned. (3) Experiences with a broad spectrum of art works will provide a rich variety of interpretations of reality against which the pupils and their leaders can test their own models and affirm or correct them.

If, indeed, experience must be "promoted"[26], then perceptual learning is a vital part of the religious education process. As Tobey states:

> Educators in recent years have laid stress on the need for perceptual experiences that will stimulate intellectual growth. Such sensory experiences involve a learner directly: it is he who does the touching, seeing, or tasting, not the teacher. As he becomes involved he learns. The more senses he uses the better he learns. As he expresses himself in the arts and languages, he clarifies and retains learning. Perceptual experiences are basic for building concepts and living a satisfying life with oneself, in relation to God, others, and the world.[27]

She describes a family Advent celebration in which persons used all their senses—tasting, touching, hearing, smelling, seeing—and comments that "The concept of the church grows with many experiences, planned and unplanned. Perceptual learning may make the concept one of warmth and happiness or it may bring negative meanings."[28] What children feel, taste, smell, hear, and see becomes part of them, and as they give expression to these experiences through color, form, word, and sound, they become art. "The foundation of scientific understanding and aesthetic appreciation and expression lies, then, in the small child's sensory experiences, which start long before nursery school."[29]

Fulfillment of the possibilities for affective learning through experiences involving many sensations can be found only if teachers and parents are willing to think of the whole person, rather than the mental faculties alone. In discussing film as one approach to affective education, Lacey states that "Even if screen education has gained a foothold, it will not be able to address the fundamental issues surrounding educational aims if teachers continue to stress grades, right answers, analytical but not expressive behavior, and the primacy of print."[30] Although religious education is not usually troubled by the restrictions of grades, it continues to be stifled by correct answers, based upon Biblical interpretations, historical traditions of the Church, or theological systems, as well as the primacy of print and almost complete dependence upon intellectual activity—in particular, memory. The suggestion here is to provide a wide variety of experiences involving the whole person. In religious education, experiences of touching, tasting, smelling, seeing, hearing, are often promoted for young children, but from the time children start to school there is a marked shift to mental experiences—hearing, reading, thinking, analyzing, writing. These are important activities, but the educative value of experiencing the wealth of the world's great art works is sadly neglected. If Babin is correct that "Modern man has experienced an extraordinary sensory development,"[31] and if McLuhan's theory is substantiated that a new kind of man has been emerging with electronic technology[32] (what Babin calls "the audiovisual man"), then art in its many forms—participation both in creating and in experiencing art works—is valuable for religious development of persons.

Experiences with art not only draw persons into the religious dimension and help to interpret religious experience, but they may provide valuable insights into the development of pupils. Recently a religious educator elicited comments[33] on several pictures from parochial school children and young people representing different developmental stages—Pre-school, third grade, seventh grade, and high school Seniors. The pictures included such acknowledged works of art as El Greco's "A View of Toledo", but also included some magazine pictures. One such picture showed trees in the forest with one falling tree in the foreground, obvious only as a blurred diagonal line. The comments of the children and youth not only corroborated the cognitive developmental stages of Piaget and others, the transition from concrete to abstract thinking becoming evident with the movement into adolescence, but also showed a shift in feelings and attitudes toward the pictures. The pre-school children answered excitedly, and their faces were usually happy. Third graders, who had recently been studying ecology, saw all the pictures from an ecological viewpoint, relating dark skies to pollution, for example. But the high school Seniors were rather indifferent to the pictures, not interested in interpreting them. As one youth commented, "I don't want to be bothered with it." Yet these same young people had responded enthusiastically to a discussion held just previously to the viewing of the pictures. Their attitude may reflect the primacy given to intellectual activity as young people develop, but it also raises a question as to whether religious educators are training young people away from responding to the visual arts, making if difficult for the arts to draw them into depth experiences and to provide clues to the interpretation of those experiences.

In El Greco's "A View of Toledo", the pre-school children saw a castle rather than a church. They saw the darkness as more "spooky" than gloom. It was "a haunted house." No comments related it to God or to the divine. The third graders exhibited much literal interpretation and concrete thought, and, of course, related the picture to their knowledge of ecology. They expressed such ideas as: "There has been a storm. Storms do damage," and "Ecology is happening." The sky was called "polluted." Again, they did not relate the picture to the divine. Seventh graders, on the other hand, demonstrated that they were becoming capable of abstract and religious thought. One boy said the picture was symbolic of hate, because of "the black and the gloom." When questioned further, he interpreted this as "not God but a lack of God." Then the rest of the class took up this idea and added the concepts of a lack of love of God, sin, and devil possession. The Seniors saw nothing of the divine, but one mockingly said that the church was "something religious." When pressed, they did see "hate" in the darkness, and one person said he saw in the clouds strength "which would remind me of God in essence." Religions are only beginning to explore this potential in art for helping persons to experience the Ultimate, to sense the real, and to find the meaning of life.

The possibilities for art to aid in interpreting life's experiences can be seen in an anecdote told about Albert Einstein. He was asked one day to describe the theory of relativity in simple words, so the questioner might catch at least a glimpse of its meaning. Einstein responded, "I cannot do what you request. But if you will call on me at Princeton, I will play it for you on my violin." Is it possible in religious education to come to the point that all experiences do not need to be verbalized, that understanding can come through feeling? Perhaps experiences with art (both involvement in creating art and with art works) can add this dimension to the religious development of the persons with whom religious educators deal.

Notes

1. Paul Pruyser, *A Dynamic Psychology of Religion* (New York: Harper & Row, 1968), pp. 139-140.

2. *Ibid.*, Chapter II, "Perceptual Processes in Religion."

3. *Ibid.*, p. 30.

4. Bennett Reimer, "The Religious in the Arts," *Religious Education*, 60 (1965), 310.

5. *Ibid.*

6. *Ibid.*

7. David B. Harned, *Theology and the Arts* (Philadelphia: Westminster Press, 1966), p. 16.

8. Editorial Introduction to the Special Issue: "Contemporary Art and Christian Education," *International Journal of Religious Education*, 42 (1966), 2.

9. F. David Martin, *Art and the Religious Experience: The "Language" of the Sacred* (Lewisburg, Pa.: Bucknell University Press), p. 91; see also Ch. 3-6.

10. *Ibid.*, pp. 27-28.

11. Roger Hazelton, *A Theological Approach to Art* (Nashville and New York: Abingdon Press, 1967), p. 31.

12. Sophia Fahs, *Today's Children and Yesterday's Heritage* (Boston: Beacon Press, 1952), p. 171.

13. Gloria Durka and Joanmarie Smith, "Modeling and Experience," *Luman Vitae* 32 (1977), 46.

14. *Ibid.*

15. Lillian Williams, "Beauty from Rubbish," *International Journal of Religious Education*, 42 (1966), 3.

16. *Ibid.*

17. Harned, p. 18.

18. *Ibid.*

19. *Ibid.*, pp. 19-20.

20. *Ibid.*, pp. 20-22.

21. Hazelton, p. 32.

22. Harned, p. 56.

23. Thomas J. Leamon, "The Search for the Real," *International Journal of Religious Education*, 42 (1966), 10.

24. Jurg Spiller, *Klee* (Dezenter: Ysel Press, Ltd., 1963), p. 13.

25. Illustrations of artists' portrayals of reality taken from Leamon, *ibid.*, pp. 8-17.

26. Durka and Smith, p. 5.

27. Kathrene M. Tobey, *Learning and Teaching Through the Senses* (Philadelphia: Westminster Press, 1970).

28. *Ibid.*, p. 16.

29. *Ibid.*, p. 17.

30. Richard A. Lacey, *Seeing with Feeling: Film in the Classroom* (Philadelphia: W. B. Saunders Co., 1972), p. 6.

31. Pierre Babin, ed., *The Audio Visual Man* (Dayton: Pflaum, 1970), p. 24.

32. See Marshall McLuhan, *Understanding Media: The Extensions of Man* (New York: New American Library, 1964).

33. A recent study conducted privately by Patricia Murphy, Assistant Director, Religious Education Division, Diocese of Bridgeport, Ct., with the cooperation of the Graduate Department of Religious Studies and the Graduate School of Communications, Fairfield University, Fairfield, Ct.

Suggested Readings

Babin, Pierre (ed.), *The Audio-Visual Man*. Dayton, Ohio: Pflaum, 1970.

"Contemporary Art and Christian Education," Special Issue, *International Journal of Religious Education*, Vol. 42, No. 6, February, 1966.

Harned, David B., *Theology and the Arts*. Philadelphia, Pa.: Westminster Press, 1966.

Hazelton, Roger, *A Theological Approach to Art*. Nashville and New York: Abingdon Press, 1967.

Lacey, Richard A., *Seeing With Feeling: Film in the Classroom*. Philadelphia: W. B. Saunders Co., 1972.

Martin, F. David, *Art and the Religious Experience: The "Language" of the Sacred*. Lewisburg, Pa.: Bucknell University Press, 1972.

Pruyser, Paul, *A Dynamic Psychology of Religion*. New York: Harper & Row, 1968.

Tobey, Kathrene M., *Learning and Teaching Through the Senses*. Philadelphia: Westminster Press, 1970.

4.
Notes on Wholeness

Paul E. Bumbar

In this essay, Paul Bumbar describes how the right hemisphere, the locus of musical expression for most people, is the domain of the non-rational dimension of human existence which includes one's emotional life. Emotions are not unique to individuals, but are characteristic of the race, and transcend culture and time. As part of our biological inheritance, and as components of our genetic make-up, emotions assume definite forms which accomplished composers can translate into musical expression and cause to be communicated to the listeners who, in recognizing and resonating with the emotions, can be made one and whole.

This is the point to which, above all, the attention of our rulers should be directed—that music and gymnastics be preserved in their original form and no innovation made . . . musical innovation is full of danger to the State and ought to be prohibited. So Damon tells me, and I can quite believe him; he says that when modes of music change, the fundamental laws of the State always change with them. (Plato, *The Republic*, Bk. IV)

Had there been any doubts or skepticism over the validity of Damon's caveat concerning musical innovations they should be dispelled and forever laid to rest in the light of events on the American musical scene over the past two decades. In particular, Elvis Presley's death, in August, 1977, was a forceful reminder of the impact which a particular type of music (rock and roll) had on the musical preferences and social mores of the generation which was growing through adolescence in the mid-fifties. News of Presley's death sent shock waves throughout the country and around the world. Stores were besieged for copies of his records, posters of his image and books on his life. Record companies and publishers could scarcely meet the demand, and furiously scrambled to make more and add to the estimated $4.3 billion produced by the sale of Elvis' records and albums during his 22 year career as "the King." More than any one person Presley changed the course of popular music in America and in the countries where it was played. He was truly a king to his legions of followers which in the end numbered not only those in their thirties when he died but scores of those not even born in 1956 when he shocked the nation and electrified a generation with his rendition of "Heartbreak Hotel" on the nationally televised "Ed Sullivan Show." Parents and adults were angered, but their indignation was no match for the adulation of the youth of America. Accompanied by their screams of delight, the generation gap took a quantum leap.

What caused the upheaval? Simply stated, Presley was a prophet. He spoke for an entire generation. His music spoke directly to his fans of the emotions (love, hate, sex, anger, fear) which they experienced every day and which, until now, lacked a musical expression which was valid for them. Along with being a frontal attack on the musical and social conventions of the time, Presley's music possessed the unique power to touch certain emotions with such force that his fans, along with their idol, were "all shook up."

The power of Presley's music to touch and charge the emotions was perceived by many (i.e., most of those well past their teens) to be insidious and irrational. "What do you see in him?" was the plaintive cry of many a distraught parent. In so phrasing the question they proved that they would never quite understand. It was not what their children *saw* (although that was part of the act), it was what they *felt* coming through the music (and movements) that had such power. For parents to seek rational explanations for their children's ecstatic response to Presley's overtures to their non-rational, emotional selves, was to miss the point entirely—much in the same vein as the interviewer who once asked Louis Armstong for a definition of jazz, and had to be told by Satchmo that if he needed a definition of jazz he would never understand it.

The emotional origins and effects of music cut across time and cultures. Presley was not entirely unique in the annals of music. The Beatles would have a similar effect on the youth and music of the sixties, and while people swooned over Sinatra in the forties, Bach's organ recitals are said to have had similar emotional impact on audiences of the eighteenth century. This essay will investigate this phenomenon from a psychological and sociological perspective. The psychology of music will be examined in the light of recent studies concerning the physiology of the brain and processes of perception, as well as "sentics," the science of the communication of emotion. Sociological observations will focus on popular American music and point out that while music is a universal language, it has distinct dialects which "speak to" and help define certain cultural groupings. Finally, some practical considerations will be drawn and related to (religious) education and worship.

In brief, there is a non-rational, intuitive and feeling dimension to the self that education and worship have traditionally neglected, and which music has a unique power to touch, give expression to, make whole, and expand. This essay explores some of the ways this is possible.

Increased research on the physiology of the brain has explored many questions on the functioning of the brain—how we assimilate, process and communicate information. In doing so, the research has left many questions unanswered and uncovered even more. From all the data and experiments two conclusions seem to have ineluctably emerged: (1) consciousness is dual in nature, that is, the human brain is composed of two hemispheres which perform different functions practically independently of one another, and (2) "the psyche seems inextricably embedded in the physiology of the brain" (Sage, 1976).

Pioneering work on bilateral specialization has been done by Roger Sperry, for Cal Tech, on end-stage epileptics whose hemispheres had been surgically severed as a means of controlling their seizures. For over twenty years he and his colleague, J.E. Bogen, as well as Philip Vogel, have investigated the physiology of the brain. Their experiments have consistently shown the left hemisphere, or left brain, to be the more "rational" hemisphere which assimilates information in piecemeal fashion, processes it in a linear way, and carries on verbal and mathematical reasoning. The right brain has been found to be "non-verbal," perceiving images as gestalts, in an holistic manner, processing information spatially in an intuitive manner, and functioning as the locus of creative and artistic capabilities and appreciation of forms of music. In terms of their functioning, the two halves of the brain are asymmetrical, yet complementary: "the left hemisphere analyzes over time . . . and possesses a phonological analyzer . . . whereas the right hemisphere synthesizes over space . . . and possesses a gestalt synthesizer"

(Neville, 1976). It might be simplistic, but not totally inaccurate, to say that the left brain specializes in language and logic, while the right brain specializes in intuition and insight.

It is a rather well-known fact that the motor functions of the right side of the body are usually controlled by the left hemisphere, and those of the left side by the right hemisphere. It has also been discovered that both hemispheres have access to, and can control, the body's motor functions, but when one hemisphere is thus involved, the other hemisphere is precluded from gaining access to the same system. Each hemisphere is capable of directing body functions (as proved by people having only one hemisphere) but they cannot perform the same function simultaneously. Moreover, while one hemisphere is engrossed in performing one of its functions, it cannot attend fully to the performance of another function. In conjunction with this, Sperry points out that "we sometimes deliberately put the right hand (left brain) to a task like doing a tic-tac-toe or sketching or rolling balls, just to keep it out of the picture so we can get to the right hemisphere" (Sage, 1976). Engaging the left brain in motor functions seems to be a way of clearing the circuits for right-brain thought. Witness the number of people who maintain that they can think better when they are doing something. It is not so much that they are thinking better, as they are engaging nonordinary thought processes.

Sperry's experiments with individuals having surgically separated hemispheres led to the discovery that each hemisphere appears to have its own sensations, perceptions, thoughts, feelings, and memories. Each seems to have its own "world" cut off from the consciousness of the other or, as he puts it, "two separate minds, that is, with two separate spheres of consciousness" (Sage, 1976). These two separate seats of consciousness exist side by side, each oblivious of the other. They both perceive through the same senses and thereby basically experience the same reality, but they perceive, process and utilize it differently. There appears to be some "cross communication" between the hemispheres of individuals with normal, i.e., unseparated, brains but exactly how this is accomplished is not fully understood as yet.

To demonstrate this silent coexistence, Sperry conducted experiments using a special lens called a "Z-lens," whereby pictures could be flashed upon the subject's retina in such a way that the visual image would fall only on that portion of the retina which relayed information, in this case, to the right hemisphere. Sporadically, in a series of innocuous photographs, a picture of a nude body would be shown to the right hemisphere only. The subject would react, e.g., blush, but verbally (i.e., with the left hemisphere) deny that anything had happened. In fact the subject was telling the truth. The left hemisphere had not perceived the provocative photo. The right hemisphere had, and communicated the awareness by using a form of "body language" (blushing) since it, unlike the left brain, cannot put words together sequentially and in an interdependent manner, i.e., speak. The right brain, therefore, can perceive or fantasize something apart from the left hemisphere which will have an emotional effect on a person and for which the person will have no "rational" explanation. This finding accounts for the truism, "There is no accounting for taste." Presley's young fans could not ever really explain to their parents what they saw in him because they could not fully explain it even to themselves. In an intuitive way, however, they knew. The fact that humans cannot verbally express roughly half of what their central nervous system might be experiencing is certainly more than an adequate justification for the existence of the arts and music. In fact it necessitates their existence.

Language's relative clarity and conciseness, however, have made logical, sequential thought the most common means of communication, especially in the Western world. This reliance on language led to the left hemisphere's being refered to as the "dominant hemisphere." The question, however, must be asked, "Dominant in what respect?" Certainly for language. Recent studies have determined that 99.6% of right-handed adults have a left-hemispheric dominance for language (Barroso, 1976). But language is not the sole reason for the brain's existence. Preoccupation with verbal expression and thought has contributed to the downplaying, and outright neglect, of the value and necessity of the functions of the "silent hemisphere." Neuropsychology views even the use of language to be "a human peculiarity which is secondary to and which makes explicit the mental processes of conceptualization" (Neville, 1976). There are other cerebral functions, equally necessary and important for human existence, for which 99.6% of right-handed adults have right-hemispheric dominance. Language is not an end in itself, nor is speech and logical thought the sole "raison d'être" of the brain.

The experiments of Sperry and others are strongly supported by the research done by Robert E. Ornstein, a psychologist, and his colleague, David Galin, a physician. Their experiments recorded the alpha rhythms produced in each hemisphere while a subject was performing different tasks. An increase in alpha rhythms signals that the brain is at rest, while a decrease is a sign of increased mental activity. They found that when subjects write letters, the electroencephalograph records a notable increase of alpha rhythms in the right hemisphere, whereas when they are arranging blocks increased alpha rhythms are recorded in the left hemisphere (Kiester, 1976). Since the initial experiments, hundreds similar have been performed, all with basically the same results.

It is also known that not all brains function exactly alike. Electroencephalograph recordings of normal individuals indicate that even they "seem to have a different brain organization from one another," that is, there are differences between left and right-handed people, those who are ambidextrous, and some simply have reversed brain functions (Kiester, 1976). In all cases, however, it was consistently found that ordinary people use their brains in an asymmetrical manner, switching from one hemisphere to the other depending on the task at hand and the cognitive processes involved.

There are no simple answers to the questions as to why and how this occurs. It is known, however, that lateralization or hemispheric specialization already exists in two-day-old infants, who seem "to be instinctively lateralized to process language" because they respond differently to speech syllables as compared to nonspeech sounds (Buck, 1976). The asymmetrical functioning of the brain, therefore, is a given of human existence and not something into which we are environmentally conditioned. It is physiological, genetically inherited, and constant.

Bilateral specialization also seems to be sexually determined. This male–female difference is noted in the different responses made to humor. Women react intuitively and make judgments on the basis of feelings. They show a right hemisphere dominance. Men, however, analyze and make judgments on the basis of conclusions. They display left hemisphere dominance. Furthermore, hearing tests give evidence that "men have a greater degree of one-sided specialization—or hemispheric lateralization (in this case usually left-hemispheric predominance)—than women, and that the difference is neurological, not cultural" (Buck, 1976). It is perhaps, therefore, not that women are more "frivolous and emotional" (read "intuitive") than men, but that men's greater degree of neurologically determined lateralization makes it more difficult for them to have access to and express right-hemispheric conceptualizations, i.e., intuition and holistic thoughts.

In addition to heredity and sex, drugs seem to affect dominance. Alcohol seems to deplete right-hemisphere related skills, while marijuana appears to produce a shift of the higher level cognitive functions (those requiring logic or verbal skills) from the sequential thought processes of the left hemisphere to the spatial and abstract processes of the right hemisphere. Low level functions (simple recognition tasks) show no such shift, possibly because these functions are processed automatically to either hemisphere (Buck, 1976). This greater accessibility to right-hemispheric thought is perhaps the motivation behind individuals' using certain drugs. Andrew Weil postulates an innate, normal drive to periodically alter consciousness. It is "a real drive arising from the neurophysiological structure of the brain" and can be satisfied in any number of ways, drugs perhaps being the most common, along with sex (Weil, 1972). In the present context, Weil's "altered consciousness" might be read as right-hemisphere consciousness, with drugs a convenient way to experience it.

There are, however, perhaps other, more acceptable and potentially less dangerous ways to enter into and heighten right-hemisphere consciousness. It does not seem merely coincidental that the rise of the drug culture of the sixties was accompanied by the birth and proliferation of hard rock music, a music which is noteworthy in its sound and intensity. Since the right hemisphere is the locus of artistic and musical processes, the Hippies stoned on marijuana or LSD and experiencing a shift to right-hemisphere thought processes would have the experience heightened and possibly prolonged by the intensity of the sounds centered in their right hemisphere.

It is an established fact that for almost all right-handed individuals the right hemisphere dominates over the left in the processing of musical sounds. Doctors Bogen and Gordon of the California Institute of Technology conducted experiments wherein they selectively and temporarily paralyzed alternate hemispheres of their subjects. When the left hemisphere was drugged, the person was able to sing normally, but when the right hemisphere was paralyzed, pitch and intonation were uncontrolled. Interestingly enough, rhythm and lyrics remained unaffected throughout. The reason adduced is that rhythm seems to be controlled by lower-level, more automatic processes common to both hemispheres. Similarly, lyrics in songs constitute what is "automatic language," that is, they require no interpretative skills, no sequential processing by the left hemisphere. There are recorded instances of individuals who have had their entire left brain removed (because of tumors) who could no longer speak, but who could still sing songs as well as ever (Buck, 1976). Other experiments have verified the locus of musical ability to commonly be the right hemisphere since time, pitch, loudness, timbre and tonal memory are more adversely affected in patients with right-hemisphere lesions (Neville, 1976).

Once again, this lateralization for sound is physiologically and genetically determined. It is present at birth. While there is some dispute as to whether the auditory system in humans is functional before birth (there are indications it is), it is generally acknowledged that newly-born infants can localize and process sound. Certain other auditory functions, however, are acquired only during late childhood (8-10), thus making the full development of hearing a relatively long process (Selmes and Whitaker, 1976). In brief, the capacity to process sound is present from the beginning, is lateralized, and, like most other human capacities, proceeds through stages of development. The same can be said of the capacity for that most sophisticated of sounds, music. The infant can certainly hear e.g., Prokofieff, but does not "understand" or appreciate Prokofieff, firstly because the infant does not have a fully developed sense of sound, and secondly, and more importantly, because the infant lacks the emotional maturity, or the matrix of feelings and experiences, which the music can touch and resonate with. This brings us to the next main point of this essay, i.e., the psychology of music or, "what's the difference between 'hearing' and 'listening to' music?"

To understand the development of musical expression and appreciation in individuals, it is helpful to recall a model of the acquisition of language which was first proposed by Eric Lenneberg and has since then been espoused by not a few notable psycholinguists (Rieber, 1976). In this model, one may look at the capacity for language much as one would view a physical capacity. Language acquisition (in line with what we have thus far discussed concerning the asymmetrical functioning of the brain's hemispheres) has a physiological foundation and is genetically determined. This does not mean to say that language as such pre-exists in the brain, something which is inherited from one's parents like the color of one's skin, or skeletal structure. What is inherited by all members of the human race (and scientists are exploring to what extent non-humans possess it) is a capacity for language, a physiological and genetically determined "apparatus" for organizing and giving meaning to the experiences of the individual. Many linguists refer to these innate mechanisms as "universal grammar." Universal grammar is not a grammar as such, and Chomsky describes it as "an underlying biological matrix that provides a framework within which the growth of language proceeds" or "a system of conditions on the range of possible grammars for possible human languages" (Rieber, 1976). The important point is that language capacity has a biological basis. It is therefore "limited" by the physiological processes of the human brain and subject to its laws of development.

Once again, this development appears to have distinct stages. There is an initial genetically determined state of mind, common to all (apart from instances of pathology), and this initial state, according to its set of experiences, passes through stages until it arrives at a "steady state," at a relatively fixed age, and then changes only marginally. "The initial state of mind might be regarded as a function . . . which maps experience into the steady state. Universal grammar is a partial characteristic of this function . . . The grammar of a language that has grown in the mind is a partial characterization of the steady state attained" (Chomsky, in Rieber, 1976). Stated in other terms, the mind, in this model, is still adequately described by the Scholastic metaphor of the "tabula rasa," but emerging issues concerning the functioning of the brain in language acquisition and utilization are making increasingly clear the critical role of the "tabula" in determining what the interactions between the subject and the world will inscribe on the "tabula." Language development is only specified by individual experience. Its possibilities are determined initially by the biological matrix of the brain, and our genetic inheritance.

Independently, but very much along similar lines, there is emerging a model for understanding the nature and function of musical expression and communication. Pioneering work in this field has been done by Manfred Clynes, a concert pianist and neurophysiologist who worked with computers after he had earned his master's degree in music and doctorate in physiology. In combining his interests and training, Clynes developed a field of study that he termed "sentics," meaning "the science of the communication of emotion through natural, biologic forms in time and space" or, more specifically, "the scientific study of genetically programmed musical expression" (Clynes, 1974, 1977). His work represents a novel and important effort to understand the physiological basis for the reciprocal causality between emotions and music.

One of the primary functions of the human nervous system is the construction of an internal model of the outside world. This internal model is necessary so that we might live in the world and communicate with everything outside of ourselves. According to neuroscientist Harry J. Jerison, the perception of sound is central to our ability to do this and "the early mammal's sense of hearing was both primary and critical in shaping human consciousness as we know it" (quoted in Fincher, 1977). Manfred Clynes attempts to explain how musical expression helps in the construction and communication of those fundamental and inseparable parts of human consciousness called emotions.

To conduct his studies, Clynes devised a special computer hooked up with an electroencephalograph which would record and average out all the electrical emanations from the brain. He called it the Computer of Average Transients, CAT for short. Using the CAT, he discovered that when individuals perceive colors and shapes, their brains register electrical patterns that are unique, reliable, and recurring. Most importantly, these electrical patterns are "the same in certain key respects for all subjects" (Fincher, 1977). In other words, by looking at the readout from the CAT it is possible to determine what was physically being perceived, regardless of who was doing the perceiving. Stimulated by this discovery, Clynes then hypothesized that the same commonality of electrical response might hold true for the perception of emotion.

To test this hypothesis, Clynes used a transducer attached to the computer to record the up-down and toward-away movements of a person's fingertips when the person fantasizes a given emotion, e.g., joy. Clynes chose to use the fingertip in an attempt to minimize body movement and therefore measure the dynamic quality of an emotion rather than its form of bodily expression. When these tracings were averaged out and plotted by the computer, there emerged separate and distinct shapes or forms for the seven emotions (anger, sex, love, grief, hate, joy, and reverence) which the subjects had been asked to imagine. These forms remained relatively constant and unique for all subjects. They were recognizable even in different cultures such as Mexico, Japan, and Bali. Because the expression of a particular fantasized emotion shows such constancy, Clynes concludes that humans possess "biologically determined expressions (of emotion) that are programmed into us." He calls these natural, biologic forms whereby emotion is expressed "essentic forms" (Clynes, 1974). They are the most basic forms of universal human emotions. To some extent, they might be compared to the "universal grammar" of the psycholinguists. It is because of the commonality of essentic forms that people from different cultures can understand the emotional state of another person speaking in a language foreign to their comprehension.

Counseling psychology maintains that the level of emotional, as contrasted with merely verbal, communication is a higher (or deeper) level of communication and represents that authentic communication which makes an individual "one-with" the other. Clynes sees a biological basis in this: "Inherent data-processing programs of the central nervous system are biologically coordinated so that a precisely produced essentic form is correspondingly recognized" (in Fincher, 1977). We know when others are upset with us, are "out of sorts," are attracted or repelled by us, etc., by tone of voice and subtle mannerisms which communicate the essentic form of the emotions they are feeling. And we tend to feel the same emotion in ourselves. Emotions are truly contagious.

Beyond idiosyncratic gestures and culturally conditioned forms of expression, there is a commonality of emotional expression which transcends time and place. It is part of our genetic inheritance, and constitutes the "universal grammar" of human emotions. Music, as shall be shown, is a universal language of this matrix of emotions.

Along with essentic forms, Clynes has tried to define the nature of the reality of which essentic forms are but the expression. In doing so he coined a word, "idiolog," and defined it as "a single, natural thought of a quality, such as sweet, red, or anger, together with certain electrical and chemical correlates in the brain" (1974). In an almost crypto-Cartesian fashion, an idiolog might be considered the "clearest idea" of that particular quality, with the clarity and distinctness of the idiolog being a touchstone of communication: "We communicate . . . qualities to one another and to ourselves through the production and recognition of precise forms" (Clynes, 1976). The two concepts, therefore, are central to Clynes' essentic model: idiologs (the clearest idea of a quality) and essentic forms (the biologically determined expressions of emotional qualities).

After he had clarified these notions, Clynes, impelled no doubt by his musical background and training, hypothesized that "a limited number of innate organizing principles were involved . . . (which) must influence the exact shape of musical images in a preprogrammed way just as our genes . . . the shape of the kidney" (in Fincher, 1977). For Clynes, there had to be a genetic base for shaping emotion and expressing it through musical images with the listener a kind of repository for the platonic archetypes of these musical images.

These hypotheses became conclusions when Clynes asked musicians to register, on a transducer attached to a computer, the movements they felt when they were thinking certain pieces of music in real time, as though they were conducting or playing them. In 1928 Gustav Becking, a German musicologist, had noted that an expert musician, upon hearing (or imagining) music, rhythmically moves a hand in the air, not aimlessly, but in patterns which, when analyzed, prove to be characteristic of that composer's work. Clynes' computer experiments verified Becking's observations. Just as fantasized emotions produced characteristic and distinct forms, the computer-analyzed movements of different sensitive musicians "feeling" the same piece of music were recorded as essentially the same curves.

Beethoven's inner pulse, for example, was measured by Clynes by having himself and other sensitive musicians (including Casals and Serkin) to imagine Beethoven's Opus 109, and to transmit the felt music by "conducting" with their finger on a transducer which recorded the musical pulse. When this data was averaged with a computer, Beethoven's inner pulse assumed a definite, constant shape, regardless of which musician was doing the "conducting." Even more importantly, Beethoven's inner pulse remained the same throughout his different compositions, so that the computer-averaged inner pulse for Opus 13 was practically identical to that of Opus 109. Similar experiments were done with the works of Mozart, Schubert, Wagner, Prokofieff, Mahler, Schumann, Tchaikovsky, Ravel, and Debussy, all with similar results (Clynes, 1974). In other words, it seems that composers do have a characteristic emotional rhythm imbedded in their works and this emotional rhythm is an essential aspect of the composer's identity which is transmitted in all the composer's works, making it thus musically impossible to insert fragments of one composer's work into another composer's. It is analogous to a writer's "style".

The inner pulse is internal to the composition insofar as it is not explicit in the notes, but felt by the sensitive ear, i.e., right brain. This pulse might be described as the psychological or existential stance of the particular composer. Composers are always expressing fundamental human emotions but from different points of view, that of actor or spectator, and either with a view toward the past, present, or future. Although Clynes found Beethoven's pulse to be substantially the same throughout the composer's works, the power of Beethoven's later music had "changed from the strength of opposition and ethical restraint, to the strength, security, and peace of being at home in the wonder of existence." Beethoven's stance is primarily that of an actor in the present, while Mozart is a spectator in the present, and Schubert is an actor with future expectations (Clynes, 1974).

The personality of a composer comes through in the compositions because, regardless of the composer or the composition, music is "a form of communication that transmits emotion and speaks about emotion in precise ways" (Clynes, 1974). Musical images are carriers of emotional qualities in themselves, but even more so insofar as they recall images of similar feelings in the perceiver. Composers make sound structures out of expressions of emotional qualities, performers recognize and reproduce them, and listeners recognize and resonate with them. The idiolog (emotional quality) that is felt by the composer finds a biologically determined and universally recognizable expression (essentic form) in a unique musical composition which in turn evokes the same emotional response from the listener, much in the same way as the string of a guitar will sympathetically vibrate when the note of similar pitch is struck on a nearby piano. It may seem to some as a rather haphazard means of communication, in comparison to the "clarity" and "exactness" of words, but Clynes' work in identifying emotional rhythms in music is demonstrating that Aaron Copland was quite correct in maintaining that music is "the unwritten Esperanto of the emotions" and that Felix Mendelssohn had an intuitive grasp of the essence of music when he said: "People often complain that music is too ambiguous, whereas everyone understands words. With me it is exactly the reverse. The thoughts which are expressed to me by music are not too indefinite to put into words, but too definite" (Fincher, 1977).

It must be remembered, however, that just as only the guitar string will resonate that is tuned to the pitch of the note struck on the piano, the listener will emotionally resonate with the composer to the extent that the listener is "in tune with" the composer. The fact that human emotions are universal and trans-cultural and the fact that music is the language of "a specific inborn design for each emotion . . . programmed into the nervous system inherently" (Clynes, 1977), should theoretically clear the way for all forms of music to be understood by all humans because we all share the same emotions of which musical forms are but the conveyors. The reality, however, is that some individuals, e.g., children, may be emotionally immature and therefore unable to recognize and resonate with the emotions(s) expressed through the composition, much in the same way as many high school students find the plays of Shakespeare tedious because they have not yet experienced, at all or not in depth, the emotion expressed therein, and the drama and meaning of the Bard become confused in stanzas of strange-sounding language. Other individuals might have the depth of emotional experience necessary to appreciate the music, but for various reasons refuse to recognize and give expression to these feelings in themselves. The response of most adults to Elvis Presley would seem to be an example of this. According to Clynes (1974), musicians use the language of essentic forms "in order to communicate emotions and qualities to others who recognize the language." Louis Armstrong was right in recognizing the futility of giving a definition of jazz.

Recognition of essentic forms by the listener is not the only touchstone of musical expression. Performers, as mentioned previously, must also express the inner pulse of the composer with precision. Musical precision refers to a musician's ability to reproduce the inwardly heard form of the emotion and not to mere faithful rhythmic reproduction of the written score. Precision of feelings must accompany precision of execution, and without the former, the latter is merely a technical exercise, not musical expression. Modestly talented amateur musicians often exemplify this, and those who have sat through children's recitals can testify that boredom is the emotion which often prevails in such instances.

The most talented musicians are those who can most faithfully produce purity of essentic forms, and the purest essentic forms are those that are most readily and universally recognizable. In other words, musical talent firstly depends on the musicians' ability to feel the emotion which gave rise to the music and then communicate it to others. The great composers are those who can create unambiguous musical expressions of emotional qualities. Emotional fidelity in both cases must take precedence over technical precision. Technical competence is necessary but not sufficient in creating authentic musical expression.

A talented musician's ability to resonate with the composer's inner pulse on the other hand can quite inadvertently culminate in technical precision to a degree not consciously attainable. Arturo Toscanini made three separate recordings of the "Brahms-Haydn Variations," in 1935, 1938, and in 1948 which were noteworthy in themselves, but also in their similarity. The total elapsed time for the first performance was sixteen minutes and forty-four seconds. Three years later, Toscanini altered his conception of one of the "Variations". The total length was 16:50.6. Ten years later, Toscanini's conception of the "Variations" had not changed and the performance totaled 16:50.3, or less than half a second difference from the recording made ten years earlier. Deliberate effort and memory cannot account for such precision. "It was the precision of feelings that led to Toscanini's precision of execution" (Clynes, 1974).

Musical precision, in execution and in feeling, in addition to communicating emotion, carries within itself the power to transform the listener, to alter consciousness. When there is correspondence between the musical sounds produced and the listener's emotional state or mental hearing, a kind of emotional ecstasy results. When the perceived sounds exceed the listener's expectations, musical experience can become mind-expanding and alter "our capacities and our sense of discrimination and our values" (Clynes, 1974). Manfred Clynes and Damon are in agreement. The fans of Presley, the Beatles, and Sinatra, as well as the devotees of Bach, all of whom were beside themselves with joy, or in a frenzy, or in a swoon, give evidence of the power of music to transform. This promise of ecstasy and transcendence (or "blowing one's mind") is perhaps music's greatest allure, and corresponds to Weil's innate, natural drive to periodically alter consciousness, or in the present context, the need to experience and express "right-hemisphere" cognitive functions. To fill this need, people will always find some form of musical expression, and some of them will always be searching out new forms. Damon's caveat, therefore, is futile.

Even though there is a commonality and universality to human emotion, not all individuals are attracted to and/or moved to the same degree by a particular type of music. Even though all persons are one in the commonality of emotion expressed by music, there are individual preferences in music. This can be explained in part by recalling Lunneberg's model of language acquisition: language capacity is determined by the physiology of the brain and its innate mechanisms, which the possibilities for human language can develop. The same might also be said for musical expression. Just as individual experience serves to specify which language(s) shall emerge from the matrix of the universal grammar, so too individual experience and cultural conditioning may be said to specify the forms of musical expression which spring from the "universal musical mode." The Phrygian mode of music, the only scale with which most Westerners are familiar, is but one specific form of musical language. Oriental music generally sounds strange to occidental ears but it is nonetheless an effective means of expressing universal human emotions. The style and type of music, therefore, that one prefers depends on a number of variables, one's experience, education, expectations, as well as emotional maturity, state and needs.

This preference, however, is not necessarily static, and can vary. It varies quite often over a person's lifetime, and it can vary from day to day. Sometimes an individual will choose to listen to semiclassical, and other times will prefer rock. Rarely does an adult's record collection contain strictly one kind of music, and often car radio buttons will be set for stations which play differing types of music. This kind of musical variation is a function of the listener's emotional state and represents an attempt to either reinforce an existing emotional state or to substitute another for it.

Since musical expression is extremely comprehensive in the range of human emotions that it conveys, the particular form which one prefers will depend to a great extent on cultural conditioning and what one has grown accustomed to. To learn to appreciate and be sensitive to new forms of music is akin to learning a new language. In fact it is often more difficult for people to change musical preferences, whose origins are buried in the "irrational" right brain, than it would be for them to learn a new language, whose rules are rooted in the "rational" left brain. The history of music bears witness to this observation. Leopold Stokowski, one of the giants of music in our, or any other century, risked his reputation in introducing the works of Stravinsky, Shostakovich and Schonberg. After prolonged initial resistance they are now a part of modern orchestral repertoire. On the popular musical scene similar delayed acceptance was accorded innovative musical styles, like Presley's and the Beatles'. There seems to be, therefore, very little basis for asserting an intrinsic superiority of one form of music over another, of classical, for example, over jazz. Both are valid means of expressing and conveying emotion. The Boston Pops under Arthur Fielder has consistently mixed popular and classical music in its repertoire, to the chagrin of some critics but the almost universal delight of its audiences. It would seem that the primary criterion for judging music ought be, a la Clynes, the precision with which it expresses the emotion which gave it birth. "The Blues," therefore, as an accurate expression of sadness, grief, loss, and hurt, is no less important in the spectrum of musical sound than the sweeping majesty of Beethoven, and to summarily dismiss one form of musical expression because it is not "classical" is to run the risk of impoverishing one's emotional repertoire. Stokowski could appreciate rock, and jazz, and Sinatra. "The history of popular music," he said, "shows that it is the true art form of the people" (in Saal, 1977). This is so because it gives expression and meaning to the felt emotions and the ineffable substratum (i.e., right-brain dimension) of daily existence.

In different cultures and in different times musical expression will vary. Thus Oriental music differs from Western and medieval differs from modern. There will also be subcultures which influence the type of music that prevails: "music preferences depend, to a large degree, on the kind of music the artist performs and the extent to which this music is rooted in the culture of the listener" (Appleton, 1973). Once again, culture influences musical preference insofar as one's subculture has specified the musical language with which one is conversant.

The sound spectrum of popular music in the United States exemplifies this. Appleton (1973) divides it into Afro-American and Anglo-American. While one can question the validity of such a neat distinction, since there are so many musical styles with so much overlap, there are observable patterns in musical preference which seem to follow distinct cultural lines. Studies have shown that Blacks as a group prefer Gospel and Jazz, while Whites prefer Rock and Country music. It is, however, also noteworthy that Aretha Franklin and James Brown, frontrunners with Black audiences, are not too far from the top of the list for Whites (Appleton, 1973). In general, more Whites will listen to Black music than vice versa. As an historically oppressed minority in American society, Blacks have a greater psychological need for self-identity than Whites. It seems logical that their music, the expression of the emotional life of a people, resist assimiliation of other forms. When one's existence is threatened, it is very difficult, if not impossible, to accept change and novelty. Whites, on the other hand, need fear losing little in accepting Black musical idioms. Prejudice perhaps is the only thing that stands in the way. A case in point is Elvis Presley's first recording, in 1953, a Black rhythm and blues song entitled, "That's All Right." As performed by Presley, it was called "rockabilly" (rock plus hillbilly) by some, but it represented a class of Black music which gave freer expression to sexual feelings than the prevailing White music. The strong sexual undercurrents of rhythm and blues could always be appreciated by pubescent adolescents but until Presley, a White man who sang Black, came along kids who could dig "soul" but not race, did not have access to Black music. A quarter of a century after Presley appeared, Whites find it much easier to cross the color lines of American music. It is still too early perhaps to tell to what extent the widespread acceptance of Presley's music contributed to the lessening of racial distinctions in American society, but it seems a bit more than mere coincidence that Presley and the Civil Rights movement are roughly contemporaneous.

Culture patterns help determine musical preferences and forms of expression; conversely, and more importantly, musical expression helps shape culture. The outraged parents whose children idolized Elvis felt this. Damon and Plato also. Many others—before, between, and after—were aware of the same thing. Given the impact which music has upon the life of individuals and society and its importance in expressing and communicating those qualities which are most distinctly human, namely, the emotions, it is always a source of wonder, amazement—and disappointment—to realize what little effort is expended in developing the musical potentialities of the citizenry. An occasional bumper sticker with a message like "Support music in our schools," is a sad reminder of the distance we as a society have yet to travel before we insure the rightful place of music and other forms of artistic expression in school curricula. The American educational system in general has been criminally negligent in providing lopsided education, one that is all but totally geared to analytical, logical, and sequential cognitive functions. Holistic, intuitive thought which is able to synthesize and express non-rational experience is equally necessary to the fully functioning person. The hills are alive with the sound of music, the Pythagoreans spoke of the "music of the Spheres," modern science has discovered that the earth itself resonates like a giant bell with a vibration of a single cycle lasting about 20 seconds, and in 1907, Ferrucio Busoni proclaimed, "music is part of the vibrating universe," but American education still seems determined to float along the currents of life like fish that are unable to perceive the water that surrounds and sustains them. Time and effort must be given to cultivate "right-hemisphere" functions, one of which is musical expression.

This is especially true for any education which purports to call itself religious. If anything, it would seem that religious education has as one of its values the integrity of the individual. This means a concern for not only moral integrity but also psychic integrity. Religious education which is concerned almost exclusively with individuals' "left-hemisphere" functions itself lacks integrity and is guilty of the sin of omission at least. Holiness and wholeness go hand in hand.

It is more important for individuals to be able to understand and express their emotional states, than it is for them to be able to repeat doctrinal statements. The Western world has always prized human thought, and this is perhaps why religious education has traditionally focused on doctrine and dogma, the basic intellectual products of the faith community. There are, however, things that are just as basic to the life of a people as are its thoughts. One of these is the emotions of community. The power of shared emotion to create oneness or unity between individuals cannot be denied, and it is hoped that by now the reader is convinced of the central (albeit "right-hemispheric") role of music in expressing and communicating human emotion. Since music, like foreign languages, can be more readily learned at an early age, a total religious education program would always include musical education beginning in the program's earliest stages and would continue along lines similar to Moran's model of ecumenical education (Moran, 1970) where the arts form a bridge between the rational and the non-rational, between primitive religion and narrow Christianity leading ultimately to ecumenical religion/Christianity. Given the fact that sound perception and discrimination are present even in new-born children and go through a process of development with critical periods, musical education cannot be started too early. And it is not too late for religious educators to begin now, for the sake of the individuals and the community which they profess to serve, to reverse the present situation wherein creative expression is systematically (hopefully unconsciously) stifled.

In incorporating music into a curriculum, care must be taken that music be experienced and understood for its own sake ("ars gratia artis") and not merely as an adjunct, audio-aid, or inducement to learning "what really matters," i.e., the ideas, the doctrine. To do so would be to fall back into the mode of thinking which produced terminology such as "dominant hemisphere," and resulted in the present state of affairs where the "non-dominant" hemisphere is hardly educated, if at all.

Most people are familiar with the Chinese proverb, "A picture is worth a thousand words." The expression is an intuitive appreciation of holistic ("right-hemisphere") conceptualization. This same appreciation also finds expression in the Roman Catholic Church's, "Qui cantat, bis orat," (Whoever sings, prays twice). It is unfortunate, however, that this insight into prayer was never quite realized in practice, or at least given the proper recognition. All too often music serves simply as accompaniment for words, and liturgical celebrations are geared almost exclusively to "left-hemisphere" functions. Prayer should be the lifting of the "mind and heart," i.e., both hemispheres, to God, and liturgies should be the occasions for the participants to celebrate their oneness as a people and their wholeness as human beings. Musical expression has a unique and indispensable role in achieving community and individual at-oneness. It does not need words for its justification and stands on its own merits as the expression and communication of emotion. All too often, however—perhaps in an effort to give verbal meaning to the community experience or else out of fear of the non-rational side of human experience—words dominate liturgical celebrations, especially the music. Church music today is practically synonymous with singing, and there is scarce opportunity for the mystical dimension of experience to penetrate one's consciousness:

" . . . the Church is still overwhelmingly didactic and verbose, both as it faces God and as it faces the world. Its liturgies consist almost entirely of telling God what to do and the people how to behave. By rationalizing the Mass and celebrating it in the vernacular instead of Latin, even the Roman Church has made the liturgy an occasion for filling one's head with thoughts, aspirations, considerations and resolutions, so that it is almost impossible to use the Mass as a support for pure contemplation, free from discursive chatter in the skull." (Alan Watts, 1971)

Within the Catholic tradition, there are many who oppose the liturgical changes and introduction of the vernacular. It is not difficult to see their protestations of having always to be listening to, speaking or singing words as an expression of resentment at having a greatly diminished opportunity for contemplation (right-hemisphere functions) during the liturgy. In a drive for meaning and relevance in the liturgy, the left-hemisphere has truly become dominant.

Musical expression, properly presented, opens the way for Watts' "pure contemplation." In this context, words used with music ought serve only to specify the emotional content for music as opposed to music's being used as a means for the congregation's reciting the same words in unison, which is generally the case at present. When music becomes an accompaniment to words, one is back in the left-hemisphere dimension of nice sounding, but still discursive, chatter. Those responsible for planning the music for liturgical celebrations should keep this contemplative, i.e., emotional, function in mind and choose music with a view towards (1) its ability to faithfully express a specific emotional quality, (2) the performers's ability to precisely reproduce the emotional expression, and (3) the congregation's ability to recognize and resonate with the expressed emotions. Depending on the purpose of the liturgical celebration, therefore, sometimes the austere, penitential sounds of Gregorian chant will be appropriate. Other occasions will call for the ornate, sensuous sounds of Baroque music, the power and solemnity of Byzantine-Slav choral music, or the free-wheeling emotional flights of modern jazz, and so on. In any case, the primary concern ought be the mood or feeling that a particular music evokes. In all cases, the music will be appropriate to the musical precision of the performers, the age and cultural background of the congregation, and to the emotional climate of the celebration. It will serve to unify those who have come together, and it will help raise their collective heart to that point beyond which all is silence.

Musical feeling is rather (like numinous feeling) something "wholly other" which, while it affords analogies, and here and there will run parallel to the ordinary emotions of life, cannot be made to coincide with them by a detailed point-to-point correspondence. It is, of course, from those places where the correspondence holds that the spell, an enchantment, points in itself to that "woof" in the fabric of music of which we spoke, the woof of the unconceived and non-rational. (Rudolph Otto, 1923)

The ability of music to express the ineffable within human experience, coupled with its power to uplift and transform those who perceive its content, has led people to always join music to their worship, and will ever keep it so.

Music will always be an integral part of human life and celebration because only half of the human mind is analytical, logical, and verbal. The other side of consciousness and religious experience cannot be denied expression or discounted as was often the case in the past. It is the task of religious educators and leaders to foster its full flowering and insure the harmonious development of the human spirit from both sides now.

Selected Bibliography

Appleton, Clyde R. "Black and White in the Music of American Youth." *New York University Education Quarterly*, Winter, 1973, 24-29.

Barroso, Felix. "Hemispheric Asymmetry of Function in Children." *Rieber* (1976), 157-180.

Buck, Craig. "Knowing the Left from the Right." *Human Behavior*, June, 1976, pp. 29-35.

Busoni, Ferrucio. "Sketch of a New Aesthetic of Music." *Three Classics in the Aesthetics of Music*. New York: Dover, 1964, p. 77.

Chomsky, Noam. "On the Biological Basis of Language Capacities." *Rieber* (1976), 1-24.

Clynes, Manfred. "The Pure Pulse of Musical Genius." *Psychology Today*, July, 1974, pp. 51-55.

Clynes, Manfred. *Sentics: The Touch of Emotions.* New York: Doubleday, Anchor Press, 1977.

Fincher, Jack. "The Joy (Grief, Love, Hate, Anger, Sex, and Reverence) of Music." *Human Behavior*, April, 1977, pp. 25-30.

Kiester, Edwin Jr., and Cudhea, David W. "Robert Ornstein: A Mind for Metaphor." *Human Behavior*, June, 1976, pp. 17-23.

Kinsbourne, Marcel. "The Ontogeny of Cerebral Dominance." *Rieber* (1976), 181–192.

Moran, Gabriel. *Design for Religion.* New York: Herder and Herder, 1970.

Neville, Helen J. "Significance of Cerebral Specialization." *Rieber* (1976), 193-227.

Otto, Rudolph. *The Idea of the Holy.* Oxford U. Press, 1923.

Rieber, R. W., ed. *The Neuropsychology of Language: Essays in Honor of Eric Lenneberg.* New York: Plenum Press, 1976.

Sage, Wayne. "The Split Brain Lab." *Human Behavior*, June, 1976, pp. 25-28.

Saal, Hubert. "A Century of Music." *Newsweek*, September 26, 1977, pp. 93-94.

Selmes, Ola A., and Whitaker, Harry A. "Morphological and Functional Development of the Auditory System." *Rieber* (1976), 125-156.

Watts, Alan. *Behold the Spirit.* New York: Vintage Books, 1971.

Weil, Andrew. *The Natural Mind.* Boston: Houghton Mifflin Co., 1972.

5.
Awakening the Right Lobe Through Dance

Carla de Sola and Arthur Easton

Dance artists themselves, Carla de Sola and Arthur Easton reflect on the process of creative dance. They suggest how dance is an aesthetic activity which is necessary for the holistic development of the person.

Then I looked, and lo, on Mount Zion stood the Lamb . . . And I heard a voice from heaven like the sound of many waters and like the sound of loud thunder; the voice I heard was like the sound of harpers playing on their harps and they sang a new song before the throne . . . No one could learn that song except the hundred and forty-four thousand who had been redeemed . . . (Rev. 14: 1-4)

St. Paul also declared that we will come to Mt. Zion, to "innumerable angels in festal gathering" (Heb. 12: 22); but instead we come to Sunday service, to sit, and kneel, and hear words. We do not hear the song, only words; we do not dance the festal dance, only sit. And the living water becomes stagnant, and the ineffable murmur is lost. There is no festal dance to awaken the soul and lift the heart.

"Singers and dancers alike say, 'All my springs are in you' " (Psalm 87). We have taken this to mean that we dance and sing out of the well-spring of God's life within us. We sing and dance when we love and are loved. But how many times is it also true that *until* we move or speak we do not even know what we feel, or where we are in relation to the world? We do not hear or know our true self. An old apocryphal text says, "Who so danceth not knoweth not what cometh to pass."[1] Our purpose in this chapter is to discuss how dancers have been able to connect themselves to sources of inspiration, and how these inner experiences have opened them and others to new perceptions of spiritual reality. We hope our observations serve to demonstrate the value of reexamining the role of dance and other arts in education and worship. Ten years of giving workshops on dance and its connection to liturgy and prayer have made it overwhelmingly clear to us that dance opens a pathway to a more personal and vivid experience of God.

We will describe how we approach the problem of creativity and the procedures we use in the process of gaining access to new ideas for choreography. For the past several years we have been participating in developing the Omega Liturgical Dance Company, which is composed of religiously motivated dancers, choreographers, and other professionals: photographers, video tape artists, and specialists in sound, lights, and stage management. Our original purpose was to tap the religious dimension in dance, and to develop ways to involve congregations in movement as part of liturgies and other services. We did not have "performances" in mind, but were trying to find ways to incorporate what dance has to offer within worship services. Only recently have we presented, as a program in its own right, our growing repertory derived from scriptural sources and from improvisations growing out of meditation.

THE PROCESS

Company members are asked to sit in a circle quietly, closing their eyes. They are able to use their own way of centering and praying; at first, this may involve focusing on one's breathing or silently uttering the name of Jesus. After about ten minutes of silence, a line from Scripture is read and perhaps repeated three or four times slowly, so that participants may absorb it. Each participant then begins to move from his or her stillness in response. There are no rules for what happens. Improvisation continues freely until the flow seems to stop naturally. Interaction between two or more dancers often occurs. Upon conclusion, the group members *consciously* recall the images and dance phrases which have come to them, writing them down so that they will be available for a later choreographic process.

The method of choosing a Scripture passage is determined by the task at hand. If we are gathered solely for an evening of prayer together, we open the Bible randomly or ask anyone present to suggest a reading. More often, we choose a reading for its relationship to a dance to be choreographed. Other sources of inspiration are also utilized, including texts drawn from the writing of saints, teachers, and sages of the world's religions. All of this is considered background work for a dance company which uses meditation techniques to inspire compositions.

Peter Madden, a member of the Omega Liturgical Dance Company and a dance therapist, offers his impressions of what takes place in the creation of a dance based on meditative preparation. First, during meditation, the right hemisphere of the brain is open to inspiration, for one is now in a quiet and non-judgmental state. The spiritual flow can then pass through, and from this arises the material out of which the dance comes. During the second stage, the left hemisphere takes over, structuring, analyzing, taking apart and reorganizing the previously intuited material. Third is the actual dance or prayer-performance. Here, the harmonious interplay of both hemispheres is required. Peter describes his experiences as a dancer:

> In a performance I go into a different reality. I feel the dancer creates a world in which it is possible to be at one with the cosmos, literally soar into new heights, creating a new reality in which, guided by the spirit, a transcendence occurs. While performing we go from a small being to a capital BEING. We go beyond our conditioning, find a "crack in the egg" and pass through it, thus changing the way reality is experienced. I feel this is done through the right hemisphere.

This is the crucial discovery of the "still point." During such experiences, Peter feels he is dancing in body, mind, and spirit—in total being. Such moments have an electrifying effect on both dancers and participants: "something new" is added to the pre-set choreography, and a flash of interpretive freshness enters. We believe that the great dancers of history—Martha Graham, Jose Limon, Ruth St. Denis, Isadora Duncan, and the great ballet dancers and choreographers—all created from the "still point." They were thus in touch with inspiration flowing from the activity of the right hemisphere.

Something unique is at work in the artistry of creative geniuses. Their followers sense this but too often form a school of "technique," in which students seek merely to imitate their teacher. Such copying is a left hemisphere activity which dampens or limits creativity. Each dancer, we believe, must find the "still point" within. When this is done, the movements arising from within will be authentic for and work for that person. Isadora Duncan, writing on "The Dance in Relation to Tragedy," says:

> . . . a dancer, who through long study, prayer or inspiration, has attained such a degree of understanding that her body is simply the luminous manifestation of her soul; whose body dances in accordance with the music heard inwardly, in an expression of something out of another, profounder world. This is the truly creative dancer, natural but not imitative, speaking in movement out of herself and out of something greater than all selves.[2]

A dancer is not just involved with the body. The body is used not only to gain an awareness of the self but also to gain a greater awareness of the self in relation to space and to the Spirit which fills that space in an unseen but intuited way. The dancer relates to surrounding space with a variety of rhythms and dynamic changes. It is not a question of becoming aware of this or that "out there," as in sensing a table or other object in relation to the body. In the artistic process, one is interested in the creation of beauty and in the unveiling of what is real but not normally perceived.

The dancer listens and becomes aware of a new speech or language which is found in quiet. Its alphabet contains silence and space, stillness and rhythm, textures and flow. This speech is apprehended in the "silent" areas of the brain, those that recognize beauty, music, song, truth and patterns of the unrecognizable and unknown.

Let us illustrate how a dancer apprehends these "unknowns" through the body, intellect, and Spirit:

Through the Body:

A dancer stands in the center of an empty space. Where does the dancer move from? What initiates the first movement? Is it a deeply felt contraction from the center of the body which sends movement rippling throughout the rest of the body? When the thoughts are stilled, the dancer simply lets the body feel its own muscles, tensions, and weight. It moves in the direction that *feels* good.

Through the intellect:

A dancer stands in the center of an empty space. First comes *thought* of what is to be done. "Let's see . . . we have to fill thirty-six measures in four quarter time. The quality is smooth . . . perhaps four gliding steps to the right as the arms slowly raise, then a turn while curving to the floor, a pause, other dancers enter . . . A. moves forward, B. moves backward . . . "

Through the Spirit:

A dancer stands in the center of an empty space, concentrating on the flow of the breath, quieting the mind, and sensing the body being open, attentive and *receptive*. The heart is lifted to the Unknown, to God. There is a pause in communion: perhaps an image comes to mind, an intuited vision or understanding . . . or simply an impulse to move. One starts, flows, and follows through.

Religious dance can be assumed to be the result of a personal, meditative experience of God; the movement's source comes from the heart's response, in an overflowing of gratitude or speech *to God*. In Christian terms, one could speak of Christ as the partner in an ever-new dance which is inspired by the Holy Spirit and offered to the Father. The highest level, point, or state would be a contemplative absorption, moving in a reality filled with God's love, realizing the words of Scripture: "In Him we move and live and have our being." However, many contemporaries describe a more transpersonal experience of God—one with emphasis on wholeness and unity—of simply being *at-one* with the cosmos. The corresponding spirituality for the dancer would be a total union of body, spirit, music, and space, forgetting the self in actualizing the dance (this is easier said than done). When this is successful, those who view the dance also become at-one and also forget themselves. For they are equally absorbed in the *aesthetic* spirituality of the prayer-dance.

The professional dancer does reach stages of at-one-ment or ecstasy in the performance of a beautiful work. Here another element, which is perceived by the audience, enters into the art. Sometimes it manifests itself as technical brilliance or as the "still point" in motion: a breakthrough occurs in time and space, as at the high point of a dancer's leap. Other times, it manifests itself as intuitional fire. Flashes of inspiration occur to the dancer on stage that are not stimulated in the studio during rehearsal. During the performance, sparked by the communication between dancer and audience, a movement is performed in a new way and catches fire. There is a sudden, unexpected contact with another force. This moment of intuitional leap is spontaneously translated into new refinements of movement. On stage, there is a pulling together and lifting of energy, perhaps analogous to the moment when water boils over heat. Something new is added in the intensity of the situation and what takes place is not thought out ahead of time. We see this flashing into awareness as an inspirational process, coming from the right lobe of the brain where "wholes" are known and the seeds of the new are born.

ECSTATIC DANCE: THE UNEXPECTED

This brings us to a discussion of other examples of ecstatic dance. We read in I Samuel 10: 5-7, 9-12:

> . . . You will meet a band of prophets coming down from the high place with harp, tambourine, flute, and lyre before them, prophesying. The Spirit of the Lord will come mightily upon you, and you shall prophesy with them and be turned into another man . . . When he turned his back to leave Samuel, God gave him another heart: and all these signs came to pass that day . . . When they came to Gideah, behold, a band of prophets met him; and the Spirit of God came mightily upon him, and he prophesied among them. And when all who knew him before saw how he prophesied with the prophets, the people said to one another, "What has come over the son of Kish? Is Saul also among the prophets?"

Greek, Vedic, and Hebrew accounts, like many "primitive" peoples today, associate dance, music, and poetry with divine inspiration. In the Hebrew Scriptures, it is understood that dance is included whenever instruments are mentioned. In fact, a state where the body moved in abandonment to rhythmic music was a sign of prophesying. Some current Sufi teachers encourage their followers to lose themselves in music while moving without thought. Whirling dervishes are known to achieve states of ecstatic union with God through the discipline of their practices. In various parts of the world—in the Philippines, in Africa, in South America, and among the American Indians—healers, sages, and prophets move ecstatically in dance to attain paranormal states of being in which energy, information and healing power are contacted. Richard Katz, in *Psychology Today*, describes how the Kung tribesmen of the Kalahari Desert dance for long hours until they are filled with a spiritual power which heals, protects and gives well-being.[3] The actions of men and women at these ceremonial occasions differ, but the experience of transcendence at the heart of the dance is the same. Both men and women share in the enhanced understanding and healing power.

In modern times, most people seem to have lost direct perception of the inner voice. Today there is more emphasis on technique based on imitation or copying the style of teachers (left lobe emphasis). Much of a dancer's life is spent doing repetitive exercises that train the body to perform actions with as little strain as possible. Most of these exercises are passed down to students from traditional vocabularies of movement. Rarely are students encouraged to add their own interpretations by tapping their own interior resources. The difficulty, or anomaly, is that training in technique *is* designed to ultimately free the dancer, for it is the ground work upon which inspiration can manifest itself as the dancer matures. Unfortunately, the dancer is seldom guided through those maturing steps from technique to performance level of interpretation and, ultimately, to spiritual understanding and freedom. Modern dance was originally a movement away from the formalized, technical expression of ballet, but in time it too became heavily influenced by standards of technical perfection.

We are not saying that technique is wrong, but the emphasis is misplaced when the goal of the dancer becomes glamorized, when the only objective is to dazzle and to prove one's worth as a performer. This imbalance results from our failure to develop and emphasize all that the right lobe can contribute. The right lobe is the transceiver of the voice of Spirit. It can be balanced with the functioning, well-developed, technique-and-habit-oriented left lobe. This creates translations which lift dance to new levels of understanding.

People rarely just dance. Self-consciousness is a serious block to inspiration for both the beginner and the experienced dancer. A non-dancer, moving for the first time, is usually at a loss for what to do next. This worry closes him to inspirational sources. Such self-preoccupation can be overcome under conditions of spontaneous play, as at parties; when judgments are temporarily suspended, we can discern glimpses of underlying joyous creativity. In another way, the purely technical dancer may become self-conscious when desiring to perform a particular step to perfection. The church can offer opportunities to both dancers and non-dancers by helping them to share selflessly in services and festive events; such participation lifts individuals from personality preoccupation to holistic experience.

The following are examples of what we may term the unexpected. They describe another type of dance which is not necessarily technical, ritualized, or communal. We preface them with some observations by C.U.M. Smith on the processes in the brain which take place when the creative imagination is stimulated:

In the creative imagination a constant rearrangement, reordering, turning-around of the representations of the perceptual world seems to occur. We can imagine . . . that this play of free association occurring in the inattentive mind has a physical correlative in the form of activity in the overlapping circuits of the cortex. Conceivably activity in one circuit "sparks off" activity in an overlapping circuit so that we become aware of "images that yet fresh images beget." With these new representations we "see" the world in a novel light.[4]

Dance is a bridge from the world of intellect to the world of imagination; through dance, we can grasp in deeper ways the meaning of religious concepts. A priest once related that when he was praying about Christ's agony in the garden he felt he could not deeply "get into it" until it occurred to him to dance the mystery. At a certain point he threw himself on the ground and, through his body, was taught new depths of meaning.

When a person has been deprived of free bodily expression for many years, often a few simple yet deeply felt motions can touch a core of being and give a new sense of significance to life. Recently, a group of older sisters were dancing the *Kiss of Peace* in a simple form. Suddenly, tears welled up in their eyes. They were responding to the element of beauty and harmony that was being introduced into the liturgy. Harmony is a graceful flowing, a juxtaposition of one element with another which produces something new and inspiring. Another time, thirty sisters, walking gracefully, touching hands, changed a sanctuary into a garden of beautiful maidens ready for the bridegroom. They danced to a simple and natural song, Reverend Carey Landry's "Peace Is Flowing like a River." The transformation of these sisters calls to mind images of the "resurrection of the body." In this sense, "resurrection" can mean a body that is tuned to seeing, hearing, and knowing God. On the other hand, a body that is sluggish, afraid to move, constricted, tight, and inhibited does not seem to fit this picture. Nor is this kind of "resurrection" to be found in a body when the person is focused on external appearances, approval and disapproval, or the need to impress others with superficial egocentric displays.

Another example of the unexpected took place in the rear of an empty church in downtown New York a few years ago. Paul, a friend of ours, slowly danced down the aisle and around the altar. There was beauty and simplicity as he moved in relation to something, someone . . . God. His movements seemed to make something invisible more visible. The space was not empty. Observing such movement, even trained dancers are taught to think of space in an entirely new way.

Once, at the closing liturgy of a dance workshop for a charismatic group, during the silence following communion, someone began to sing in tongues. A young priest got up and began to move, dancing as the spirit of the song led him. It was a wordless, non-literal dance, coming from the same unexplainable source as the song; and it was both beautiful and healing.

When a prayer during liturgy is offered with movements of arms, hands, and torsos, a new energy seems to enter the sanctuary. The movements may include simple hand gestures, lifting the arms in praise, or lowering the torsos in deep bows. These movements are done reverently and as the Spirit suggests. On a number of occasions people reported "seeing" the waves of arms lifting even though their eyes were closed. It was as though layer upon layer of branches in a forest, or stalks of wheat in a field, were swaying to the movement of the wind and a healing power seemed to flow from the tips.

Sometimes the strong, dramatic, and startling occurs. Once, at a liturgy celebrated after endless discussion and argumentation, when it seemed that there would be yet more verbalization all through the liturgy, the unexpected happened. During a momentary pause, a young man arose and dramatically entered the open space before the altar. Then, without a word, he mimed, danced, and acted out a moving comment on the morning's conflict, cutting through with strong gestures all that was unessential. A gasp of astonishment passed through the congregation; it was reminiscent of other times when the Holy Spirit seemed to suddenly move and be present in unexpected ways, causing all to take note and be changed.

The good hearty folk dances of the world are very close to the Holy when they allow the sharing of individual expression, human foibles, and playfulness. A circle of people clapping and cheering at the conclusion of a Spanish Mass, an Irish priest dancing with a hat in his hand, passing it on to the next—these bring out the best in human nature. Judgments are bound and people become unified in their shared enjoyment.

EDUCATION OF THE YOUNG

We have found that a mixture of ages enriches such experiences in the life of the young. Little hands can be raised in prayer as well as big hands. Little beings often ease the way for the older to participate. But they too are shy and need the support of older people around them. Children become self-conscious at very early ages unless they are encouraged to participate in experiences where everyone shares for better or worse in enjoyable occasions, where it is understood that all make mistakes and are not judged wrong. Everyone needs the other for wholeness. When a five-year-old child holds a huge white scarf and sails around the room dancing in wonderment and glory to some beautiful music, has not another dimension of life been sensed? In a Christian dance, in the church, people are not taken out of society to form their own subculture; instead, they celebrate life in all its ups and downs, in the seasons of the church year, in this world, and in relationship to the resurrection.

All of us who are responsible for the education of young children must take a fresh look at the potentials for creativity which lie hidden within each being. By our culture's emphasis on linearity in thinking, by categorical imperatives, by our fear of the nonsensical, and by our preoccupation with discipline and order, we perhaps by example inhibit the right hemisphere from opening into full functioning in educational experiences.

Is it an accident that when a budget crisis arises in schools, public or private, the first subjects to be eliminated have to do with the creative in life? Courses in music, art, and dance are early casualties when administrators—generally linear, left hemisphere types—are allowed to have the final decision about priorities given. Perhaps we need committees to make such decisions, with weight given to the less vocal viewpoint of those whose speech is not primarily verbal, but who speak the language of the soul—those whose language is organized on the mystical, intuitive, musical, and imaginative elements of life.

We believe a new balance must be attained. The curriculum for the formative years must be designed to help children to find their spatial relationships; to experience and participate in music, song, and dance; to move in relation to one another so that they may feel their boundaries and extents. Our education, so geared to commercial success, manages to create computer-like beings, skillful in storing environmental input from teachers, television, and parents; it also creates the opposite kind of human being, one who is "turned off" and drops out one way or another. What gets lost along the way is the means to open the door to inner creativity, intuitive perception, and the self-body-universal language of imagery and symbolism. The door is shut prematurely, and potential creativity dies for lack of the water of the spirit. By the age of fifteen, our well-conditioned children become the best consumers of things in the world; but they have lost confidence in visions, dreams, and the awareness coming from the right hemisphere of the brain.

Howard Gardner writes in *The Shattered Mind*:

> Thus, in early life, each hemisphere of the brain (or the whole brain, if you like) appears to participate in all of learning. It is only when, for some unknown reason, the left side of the brain takes the lead in manipulating objects, and the child begins to speak, that the first signs of asymmetry are discernible. At this time the corpus collosum is gradually beginning to function. For a number of years, learning of diverse sorts appears to occur in both hemispheres, but there is a gradual shift of dominant motor and speech functions to the left hemisphere, while visual-spatial functions are presumably migrating to the right. In those infrequent cases where the corpus collosum fails to develop, the individual develops two independent brains, each of which appears capable of spatial, linguistic, and other functions. But in the normal person, the division of labor grows increasingly marked until in the post-adolescent period, each hemisphere becomes incapable of executing the activities that the other hemisphere dominates, either because it no longer has access to its early learning or because early traces have begun to atrophy through disuse. [5]

Joseph Chilton Pearce stresses the need for us to keep a path open to the unknown and the unexpected, that which cannot be put into ordinary dualities and categories of knowledge:

> Our cosmic egg is the sum total of our notions of what the world is, notions which define what reality can be for us. The crack, then, is a mode of thinking through which imagination can escape the mundane shell and create a new cosmic egg . . . the crack is an open end, going beyond the broad statistical way of the world. [6]

Perhaps this crack was found when John ecstatically received the words and images of Revelation:

> After this I looked, and behold, a door *was* opened in heaven; and the first voice which I heard *was* as it were of a trumpet talking with me; which said, Come up hither and I will show thee things which must be here-after. (Rev. 4:1)

In prophetic revelation, we constantly find references to sounds of music, of rushing waters, of lyres, of trumpets and flutes. Research in our modern era has demonstrated beyond doubt that music and singing are apprehended and experienced in the right hemisphere of the brain. Singing, musical comprehension, discrimination of pitch, and discrimination in memory of musical elements are functions of the right lobe. A trumpet talking makes sense to a right-lobe-oriented individual, for such people can treat parallel elements simultaneously and do not have to reduce input into preexisting structures in the mind. The right lobe is known to be superior in dealing with "nonsensical" or random patterns; it deals with totalities of experience and can integrate dissimilar units.

Phil Lansky, writing in the *East West Journal*, comments:

The present technological imbalance in Western culture may be seen, in one sense, as an overvaluation of left-hemispheric function with a concomitant devaluation of the right hemisphere. Left hemisphere compartmentalization of knowledge has not been sufficiently balanced by right hemispheric unification and holism. [7]

A number of observers of brain functioning think that the use of both hemispheres increases brain efficiency. Both are used in walking and dancing. Music seems to involve the left lobe as well as the right. In twirling the body, as in certain Sufi dances or in ice skating, there seems to be an intermingling of the functions of the lobes. Various means of balancing the hemispheric functions have been suggested, including activities where pattern thinking is involved; for example, crafts like pottery, weaving, and other artistic work. Here, the digital-analytic and verbal functioning is temporarily silenced. It has also been found that paradoxical stories amplify right lobe functioning. When we meditate or use biofeedback relaxation methods, there are opportunities for the subtle communications of the right hemisphere to be heard.

The creative person is probably one who has been able to develop a dynamic balance in the functioning of both hemispheres. In his *A Vision*, W. B. Yeats suggests that "when Creative Mind is separated from Spirit, there is abstract thought, classification, syllogism, number, everything whereby the fact is established, and the sum of such facts is the world of science and common sense, Creative Mind united to Spirit brings not fact but truth, not science but philosophy."[8]

Dance springs from a deep and spontaneous source. Its essence is free and perhaps analogous to the unfettered, spontaneous creativity of God in creating the world. In Hindu mythology, Lord Shiva set the world in motion through his dance. Following Jesus's advice to "be . . . as little children" may involve reestablishing harmonious relationships between the two spheres or lobes of our brains. A modern dancer, Joseph Drexel, puts it this way: "Beginning with the most elemental childhood ecstasy-generator, the spinning or whirling dance, I proceed to consciously regain, amplify and modulate that childhood energy so rich in peak experience to . . . childhood states of consciousness by . . . reengaging the clutch of our inner gyroscope . . . setting us humming once again in the eternal play of the orbital flight of the Dance."

As we trust the intimations from our intuitive center, we can hear more deeply, see more holistically, and move more spontaneously. We can thus hear the inner voice, sound, and vision of God. This can only help us in our quest to find richer meaning in our lives and, in deeper humility, to understand our place in the larger scheme of things.

Notes

1. From *Apocalyptic Acts of John*, "Hymns of Jesus"; cited in Margaret Fisk Taylor, *A Time to Dance: Symbolic Movement in Worship* (Philadelphia: United Church Press, 1967), p. 71.
2. Isadora Duncan, "The Dance in Relation to Tragedy," *Theater Arts Monthly*, 2 (Oct. 1927), 757.
3. Richard Katz, "The Painful Ecstasy of Healing," *Psychology Today*, 10 (Dec., 1967), 81-86.
4. C.U.M. Smith, *The Brain: Toward an Understanding* (New York: G.P. Putnam's Sons, 1972), p. 329.
5. Howard Gardner, *The Shattered Mind* (New York: Borzoi Books, 1974), pp. 385-386.
6. Joseph Chilton Pearce, *The Crack in the Cosmic Egg* (New York: Pocket Books, 1971), p. xiv.
7. Phil Lansky, "The Alchemy of the Nervous System," *East-West Journal* (Feb., 1977), pp. 37-38.
8. William Butler Yeats, *A Vision* (New York: Macmillan, 1961), p. 195.

III
WORSHIPING AESTHETICALLY AND EDUCATING THE AESTHETIC SENSIBILITY

6.
A Program for Affective Liturgy

Ken Meltz

As a liturgist and musician, Ken Meltz submits that the new liturgy has as yet failed to achieve a degree of attractive emotion and affectivity. Using the categories of audience, script and symbol, he offers concrete suggestions to remedy the situation so that an affective style of liturgy could be developed.

"I do believe that feeling is the deeper source of religion, and that philosophic and theological formulas are secondary products, like translations of a text into another tongue."[1]

—William James

INTRODUCTION

Few changes in the past twenty-five years have been as far-reaching, as well received (or ill received depending on one's perspective) and as significant as that of liturgical renewal and revision. The worship forms of most churches, relatively unchanged since the Reformation period, have undergone extensive change and adaptation. Nowhere has this been more obvious than in the Roman Catholic Communion which has lived through a virtual Copernican revolution in its rites and worship. Indeed, few church groups have been untouched by this liturgical movement for renewal and reform. For the most part, this renewal has been flamed by two sources: scholarly research into the history of worship and the desire of the various churches to make the rites more understandable to their members. Historical research has laid bare the roots of Christian worship and how it has evolved throughout the centuries. In many cases this has led to the restoration of more primitive liturgical structures and forms. The complementary desire for intelligibility has led to ritual simplification and the peeling away of churchly accretions which have tended to obfuscate the original meaning and significance of Christian worship.

While the revisions in the rites, the simplifications, and the liturgical adaptations have been intended to cure the misunderstanding and the perfunctory participation of the average congregation, one can honestly and seriously question the extent of their success. For many Christians, the Sunday service is still very much an obligation and, at times, a rather unpleasant one. The perfunctory atmosphere of the past has become the banal environment of many current liturgical celebrations. And if one looks for signs of religious vitality today, one is hard pressed to find them in the worship of the established churches. Vitality, interest and enthusiasm are more likely to be found in charismatic prayer meetings, home rituals and certain forms of revivalism. In brief, the liturgical renewal has not been as successful as was hoped.

One can rightly ask: "What's going wrong?" There is no single answer to this question, a handy scapegoat we can brand and drive into the desert. Many possible answers have been suggested: that people did not want the present changes, therefore, what we are experiencing today is a gut level reaction against change imposed from outside; or, that people were not adequately prepared, in which case the churches are really suffering from a kind of educational-formational backlog. Still again, some will argue that the lack of vitality is a product of the trivialization and de-mystification of the ancient rites; in which case the cure is to be sought in a rediscovery of the Transcendent through more elaborate and solemn liturgical celebrations. Surely, all of these are contributing factors. While it would be simplistic to attribute the present situation to any one factor, I would like to suggest in this chapter that our liturgical renewal has not fully succeeded because it has lost sight of what could be called the "affective" dimension of liturgy.

THE ISSUE

When I speak of "affective" liturgy, I am referring to that capacity in ritual action to address the whole person, that is on a feeling as well as on a more purely rational level. Worship which is affective elicits a response from the human participant which is marked by feelings more than thoughts, by intuitive reaction more than cool logic. I carefully use the words "more than" for the issue here is one of balance rather than one of some "either-or" dichotomy. Clearly, to stress feeling, emotion, and affectivity in the human person to the exclusion of rationality, logic, and intelligibility would lead to the classic *reductio* known as Intuitionism or, in its theological raiment, Fideism. To reduce the human personality entirely to emotion and intuition would be as erroneous and unbalanced as the various forms of naive Rationalism which stress the intellect, the role of reason and logic but exclude the more affective dimensions of the human person. While there is need here for a proper balance, certain aspects of the liturgical renewal have tipped the scale in favor of intelligibility over affectivity.

I would like to suggest that this underplaying of affectivity in the liturgy has created its own set of problems. Our revisions and simplifications, while most needed and overdue, have produced in many cases a rather sterile, overly conceptual, and highly intellectualized liturgy. I believe that the absence of affectivity is precisely the point at stake, for example, when Roman Catholics harken back nostalgically to the "good old days" of the Latin mass. It is not so much a case that these people understood the liturgy better then or had a deeper theological insight into Christian worship. If anything, this kind of rational comprehension was obviated by a foreign tongue and a proliferation of gestures. While one can fault this "old" liturgy for these drawbacks to intelligibility, it possessed what the new liturgy has, as yet, failed to achieve—a degree of attractive emotion and affectivity.

There is, then, in our current renewal this decided preference for the intelligible over the affective, a preference which can be traced to two sources. The first is a prevalent and almost ecumenical distrust and disparagement of the emotional and affective in the religious life. In the past, emotion was often viewed as ungrounded, unreliable, and conducive to all sorts of enthusiastic excess. Catholics, in reaction to the seeming subjectivism of the Reformation, and mainline Protestants, partly in reaction to the experiential theology of Schleiermacher and partly to the excesses of revivalism, became strange bedfellows in learning to distrust the emotional and affective side of the religious life. Clearly, religious affectivity could not be removed any more than human emotion in general. But where it was recognized, it was carefully monitored and officially channeled as, for example, in approved devotions, public missions, structured revivals, voluntary associations, etc.

The second source for the decided imbalance I have been describing derives from the Enlightenment and its preference for clear rational forms. When "reason" and the empirical sciences become the dominant arbiters of reality, religious emotion becomes at best a shaky step on the way to religious clarity, often seen in rational Deistic terms. At worst, religious affectivity is perceived as the by-product of some cranial body and given as much credibility as any hormonal operation. Both of these sources have exercised a kind of residual influence in the recent liturgical reforms where so much attention is given to understanding and comprehension and so little to feeling and experience.

The remainder of this chapter will attempt to outline some of the ways that the affective dimension of the liturgy may be enhanced. The intention here is to suggest a practical program and point out certain aspects of communal worship which may become avenues for vitalistic religious feeling and emotion. The result will happily be not only an appreciation of the value of intelligibility in worship but also a respect and care for the more affective side of the liturgy.

THE AUDIENCE

As a first step in dealing with the affective dimension of liturgy those responsible for the worship life of the various churches will have to become more aware of who constitutes the worshipping audience. Liturgists, religious educators, ministers and musicians alike will have to see that in communal worship we are dealing with whole persons, not disembodied intellects. This is to say that too often the liturgy has favored the more rational, intellectual side of the human person to the sometimes neglect of the more physical and emotional. A few examples can help make this point.

First, the human body, the physical, is not completely at home, even today, in the public worship of the churches. This can be traced to a very influential yet errant current of Christian Platonism which throughout history has overly dichotomized the relation of "body and soul." This stream has grown up alongside of and has some-times dominated the more biblically grounded mainstream which sees the human person as an integrated unity of body and spirit. At its best, the Christian theological tradition has upheld this basic unity and has repudiated any attempt to view the soul as the "good", immortal, spiritual component somehow imprisoned in the "evil", transient, physical body. This distorted theological anthropology known as Manichaeism or dualism has been a constant factor in the history of Christianity, one which has been vigorously and consis-tently contested. Nevertheless, its influence and residual effects have tinged Christian manners and practices. Many talks and ser-mons, for instance, have been delivered on "custody of the eyes" which implied and suggested that there was something intrinsically evil about human corporeality. Many religious persons were raised on diets of ascetical practice aimed more at taming recalcitrant bodies than at holistic renewal and personal transformation. Not surprisingly, this depreciation of the physical and corporeal has had an effect on liturgical practice. The church building was the place where we went to pray, that is where we "lifted minds and hearts to God." The body was often perceived as a necessary but annoying encumbrance which, through its limiting pains, pleasures, needs, and desires, hindered this raising up of the mind and heart. The body brought people to the church but, once there, it was virtually ignored until it was time to go home. The current liturgical reforms have done little to remedy this situation.

Even with the present ritual revisions, one gets the impression that the liturgy is still primarily designed for the two human ears and especially for the gray matter lying in between. In the Roman Catholic celebration of the Eucharist, for example, the entire liturgy from penitential rite, through creed, to final blessing and dismissal often comes across as a solid barrage of words and concepts aimed primarily at the human intellect. Like a classroom situation, the physical body remains largely inert, passive, and inconsequential. It is almost as if it has been forgotten in the midst of the current liturgical renewal that ritual is *action* and demands the attention and participation of the whole person—body, mind, and heart. A liturgy program which aims to be affective will strive to be more aware of the physical dimensions of the worshipping audience. It will move from awareness to action in that it will try to develop means to bring the body more fully into the liturgical prayer experience. The means will vary but two can be mentioned which have initially proven rewarding. From the East, the liturgy will continue to learn much about the posture of the body for prayer. Yoga and its related forms can point out how the body can be a springboard and resource for prayer experiences. The suggested liturgy program will build on this insight, allowing ample time and opportunity for Christians to experience the spirituality and prayerfulness of their bodies within the act of worship. Secondly, a program for affective liturgy will continue to build on the pioneering efforts of artists like Gloria Weyman and Carla DeSola who have once again reminded us that bodily dance is a form of prayer.[2] They and others have shown us that dance, as movement, has a religious origin and essentially a religious character. Though often overlooked in the past, this insight will expand the definition so that prayer can be seen as the lifting up of the heart and mind and body to God. The program for affective liturgy will invite the body to dance and pray through gesture, movement, posture, and ritual activity. The rediscovery of this aspect of prayerfulness will go a long way toward achieving the liturgical goal of full participation, seen now as the involvement of the whole human person, not only the human intellect.

In the current renewal, there is a similar need to address the more emotional and intuitive dimensions of the human participants. As suggested above, religious emotion has frequently been a bit suspect in ecclesiastical circles. While abuse due to overemphasis on the side of human feeling is possible (Intuitionism), possible abuse should not preempt legitimate and healthy emotional expression. Yet, as one views the worship scene today, practitioners of the revised liturgy seem to distrust the emotional and affective dimensions of the human person almost as much as those of the past. Another example may prove helpful here.

One of the most popular developments in the wake of the renewal is the so-called "thematic" approach to liturgy. Uppermost in the minds of celebrants, preachers, planners, and musicians alike is the question: "What is the theme of the liturgy?" Now there is a sense in which this is a healthy and beneficial development, to the extent that it lends a certain focus to the liturgical celebration. A theme can provide the frame of reference for the unity, coherence, and emphasis in the liturgy that the rhetoric books still commend for writing. Clearly, much of the current preoccupation with "theme" in the renewal has been to correct the verbal meanderings and diffusion of thought that marked so many sermons in the past. To the extent that it has alleviated some of these homiletic shortcomings, the "thematic approach" should be accorded some congratulations.

Nevertheless, in many cases the "thematic" knot has been drawn so tightly that it has created a liturgy that is overly conceptual and intellectualized. One almost gets the feeling that the statement of theme which has become normative for many Sunday celebrations is very much akin to the scholastic's thesis. Once stated, it is argued, supported, and defended throughout the various parts of the liturgy as if Sunday worship were more a disputation than an experience of prayer. There is a difference between theologizing "about" God and praying "to" God, a distinction which must be respected if the liturgy is to engage the whole person and not simply his/her mind. Liturgy is not the celebration of an idea but rather the prayerful remembrance of a person, Jesus Christ. When over-thematizing does occur, the liturgy becomes more concerned with content than with the actual experience of the gathered community. This leads to an act of worship which appears heady, cold, and basically removed from human emotion and sentiment.

The suggested program for affective liturgy stresses that while content is important in our celebrations, the actual experience of communing with God and other persons is more important. In other words, while worship does include the notional, that is the rational and the conceptual, it is more so an act of devotion. Liturgy is central to the Christian life not so much because it convinces us of some article of faith but because it moves us to deeper belief. It is important not simply because it teaches us something but because it invites us to proclaim, celebrate and experience God's presence through the words and signs of that presence. Like good drama and good art, affective liturgy will invite the audience to respond and participate not simply because they rationally comprehend all that is going on but more so and more importantly because they are touched and drawn by the experience itself.

THE SCRIPT

Since the goal of the suggested program for affective liturgy is to engage the whole person in the act of worship, especially on an affective and emotional level, this has implications for the actual celebration of the liturgy. While some of these have already been suggested, in this section I would like to focus on three distinct but related liturgical elements—preaching, symbol, and music to see how they might function in the proposed program.

Preaching

As Clarence Rivers is fond of pointing out, it is most ironic that a Church whose worship gave birth to the theater needs to be reminded that its liturgy is a kind of drama.[3] The suggested program for affective liturgy stresses the dramatic nature of religious ritual to the extent that good drama and good ritual both strive to put men and women in touch with the depths of human experience. This is to say that our liturgy becomes a holy play, a *sacer ludus*, when we experience in it the ongoing drama of God and the human community. This is highlighted primarily through the dramatic word of preaching.

Affective liturgy will require certain adjustments in current preaching styles. At present, a liturgical homily requires three steps: research, composition, and delivery. In the first, the preacher reads the lessons, reflects on them, and confers with a respected biblical commentary for further insight. In the process of composition the thoughts are ordered, arranged, and given verbal expression. Finally, the sermon or homily is delivered to the audience. Intrinsic as they are to all preaching, these three steps are retained and refined in the program that is being suggested.

In the research stage, the attempt will be made not only to engage in the work of exegesis strictly speaking, but to move beyond this to what could be called a level of personal significance. While competent and scholarly exegesis is extremely important and a most needed corrective to an often shallow and moralizing approach which marked the past, the affective preacher will try at the outset to answer the question: "What does this text mean to me?" S/he is thus moving to a level of personal import almost immediately. The affective preacher realizes that if s/he cannot make much sense of the text for his/her life at this initial stage, it is unlikely that it will make much sense to a listening audience in its final form. Liturgy which aims to be affective does not shy away from the personal reactions of the preacher. The questioning, the clarification and indeed the whole feeling level response of the preacher to the Word of God are seen not as unscholarly intrusions into the task of research. Rather, the quest for the personal meaning of the lessons is an integral part of this stage. If it is missing, then the exegetical research and study may be complete and compelling but they will come across as cold and distant facts of biblical science.

The task of composition will likewise require some adjustment in the light of this program. If one were to sum this up in one phrase it would be that preaching must become more poetic and less prosaic. Some homilies heard in churches today have little artistic appeal and consequently little or no affective impact on the worshipping congregation. There are many reasons for this. Often the form of preaching is overly didactic, which style is more appropriate for a lecture than a liturgical homily. Often the sermon is permeated with terms and phrases which come across as theological jargon. Frequently the length or, in rare cases, the brevity of a homily is a major factor in the failure of preaching. The point is a simple one. The suggested program calls for homiletic composition which is literate, well thought out and humanly attractive. This is to say that our preaching must not only be a product of scholarly research but an object of attractive art as well. Its choice of words, its rhythm, its emphases must strive to go beyond the sharing of information to the deeper level of touching the human spirit. This kind of liturgy calls for a style of writing which stirs, which inspires and which gently urges the human person to respond and participate on all levels. It is aimed more at stirring the heart than at convincing the head. Its form is poetic inspiration more than didactic information.

Finally, even the style of delivery should be adjusted. For the most part, preaching courses have stressed poise, vocal quality, and gesture as the basic building blocks of effective delivery. For affective preaching one should add a fourth qualification which could be called "personal filter." I use the term not to sustain the truism that everyone views reality through his/her own set of filters. Rather, it is an issue of style and pre-eminently of attitude. In affective liturgy, the homilist will make special efforts to proclaim the Gospel especially as filtered through his/her own personal experiences. Whereas objectivity and a degree of distance were the recommended values in the past, the program for affective liturgy will encourage and even require that preachers reveal their own experiences and how the Scriptures have informed, challenged and even judged them. This is not meant to suggest that "personal witness" replace Christian homiletics but it is proposing that current preaching models become more down to earth and personally revealing. By mediating the Gospel message through his/her own experiences and feelings, the preacher will communicate a new dimension to the Gospel's universality, namely that it is addressed to the totality of the human person, the affective as well as the rational. Affective liturgy, then, does not shun the personal filter of the preacher. Rather it holds it up as a value without which a sermon might appear well researched, well written, and well spoken but never quite convincing.

Symbol

The suggested program for affective liturgy has one cardinal principle when it comes to symbol, namely that our ritual symbols should primarily be experienced, not described. The above statement might appear a commonplace except when one realizes that Christian liturgy has for some time suffered from what could be called "sacramental minimalism," a kind of sacramental synecdoche in which we rely on the smallest possible unit of the ritual symbol to stand for the whole. For example, both the New Testament and tradition view the ritual symbol of Baptism as a saving bath which plunges us into the death and resurrection of Christ and incorporates us into the body of believers, the Church. Despite this, we have come to settle in our practice for a few drops of water, the sacramental minimum, rather than the full symbolism of immersion as ritual dying and rising. The sources of this sacramental minimalism are historically difficult to discern but two contributing factors should be noted here. The first is fundamentally theological and emerges from the "ex opere operato—ex opere operantis" debate dealing with the validity and efficacy of the Church's sacraments. "Ex opere operato" affirms that sacramental validity and efficacy depend on God rather than on the subjective disposition of the human participant ("ex opere operantis"). While this has been a necessary safeguard against a kind of sacramental Pelagianism, if stressed too far, "ex opere operato" can lead to an unfortunate overshadowing of the very important and legitimate subjective predispositions addressed by the term "ex opere operantis." When this happens, as for instance in the example of Baptism already cited, the form of the sacramental symbol, how it is administered, becomes less significant. Since God assures the efficacy of the baptismal rite, it makes little difference whether it be performed in a river or with a single drop of water.

Affective liturgy, while not denying the traditional position of "opus operatum" is more concerned with the subjective feeling and disposition of the sacramental recipient, the area of human affectivity. In affective liturgy, how the sacrament is administered takes on a new importance since it is here that the human participant grasps the meaning and significance of the sacrament. The believer experiences the significance of the sacrament through his/her subjective perceptions of the symbol's meaning. This is another way of stating the classic axiom that a sacrament effects what it signifies. Whereas in the past sacramental efficacy tended to be the central issue, today the problem is more one of symbolic significance. Put rather bluntly, our symbols do not fully signify what the sacraments are saying. A few drops of water can hardly signify the ritual dying and rising with Christ that Baptism proclaims. A formula of absolution hastily recited cannot signify the fullness of God's saving mercy and the gift of reconciliation.

The second factor which contributes to sacramental minimalism could well be termed "pastoral pragmatism." Its arguments against a possible enactment of symbolic fullness are often couched in phrases such as: "It's inconvenient," "It takes too long," "It's messy." So, for example, even though the instructions for reception of communion in the Roman Catholic Church suggest that the sign is more complete when given as both bread and wine, and grants ample permission for its implementation[4], this has largely been ignored on the basis of the pragmatic approach described above. While we have become more aware in recent years of the social significance of symbols[5], the archetypal power of symbols[6], indeed of the indispensability of symbol for human communication[7], it would appear from current practice that the churches are still not disposed to making the liturgical symbols more complete and humanly attractive. A program for affective liturgy calls for a concerted effort on the part of liturgists and religious educators alike to bring about the full expression of the ritual symbols of water, oil, bread, wine, word, and imposition of hands. This will slowly lead from the current practice of minimalism to one of sacramental fullness and symbolic plenitude. Why is this fullness such a concern for affective liturgy?

When sacramental minimalism occurs, as it does in many of the rites, one compensates for the lack of symbolic experience by describing the symbolic significance. In other words, instead of experiencing the power and beauty of the symbol directly, instead of immediately grasping its meaning, the attempt is made to mediate the symbol's significance through descriptive and explanatory prose. When this happens, we once again opt for intelligibility over affectivity and direct experience. For example, one proceeds to describe and explain that the Eucharist is a sacred meal of God's people. Now if this cannot be grasped directly from the context and the meal symbols of bread and wine, then there is something terribly deficient about the symbols. Briefly put, the problem today is not a question of whether the sacraments effect what they signify; rather, due to prolonged sacramental minimalism, it is more a question whether they signify what they claim to effect. As long as we continue to describe the significance rather than improve the quality of the symbol itself, its meaning will not be experienced directly. Only when the symbols are made adequate to their meaning will people fully grasp their liturgical significance. Then, worshippers will not have to be taught it; they will know the meaning directly, forcefully, and affectively from symbolic experience.

Music

Whether it be the chanting of the psalms, a Bach organ work or the rhythmic accompaniment of a jazz ensemble, music is certainly one of the oldest and most consistent components in the Church's liturgical tradition. Its antiquity but more so its intrinsic relation to ritual moved the religious historian van der Leeuw to write: "With the possible exception of architecture, music of all the arts stands the closest to religion."[8] Throughout human history, music, even in its most primitive form of rhythmic cadence, has permeated almost all manifestations of religious ritual. The suggested program highlights music as an indispensable means for bringing about affective liturgy. This is said for three related reasons.

First, in worship, music is a very real and powerful form of prayer. The oft quoted dictum of St. Augustine that whoever sings prays twice is at the heart of this musical appreciation. In affective liturgy, hymnody and psalmody are in no way seen as intrusions into the "real prayer" of spoken worship. Rather, they will be experienced as sung prayer, as musical liturgy. Why is this so? It is because music has the capacity to point beyond itself, that is, to free the human spirit for contemplation and religious imagination. As one author states: "An imaginative mind is essential to the creation of art in any medium, but it is even more essential in music because music provides the broadest possible vista for the imagination since it is the freest, the most abstract, the least fettered of all the arts."[9] Translated into a more strictly religious context, this is to say that music can open the door for the human participant to experience the act of religious imagination which we traditionally call prayer and contemplation. Music can set a mood, an atmosphere conducive to personal and communal prayer alike. Like the proverbial music that soothes the savage breast, our liturgical music can help calm the restless heart and gently draw it into a prayerful posture. This was certainly the case with Simone Weil, the brilliant French activist, who is said to have found relief from her chronic headaches and to have experienced prayer through the music of Solesmes. Affective liturgy aims to set such an atmosphere in which the religious imagination may move into an experience of prayer and music is one of the basic ingredients of this environment.

The second reason for stressing music in a program for affective liturgy is that music has the capacity to enhance and give emphasis to the words of ritual. It has the capacity to transform what might appear as a simple declaration of faith into a resounding proclamation of praise. Liturgical hymnody is a case in point. Its form is the fortunate marriage of text and melody punctuated by rhythm and seasoned by harmony. Its offspring is a product which is more potent than the text alone and less abstract than the simple melody. For this reason, hymnody has been extremely influential in the western churches, especially those of Protestantism. There is the perhaps apocryphal story about Cardinal Cajetan, Luther's great adversary, looking back toward the end of his life on the victories and defeats of the Reformation period and attributing much of the reformer's success to his powerful and inspiring hymns. Whether grounded in history or not, the story points up in a vivid way the extensive formative power of music when applied to texts in hymnody. Hymnody is a text which expresses the faith of the believing community but it is more so a melody which deepens and makes more forceful the meaning of the text.

There are two consequences which follow directly from this. First, the text and melody of a hymn are an extremely effective way of religious formation. The way we pray is the way we believe (*Lex Orandi, Lex Credendi*) and for this reason composers, performers and those responsible for church music programs should take special care that the text really does represent the faith of the community. But secondly and beyond this, care should be taken that both the text and melody of our hymnody be affective in that they elicit a response of aesthetic appreciation and devotional fervor from those who enter fully into it. It is this affective capacity to inspire and please which makes church hymnody so influential and so much a part of the suggested program.

Finally, music is highlighted because of the way it functions in the liturgy as a unifying social force. Thus, with reference to a liturgical gathering in a given place, the French liturgist Lucien Deiss writes: "The faithful, who were previously only a crowd, become a liturgical congregation through song."[10] The point is a simple one. In the liturgy, hymnody and musical accompaniment are a pre-eminent way of bringing people together who, by being of one voice, learn to become of one heart and one mind. If the liturgy in the past has been known for its overemphasis on private prayer and an almost isolated individualism, the task today is still a rediscovery and reemphasis on the communal nature of Christian worship. This experience of community, this feeling of belonging to other Christians is an important goal of the suggested program. Toward its realization the importance of liturgical music is stressed for it calls individuals out of themselves into such a feeling and such an experience of communal prayer.

CONCLUSION

The attempt to achieve a modicum of affectivity in the current liturgical renewal of the churches is not a goal shared equally by all. For some, human emotion and affectivity have little place when speaking of worship and prayer. In such cases, the liturgy may well be seen as a formalized ritual response to the rational content of a belief system. For still others, human feeling and affectivity are seen as somehow less respectable, less important than the more highly regarded human rational capacities. In such cases, human affectivity is tolerated but hardly encouraged in prayer and worship.

This article has been an attempt to argue that more attention should be given to affectivity in the ritual renewal of the churches today. The argument is based fundamentally on a more holistic view of the human person, one that accounts for the more affective as well as the more rational human dimensions. The present article consequently has sought not only to expose the issue of affectivity but also to suggest concrete ways in which an affective style of liturgy could be developed. As such, it is by no means a panacea for liturgical ills nor a comprehensive blueprint for ritual reform. Rather, as a limited program for affective liturgy, it will serve its purpose if the various churches become more aware of the question of affectivity and seek creative and purposeful liturgical solutions.

Notes

1. William James, *The Varieties of Religious Experience* (New York: Collier Books edition, 1961), p. 337.

2. Carla DeSola, *Learning Through Dance* (New York: Paulist Press, 1974); Lucien Deiss and Gloria Weyman, *Dance For The Lord* (Cincinnati: World Library Publications, 1975).

3. Clarence Rivers, "Catharsis In The Drama of Worship," *Liturgy*, 22, (1977), 11-17.

4. Roman Missal, *General Instruction*, nos. 240-242.

5. Mary Douglas, *Natural Symbols* (New York: Pantheon Books, 1970).

6. Carl Jung, *Man And His Symbols* (New York: Doubleday, 1964).

7. Susanne K. Langer, *Philosophy In A New Key* (Cambridge, Mass.: Harvard University Press, 1957).

8. Gerardus van der Leeuw, *Sacred And Profane Beauty: The Holy In Art*. tr. David E. Green (Nashville: Abingdon Press, 1963), p. 225.

9. Aaron Copland, *Music And Imagination* (Cambridge, Mass.: Harvard University Press, 1952), p. 7.

10. Lucien Deiss, *Spirit And Song Of The New Liturgy* (Cincinnati: World Library Publications, 1970), p. 17.

Further Readings

Keen, Sam. *To A Dancing God*. New York: Harper and Row, 1970.

Killinger, John. *Leave It To The Spirit*. New York: Harper and Row, 1971.

Micks, Marianne H. *The Future Present*. New York: Seabury Press, 1970.

Snyder, Ross. *Contemporary Celebration*. Nashville: Abingdon Press, 1971.

7.
Community: An Aesthetic Perspective

Gloria Durka and Joanmarie Smith

Durka and Smith contend that attention to the quality of community rather than its concrete elements may be a helpful contribution at this time. Their esthetics is worked out in the pragmatic tradition. They also pay special attention to celebration as the unique expression of community.

INTRODUCTION

The fostering of community has been seen as a major task of religious educators. The flowering of community has been viewed as a sign that religious education has occurred. The term community, however, is an ambiguous one. It is used in many contexts. On the one hand, for example, nothing can exist outside of community; *we are* to the degree that we are related. To speak of building a community in the face of this view is redundant. On the other hand, community can be used to designate a geographical location. Yet surely when we speak of constructing a community we do not think that community exists simply because people are living in the same neighborhood. Neither are persons who share many common values (the scientific community, for example) necessarily a community in the normative sense in which it is so often used today. If it were, then a band of thieves could be regarded as a model of community. They exhibit at least a minimal degree of community. "They have aims in common and the activities of each member is directly modified by knowledge of what others are doing."[1]

As in so many instances, it is much easier to say what we do not mean than what we do mean. We think, therefore, that the very attempt to identify those elements which constitute a community in the aspirative sense in which it is frequently used would be a contribution. In this article we make that attempt.

We examine the notion of community from an aesthetic perspective. What distinguishes community as it is embodied in a band of thieves from a community as it is idealized is its quality. We think that this approach has at least as one of its advantages the freeing of the imagination. There is a tendency in our efforts to effect community to discuss such specifics as the minimal or maximal number of persons that can be involved and the kind of communication which must occur as well as the strategies which will bring about that communication. While this can certainly be helpful it may also be analogous to telling an artist what materials to use and how they should be arranged. Such information undoubtedly contributes to the artist's education, however many breakthroughs in the arts occur by using heretofore rejected materials or by arranging the elements in previously unimagined modes. Scrap metal art and electronic music represent two such breakthroughs. Whether or not something is art is determined by its quality, not its concrete elements.

By concentrating on the quality of community therefore, we suggest that perhaps community can occur among much larger numbers than we have suspected. Perhaps it can also occur through modes of communication that have not yet been conceived.

We will also attempt to identify those elements of community in a framework that "reflects our original relation to the universe." Many current theories of community are European imports and to some degree alien to our history. An authentic theory of community for us will be one that is grounded in our peculiar experience and the interpretation of reality that flows from it. We propose that the categories of the pragmatic tradition provide a structure for such an indigenous theory of community.

The North American temper especially as it is localized in the United States has been characterized as notoriously practical. That might be expected in a people who carved a nation in the wilderness. The technological seems to be exalted over the theoretical and the aesthetic. "Build a better mousetrap," has been seen as a more compelling ideal than, "Compose a more beautiful symphony." It should not be surprising, then, that when a philosophy organic to our history is generated, it is called pragmatism. It may also be understandable that this philosophy is mistakenly described as equating the useful with the good and the workable with the true. We hope that the correction of this mistake may be a by-product of our discussion.

THE PRAGMATIC TRADITION

For many of us John Dewey *is* the pragmatic tradition. It was through his long years of publishing and influential teaching, first at the University of Chicago and then at Columbia Teachers College that most of the ideas of the pragmatic school were popularized and disseminated. During his life he was constantly attempting to refute the misunderstanding of pragmatism.

Pragmatists and non-pragmatists alike concede that the scientific method is at the heart of the pragmatic stance towards reality. Non-pragmatists, however, usually fail to remark that the scientific method as proposed by Dewey is essentially an esthetic endeavor.[2] Consider, for example, his definition of inquiry; it might describe the work of an artist:

> Inquiry is the controlled or directed transformation of an indeterminate situation into one that is so determinate in its constituent distinctions and relations as to convert the elements of the original situation into a unified whole.[3]

Science and **art** was one of the many unnatural divisions that Dewey sought to overcome in his work.[4] For him reality is a continuum. It is our task to note how, why, and to what effect distinctions are made in the whole.[5]

When he addresses himself to the specifically esthetic, he cites as his primary task to restore the continuity of esthetic experience and all other experience.

> Mountain peaks do not float unsupported; they do not even just rest upon the earth. They *are* the earth in one of its manifest operations. It is the business of those who are concerned with the theory of the earth, geographers and geologists, to make this fact evident in its various implications. The theorist who would deal philosophically with fine art has a like task to accomplish.[6]

Dewey alludes only to the traditional materials of the artists such as watercolor, oil paint, stone, in his discussion but it does not seem a distortion of his thinking to apply his esthetic theory to another of his dominant concerns, the construction of community.[7]

THE QUALITY OF COMMUNITY

How community comes into being is no problem for Dewey because nothing exists outside of community. Things do not *have* relationships; they *are* their relationships. Therefore, "community" in itself is not necessarily an aspirative term;[8] it is simply a description of the nature of reality. But at the heart of our experience is the conviction that reality is raw potentiality; that its quality can be transformed and augmented into something more desirable. An esthetically reconstructed community of persons would be an example of that possibility realized. In our references to quality we obviously do not mean to the primary qualities of experience: extension, shape and motion or even the secondary qualities: taste, smell, color and sound. We are speaking of a third type of quality. Dewey borrows this notion of a tertiary quality from Santyana.[9] "A tertiary quality qualifies *all* the constituents to which it applies in thoroughgoing fashion."[10] This type of quality is exemplified in the resemblance we can detect among family members who may not even share similar features. It is the affectional and emotional hues that pervade an interaction and constitute it *a* situation, *an* experience, *a* substance.[11] While this quality is always esthetic in the broad sense because it constructs wholeness it can be esthetic in the more traditional sense when the experience of wholeness is consummatory. For Dewey the *explicitly* esthetic quality is characterized by a wholeness which is final and which arouses no search for other experience.[12]

ARTFULLY CONSTRUCTING COMMUNITY

In *Art as Experience* Dewey identifies the conditions of the esthetic as *conservation, tension, cumulation, anticipation,* and *fulfillment.*[13] We will briefly describe these conditions and suggest that their implementation by a group of persons would constitute a community of such compelling quality that it could only be called a work of art.

In *conservation* the artist attends to the preservation of the individual elements of the art work. Dewey quotes Matisse on this point:

I put on the canvas the particular red that satisfies me. A relation is now established between this red and the paleness of the canvas. When I put on besides a green, and also a yellow to represent the floor, between this green and the yellow and the color of the canvas there will be still further relations. But these different tones diminish one another. It is necessary that the different tones I use be balanced in such a way that they do not destroy one another. . . . The relationships between tones must be instituted in such a way that *they are built up instead of knocked down*[14]

In a community it is the individual selves which must be preserved. Dewey frequently expresses impatience in discussions of the relationship between the self and community.[15] For him this is a pseudo-problem. There are not two entities. As there are no communities without the persons who comprise them so there are no selves except as they emerge in the interaction called community. But he does speak of individuality as interchangeable with choice or interest or perhaps, more accurately, the potentiality for choosing.[16] The mode of responding to these needs and the preferential bias they reflect is the "incommensurable" about each of us.[17] It is this individuality which must be conserved.

Tension is the method by which the individual units are conserved. Preserving the "otherness" of others involves a conflict which is not opposed to the esthetic. In fact, Dewey refers to the conversion of resistance and tensions into a fulfilling close as a distinguishing note of the esthetic.[18] In searching for a principle of organizing tensions in community, Dewey concluded that in the notion of democracy we have a method of association that will not only release and sustain the power of individuals, thereby generating tension, but which can effect the resolution of tensions through integration of these individuals. Democracy is not to be equated with majority rule. Its central concern is how the majority has come to value as it does. Tension is not desirable in itself. Its value lies in that it unleashes novelty by surfacing new possibilities.[19] Democracy is the commitment to the participation of all members in the construction of those values which regulate their lives.

It is probably on this point more than on any other that would be communities flounder. The ideal of shared values which any community must have is too often confused with the notion of uniform values. Where there is no conflict, there is no questioning. Where values are not questioned or critiqued mature commitment to them is impossible. In fact, it is debatable whether that which is held in common can be called values if no alternatives are considered.[20]

The principle of *cumulation* is operative whether one is talking about the colors in a painting, the characters in a drama or the themes and harmonies of a musical composition. The elements must be so promoted that not only do they significantly contribute to the whole but they become more significant than they are in isolation or even surrounded by less dominant elements. Moreover, the whole itself becomes greater than the sum of its parts. We are proposing here that cumulation is also operative in a community that is esthetically constructed.

Anticipation is the fourth condition of the esthetic in Dewey's theory. For him art is nature transformed.[21] Art, says Dewey, is an immediate realization of intention.[22] The work in progress as well as the finished product is marked by anticipation of the end. This anticipation acts as a regulative ideal throughout the esthetic endeavor.

"The end-in-view is present at each stage of the process; it is present as the *meaning* of the materials used and acts done."[23] It is not that the completed product can be imagined in detail but that there is some sense which allows the poet for example, to say which words are inappropriate to the overall design. Similarly, although a community's vision of itself may lack completeness the members share a sense of what is at least incongruent with that vision.

Of all the qualities we associate with an esthetic experience surely the most prominent is *fulfillment* or consummation. Consummation encourages us that events are not mere means to other events *ad infinitum*. But as Dewey remarks, "Under some conditions the completeness of the object enjoyed gives the experience a quality so intense that it is justly termed 'religious.' "[24] The relatedness experienced can only be called communion. That is, the wholeness is so profound and extensive that no one and no thing is excluded from one's sense of self.

It seems that a community which embodied this quality could quite properly be called a "holy" community. It is "wholly" community because its essence is communion. It is "holy" community because communion is the essence of religious experience.

CELEBRATION

Celebration is the unique expression of the community we have been describing.

In celebration the five conditions of the esthetic community are present to a pre-eminent degree. One of the most common celebrations in which the community expresses itself is by the recognition of the birthday of its members. Remarking a person's date of birth as a cause for celebration implements the conviction that the uniqueness of the members must be *conserved*. *Tension* is promoted by the anti-authoritarian character of the celebration. There can be no "bosses" at a real party. Celebration is radically democratic, even anarchical at times. And sometimes because of this quality, celebration degenerates into chaos. Fear of this ever happening sometimes underlies our hesitation to celebrate.

The spontaneity that reflects the anti-authoritarian character of a celebration is creatively organized with the rituals that are peculiar to different causes for celebration. We see this as a sign of *cumulation*. Regardless of how innovative a birthday party aspires to be, the observance of the traditional gift giving, birthday cake/candle blowing, and the singing of the song "Happy Birthday" seem to be invariables. By participating in these rites the members of a particular community plug into every person's birthday that has been similarly celebrated. Ontogenesis mirrors phylogenesis.

In a celebration the *anticipation* of fulfillment is so intense that "all business as usual" is suspended. It may seem puzzling to consider time in a discussion of fulfillment. But celebrations are very time-oriented.

The first thing celebration does is to affirm the event at issue. To celebrate anything is to say "Yes" to the moment; it is to act the judgment: *this moment in history is good*. In fact, however, it also affirms all of time; it affirms history itself. To sing "Happy Birthday" is to say, "I am glad for your entire history. I am glad that you were born; I am glad that you are here today; I am glad that your mother and father met, that their parents met and theirs," and so on, *ad infinitum*. It is also to say, "I hope you will be here tomorrow and tomorrow—indeed I hope you will live forever." For if we examine our sentiments when we sing "Happy Birthday" or "Happy Anniversary" we will see that there is no limit to our good wishes. We may sing, "May you have many more." But, even if we do not, we probably do not restrict our good wishes to two more birthdays or even fifty more birthdays. What we sing, if only implicitly, is an unlimited affirmation of a particular past history and future history.

Celebration then, is quite time oriented. In selecting some moment of time on which to concentrate, our attention is called to time generally but with very different results from the reminders of time which come from looking at a watch or calendar. Our attention to time is usually harrying if not harrowing. We feel rushed at the least and sense our mortality more often than we wish. But celebration is an experience of our immortality. It attends to time but refuses to be intimidated by time. In celebration we implicitly acknowledge our superiority to the temporal that is, our conviction that we transcend it, because in celebration we WASTE time. A central element of celebration is that it is non-productive. There is something heroic in the decision to celebrate a birthday because by all calculated standards the time might be better spent in a more productive way working to make one's remaining years count. But, paradoxically again, when we celebrate a birthday while we are saying, "It is great to be alive," or "This is a great achievement," we are also saying, "It is not *so* much; it is not *everything*." In celebration we experience an aspect of "everything." We experience a peak moment of existence. We experience fulfillment in and of others. Another way of saying it is: every authentic celebration culminates in communion. Every real celebration is the liturgy of a holy community.

106   GLORIA DURKA AND JOANMARIE SMITH

Notes

1. John Dewey, *Democracy and Education* (New York: The Free Press), p. 21.

2. We also speak of this point in Gloria Durka and Joanmarie Smith, *Modeling God* (New York: Paulist Press, 1976), pp. 12-17.

3. John Dewey, *Logic: The Theory of Inquiry* (New York: Holt, Rinehart and Winston, 1938), pp. 104-5. Martemer Kadish calls attention to this point in "John Dewey and the Theory of the Aesthetic Practice." *New Studies in the Philosophy of John Dewey*, ed. Steven M. Cahn (Hanover, New Hampshire: The University Press of New England, 1977), p. 115.

4. John Dewey, *Experience and Nature* (New York: Dover Publications, 1958), p.XV

5. *Ibid.*, p. 9.

6. John Dewey, *Art as Experience* (New York: Minton, Balch & Co., 1934), p. 9.

7. This is done at great length in Joanmarie Smith, "John Dewey and the Ideal Community," Unpublished Dissertation, Fordham University, 1971.

8. We will use the term aspirative community to refer to the community which has the esthetic qualities we are describing.

9. John Dewey, *Quest for Certainty* (New York: Minton, Balch & Co., 1929), p. 214.

10. John Dewey, *Logic: The Theory of Inquiry*, p. 69.

11. *Ibid.*, pp. 128-9; Dewey, *Experience and Nature*, p. 259.

12. Dewey, *Quest for Certainty*, p. 235.

13. Dewey, *Art as Experience*, p. 145.

14. Dewey, *Art as Experience*, p. 136.

15. Dewey, *Individualism, Old and New* (New York: Minton, Balch & Co., 1929), pp. 168-9.

16. Dewey, *Democracy and Education*, p. 121.

17. Dewey, *Art as Experience*, p. 56; Dewey, *Experience and Nature*, p. 90.

18. Several important authors who have addressed this topic are: Lewis Coser, *The Functions of Social Conflict* (New York: Free Press, 1956), and Rollo May, *The Courage to Create* (New York: W.W. Norton & Co., 1975).

19. Louis Raths *et al.*, *Values and Teaching* (Columbus: G.E. Merrill, 1966).

20. Dewey, *Art as Experience*, p. 79; Dewey, *Experience and Nature*, p. 154.

21. Dewey, *Art as Experience*, p. 85.

22. Dewey, *Experience and Nature*, p. 374.

23. Dewey, *Quest for Certainty*, p. 235.

8.
Process Thought, Worship and Religious Education

Randolph Crump Miller

With its incorporation of the scientific and aesthetic modes of thought, process theology appears to offer one of the most adequate interpretations of contemporary experience. It has become an exciting alternative to traditional theology. One of the earliest and best known proponents of process theology and its implications for religious education, Randolph Crump Miller, examines the ideal of worship.

Worship has a dual relationship to religious education. The experience of worship in itself has a primary educational value, for built into worship are many functions which are directly educational, such as words from the scripture, the words of the prayers and hymns, and the content of the sermon or homily. There are also the physical reactions, the liturgical practices, and the sense of participation with others. The response of worship is often visceral and emotional rather than mental and intellectual, and one's attachment or addiction to worship as a habitual practice is a right lobe form of behavior.

Whitehead tells us that religion is primarily a vision of something. The response to that vision is worship. We are drawn to God as the lure of feelings, as a claim on us for assimilation. We respond to a deity who does not overrule us but who draws us into the harmony of persuasive love. "The power of God is the worship he inspires."[1]

A vision is not an intuition but is an intense mental operation. There is "a unity of aesthetic appreciation immediately felt as private."[2] Yet in worship this appreciation is shared with the believing community. The vision points to "something which stands beyond, behind, and within, the passing flux of immediate things,"[3] which includes the content of "everlastingness."[4]

One task of philosophy or theology or education is to look at religious concepts in the light of experience. Religious teachings, as intermediate representations, are essential to our understanding of and practice of worship, provided that they do not become static and uncriticized. Worship is an adventure that involves risk as a response to the primary vision, and therefore is open to constant reconstruction of beliefs and forms.

WORSHIP

The religious vision comes from the experience of solitariness. This experience may be when one is isolated from other persons or it may occur in the midst of a congregation, but it is an individual's personal response to the vision. Religion, like philosophy, begins in wonder, which is both an emotional and a perceptive experience. As one goes through the "transition from God the void to God the enemy, and from God the enemy to God the companion"[5] what should emerge is a sense of individual worth, either as good or bad. If it is the latter, the results may be evil without reconciliation, for there is always the possibility of degradation, but in any case the experience is one of "transcendent importance."[6]

But one never remains in solitariness, for one belongs to a community. The vision vouchsafed to the individual must be enjoyed and verified within a community, and thus corporate worship becomes essential. The good news is understood as the possession of the community and as universal in application. In this form, if it remains static it can die but if it remains flexible it can face the transformations of history.

There is a dual basis for worship in process theology. There is the incorporation of the individual believer within the community as a means of validating the experience of solitariness; there is also the experience of the individual in community as one shares in the prehension[7] of God and God's prehension of the worshipper and as the others mutually prehend each other in their prehensions of God. Thus our personal prehension of God is strengthened by our prehensions of others who are also in the act of worship. This is an intricate experience, catching hold of the worshipper in the unconscious as well as the conscious awareness of that happening. Thus the worshipper may be only partly aware of what others experience. The appreciative consciousness may sense a depth of meaning which cannot be articulated, while the critical consciousness may be at rest. The primary response is in the affective realm.

This corporate experience is primarily a human form of relating, not different in kind from many secular gatherings such as political meetings or athletic rallies, except for the primary focus on God. The acknowledgment that we are in God's presence in some unique way (for we are always in God's presence) marks worship off from other human gatherings. There are still special occasions in human experience where a human gathering is worshipping, such as celebrations of birth, baptisms, confirmations, ordinations, weddings, and deaths, which highlight not only the sense of togetherness but also the vividness of God's presence.

In the more primitive forms of worship, the response to the central vision is clearly primary. Often the imagination has been crude and barbaric, but there has been an upward trend which fades and recurs as far as beliefs are concerned. Worship has been enriched through the ages by new insights and refined practices. Whitehead sees this central fact of the religious vision, and especially of its increasing enrichment and expansion, as "our one ground for optimism. Apart from it, human life is a flash of occasional enjoyments lighting up a mass of pain and misery, a bagatelle of transient experience."[8]

Worship is a response not only to a vision but to an actual entity.[9] Worship is the only possible response to this vision. It is an "intuition of holiness" which finds increasing expression in every advancing civilization and when lost leads to civilization's decay. Worship is a surrender, not in terms of passivity but in mutual love. It leads to a response in terms of reverence and duty. We do have some control over the course of events, and worship is a primary inspiration for moral action. In worship we are aware of "a character of permanent rightness."[10]

This is what Whitehead calls "an apprehension of commanding vision."[11] It is a vision of the power of love which never coerces or overrules, and yet it presents a command to achieve harmony in a complex world. So we enter into an adventure of the spirit and seek what is potential and yet beyond our grasp. We share "the habitual vision of greatness." We can see such greatness in a few people throughout history, for novel intuitions are unique and such primary insights are usually limited geographically and are not well formulated, but they have a vitality that can be shared in time, provided they do not become dead formulae. We need to see behind the formulae to the fruitful meaning of the novel insight and then interpret it for our world.

In worship, memory and hope belong together. The past which has perished is the basis for our understanding the present that is becoming. We build upon the past and yet we are not slaves to it, for in the becoming there is the emerging novelty, the unpredictable chance, the intended change for which we are responsible. Thus all things become new. This is particularly true of the sacrament of Holy Communion, in which the memory of the Last Supper is brought to bear on the present and points to the unknown future with hope. We recall the past which has perished but which is prehended everlastingly by God, and in our prehension of God the past comes alive as the basis for our present. The emergent novelty which came into actuality in the life of Jesus and is everlastingly prehended by God becomes available to us through the sacrament. Thus we see more clearly the suffering and persuasive love of God at work in our lives.

The non-sacramental services of the word also bring memory and hope together. In this case, there is greater emphasis on the biblical story and on preaching. The response to the vision is more clearly verbal in its primary form, although it leads to moral and social action afterwards. Thus the subjective aim[12] of God is clarified for the congregation through story and proclamation, so that the subjective aims of the members may be aligned with God's aim. This clarification is more obviously educational in intent.

GOD

"The power of God is the worship he inspires."[13] God is accessible through our worship. Process theology provides the regulating concept of God which makes God religiously available through our worship. God is to be understood as the unity of a dipolar nature; we do not experience half of God, for the primodial nature is to be understood as within the consequent[14] nature. So we speak of God as "the lure of feelings, the eternal urge to desire,"[15] as relevant to each creative act. God provides "a tender care that nothing be lost," or God judges the world with "a tenderness which loses nothing that can be saved."[16] This emphasis on tenderness must not make us lose sight of God's remorselessness, for there is an inexorable aspect to God's initial aim as the principle of concretion and God's working may be seen as a righteous judgment on human behavior. God seeks to save the world "or, more accurately, he is the poet of the world, with tender patience leading it by his vision of truth, beauty, and goodness."[17]

There is redemption in God's activity, for suffering love can take sorrow and pain into itself and transform them. God is not static. His everlasting nature is related to the world in such a way that God's consequent nature changes, and thus evil is overcome by good. Because God prehends us, God shares our sufferings and joys in a way that a static deity cannot. In order genuinely to suffer, to be moved by human joys and sorrows, to be pained by the evil in the world, God must be capable of change, of being affected by human experiences. This interrelationship of God and the world, this mutual immanence, is essential for understanding process theology, and it makes possible a concept of a deity worthy of our worship (worship-worthship).

Hartshorne describes a dipolar deity in slightly different terms. A perfect deity is unsurpassable, but logically this means that he may be capable of surpassing himself. God's perfection is surrelative. God is absolute in some ways and relative in other ways, so that God is both everlastingly absolute and temporally involved in the process of change, of becoming and perishing, which is life as we know it.

God is persuasive and not coercive. To be human means to be responsive to persuasion and, therefore, to be free to choose. This leads to the view of mutual immanence and mutual prehension. God is immanent in the world and the world in God. "What is done in the world is transformed into a reality in heaven, and the reality in heaven passes back into the world. By reason of this reciprocal relation, the love in the world passes into the love in heaven, and floods back again into the world. In this sense, God is the great companion—the fellow-sufferer who understands."[18]

In worship we are in the presence of an ideal companion, who is like a "mirror which discloses to every creature its own greatness."[19] "The power by which God sustains the world is the power of himself as an ideal."[20] The response of worship, we have said, is to a commanding vision. It is a free response to persuasive love. Thus our range of values is extended beyond ourselves to others, and we begin to understand that the attainment of values for others is transformed into values for ourselves. This is the basis for an ethics which is both personal and social, for we see ourselves as interrelated to both the organic and inorganic worlds, with responsibilities to both.

The world fits a paradigm that allows for chance, the emergence of novelty, and freedom. The creative processes that emerge into novelty are not fully predictable. An actual entity may be internally determined but eternally it has a degree of freedom. This is the basis for moral responsibility at the human level, whereby God's subjective aim is aligned with that of a human being. But there is freedom for an actual entity to disregard God's subjective aim, and this leads to alienation.

In this world there is evil, which is "the brute motive force of fragmentary purpose, disregarding the eternal vision. Evil is overruling, retarding, hurting."[21] When things are mutually destructive, there is a danger of loss, and the challenge is to provide ways of overcoming evil within a complex structure of harmony. We see evil in all kinds of suffering and in the loss of higher levels of experience. It is a destructive agent, but it is positive and not negative. It tends to eliminate itself "by destruction, or degradation, or by elevation."[22] "There is evil when things are at cross purposes."[23] "The fact of the instability of evil is the moral order of the world."[24]

Evil is opposed to God. God is not a predestinating deity of both good and evil, but rather is a persuasive force for good and beauty and value. "The purpose of God is the attainment of value in the temporal world."[25] Charles Hartshorne suggests that "instead of saying that God's power is limited, . . . we should suggest that his power is absolutely maximal, the greatest possible, but even the greatest possible power is still one power among others, is not the only power. God can do everything that a God can do, everything that could be done by a being with no possible superior."[26] God prehends the evil in the world, but within God's nature evil is overcome with good. The evil from which we suffer is shared by God, who is suffering as well as persuasive love, and thus evil remains genuine and real in this world. But evil is transformed when prehended by God and thus may be woven into the nature of things and become the basis for future goods.

If worship is the human response to the vision of a God at work in the flux of things and also standing behind all things as the ideal, a deity who is good and who is opposed to evil, a God who is suffering and persuasive love, and if this is the basis for understanding the God who is "the chief exemplification" of all the categories of reality, we can understand the value of a process view for the validity of such worship.

Such concepts need to be incorporated into the rituals and preaching of our churches, for there are some fundamental themes that cry out as ways of meeting people's religious needs.

PREACHING

Preaching is the attempt to make relevant the insights of religious living. This relevance comes to a few in moments of insight, but for most of us only after having it suggested to us. This is the justification for both preaching and teaching, and it may also serve as the basis for the revision of ritual. The first principle is to point to "a wisdom in the nature of things."[27] This "production of active wisdom"[28] finds its inspiration not in dogmas but in the "primary expressions of the intuitions of the finest types of religious lives."[29]

Preaching that deals with history might well begin with the recognition that "there stands the inexorable law that apart from some transcendent aim the civilized life either wallows in pleasure or relapses slowly into a barren repetition with waning intensities of feeling." This might be followed with the notice that "the iron compulsion of nature" requires "that the bodily necessities of food, clothing, and shelter be provided." Third, "the compulsory domination of men over men has a double significance. It has a benign effect so far as it secures the coordination of behaviour necessary for social welfare. But it is fatal to extend this dominion beyond the barest limits necessary for this coordination." The fourth factor is "the way of persuasion," which is the basis for community living, in family, human relations and dialogue, and in commerce. Beyond all three, of course, there is the need for "the growth of reverence for that power in virtue of which nature harbours ideal ends, and produces individuals capable of conscious discrimination of such ends."[30] Thus we can have liberty of thought and action.

Such preaching would stress the love of God, the understanding of evil and suffering as not willed by God but prehended by God and thus overcome by God within God's objective for immortality.[31] It would point to "the essence of life" as "the teleological introduction of novelty" which in turn requires "human novelty of functioning and freedom of choice to adapt to it."[32] All that we have said about God in the previous section would be pertinent to teaching, preaching, and ritual.

The sense of deity leads to an awareness of the sense of worth beyond ourselves; this leads to the sense of worth of others and then of ourselves. We are enabled to entertain ideals, to aim at them, to achieve them, and also we can fail or turn against them. "The ultimate motive power, alike in science, in morality, and in religion, is the sense of value, the sense of importance. It takes the various forms of wonder, of curiosity, of reverence, or worship, of tumultous desire for merging personality into something beyond itself. This sense of value imposes on life incredible labours, and apart from it life sinks back into the passivity of its lower types."[33]

Worship is the one experience that captures the nuances of what it means to wonder, to be curious about ultimate things, to be reverent in the face of mystery and to be merged in some way with deity without losing one's own identity and sense of importance. The incredible labors to which worship points are focused on a commanding vision, an initial aim that is vital and exciting, that promises novelty and change for the better. Worship is a call to risk and adventure, a facing of the future that builds on memory of the past but points to an uncharted and open path, and yet finds security in the love of God. As Whitehead says, we can sing "Abide with me" and "Fast falls the eventide" as we are aware of both permanence and flux.[34] Becoming and perishing are seen in relation to that objective immortality by which all that we stand for is prehended by God as a fact for the future. In this sense, "as we perish we are immortal."[35]

EDUCATION

Worship, because it is a primary experience involving the appreciative consciousness, affects the right lobe of learning. It is when worship becomes an automatic routine that the results are deadening. The balance between the appeal to the intellect and the emotions varies with different liturgical traditions, but if either side takes over completely either motive power or direction of action will be lost.

Worship, as we have described it, is a means for keeping alive the vitality of the religious dimension of life. Where wonder, reverence, awe, and the sense of duty coalesce, religion remains vital. Within the framework of worship, chiefly through scripture, hymns, and preaching, this vitality is interpreted and, therefore, kept alive and relevant. As liturgies and creeds are revised, the inert ideas that have lost their significance are excised, often to the dismay of traditionalists but for the good of those who try to live in today's world and worship within a historic tradition that remains relevant. Thus, we are being educated as we worship, although worship is a vital end in itself as the response to the religious vision.

The background of worship as a basis for reflection is an equally important element in religious education. When students and teachers have shared in worship prior to a class session, there are data of experience open to interpretation. Furthermore, there are experiences to which propositions may be applied. Worship provides the data for reflection and also the practical outcome of the application of the study of worship, so that we understand more fully what we are doing when we worship.

Worship is also related to what we do in the world. It is a source of vitality and motivation for ethical and political action. We are moved by the experience of worship to deal with the human condition, in so far as our abilities permit. Education and worship come together in "the production of active wisdom."[36] The deep feeling that we have for others is translated into action by our use of critical and constructive analytical reasoning. This will lead to action and, therefore, to knowledge that we can use. Such knowledge will be reinforced by our efforts and particularly by our successes in applying our insights to assisting others.

Worship seen from a process perspective opens up many theological issues that have practical consequences. The liberation theologies, especially those coming from blacks, women, and Third World countries, fit into a process way of thinking, acting, and worshipping. The emphasis on freedom is not restricted to democracies but is relevant to the concern for human rights everywhere. Freedom involves us in seeking those general ends whereby human beings can live in peace and righteousness. When worship leads to the formation of a sense of community, when the will to belong is satisfied by actually belonging, it is possible to feel at home in the community and in the universe. We begin to see our experiences as a ground for optimism because we live under the religious vision. Someone shares in the misery and meaninglessness of much that happens in the triviality of transient experience.

Worship as we have interpreted it leads to being in the presence of a suffering and loving God. Suffering means having the capacity to be acted upon, to bear another's burdens or happiness. As God is acted upon through the prehension of our feelings and thoughts, a change may be wrought in God. He is "a fellow sufferer who understands."[37] This loving God wills the freedom of others, although in the nature of things God's power never overwhelms our freedom. Because every actual entity has power, God has an external environment and is related to all other actual entities.

At the center of worship is the experience of forgiveness and reconciliation. Traditional views of the atonement have tried to explain how Jesus' death has saved us, but none of these theories starts from the concept of God's love. Reconciliation begins with an awareness that things are not right and that love desires such reconciliation, and this may involve suffering on both sides. The suffering of Jesus exposed some sources of evil, revealed his opposition to the evil that led to conflict and finally violence, and then ultimately opened a new response of love through suffering. What is clear in process thought is that God prehended Jesus' suffering and therefore suffered with Jesus on the cross, just as God suffers with us in our joys and sorrows. The words from the cross become a model of what forgiving love is all about. The healing power of worship turns on the confession and absolution that are part of almost all formal worship. "The uniquely creative element in Christian experience is just the overflow of new life and power which comes from the depths of that experience in which our human despair is met by the suffering love of God in all its majesty, humility, and holiness,"[38] as Daniel Day Williams summarized it.

We come back to the vitality of religious faith kept alive in the worshipping community by the power of the Holy Spirit. The religious vision is the ground of our optimism, the basis for our sense of worth, and the foundation for our work toward liberation. Such a vision is a lure which attracts and repels us at the same time. God becomes an enemy when our aims are not aligned with God's aim for us; we have freedom to turn from God, from the vision, from the adventure and risk of worship, and thus we can experience the death of religious faith in ourselves.

But what passes for worship is often not worship in the sense we have defined it. Much so-called worship is locked in the bonds of tradition, with outmoded teachings and inert idea, and repressive of "the high hope of adventure."[39] Our problem is to work for the reformation of such worship, to align our practice of worship with the high hope of adventure, with the flight after the unattainable, and with God as the one who inspires it.

The reformation of the practice of worship will lead to liturgical changes. If we are correct in the use of the concept of God in process theology, we may have to restructure the language of worship. References to God as impassible or omnipotent, who predestines individuals in their activities and their destinations, who wills that humankind should suffer from genuine evil, who is a god of war and destruction, as found so often in traditional prayers, would be abolished. The emphasis would be on God's persuasive and suffering and forgiving love, on God's initial aim for humankind and on the need to align our aims with his. The language would not be reflective of a one-on-one relationship but on the multirelational nature of God and our experience of God as an actual entity known in a myriad of ways. The themes of forgiveness and reconciliation, liberation and freedom, suffering and love, and the sense of worth of each individual would resound throughout such worship, both in the liturgy and in the preaching. These would also be the major themes in the educational program derived from the experience of being together as a community at worship.[40]

Religion, we have said, is a vision. The response to that vision is worship, and this includes the apprehension of a commanding vision, so that our worship is more than ritual; it is an adventure of the spirit as we seek the kingdom of heaven on earth. Because the power of God is the worship he inspires, we are persuaded, not coerced, to respond in our freedom to those values which may come to be, so that as we prehend the value in God we may apply it to the value of other entities and finally to ourselves. Thus we learn to love God, and to love our neighbors as ourselves.

Notes

1. Alfred North Whitehead, *Science and the Modern World* (New York: Macmillan, 1926), Mentor Edition, p. 192. Hereafter cited SMW.

2. Alfred North Whitehead, *Process and Reality* (New York: Macmillan, 1929), p. 323. Hereafter cited PR.

3. SMW, p. 191.

4. PR, p. 527.

5. Alfred North Whitehead, *Religion in the Making* (New York: Macmillan, 1926), pp. 16-7. Hereafter cited RM.

6. RM, p. 18.

7. "There is a 'vague affective tone' at the basis of experience. There is a feeling or concern or grasping which is an activity of the whole body and not just the senses. Whitehead calls this feeling a 'prehension.' It is a feeling by which one entity is related to another; it can become very complex. The use of the word *know* in the Bible to refer to both sexual intercourse and to knowledge of God indicates something of this feeling tone of a prehension. It is a kind of empathy for others. In its physical form it may be unconscious; in its mental form, as when we grasp the objective form of a potential that is not yet actual, it is conscious. The whole body experiences, and there is a feeling of closeness, as when we are told, 'You will know that I am in my Father, and you in me, and I in you' (Jn. 14:20, RSV). In this usage, we can say that we prehend God and God prehends us." (From my *This We Can Believe*, New York: Hawthorn, 1976, pp. 27-8; see PR, pp. 337-8.)

8. SMW, p. 192.

9. "The real world is made up of actual entities. 'There is no going behind actual entities to find anything more real.' . . . We never get behind these final facts, which are 'drops of experience, complex and independent.' . . . Actual entities are linked together into societies which give historical continuity to the world, but they retain their individuality and novelty, differing in richness or degree of quality." (From my *The American Spirit in Theology*, Philadelphia: Pilgrim, 1974, p. 150; see PR, pp. 27-8.)

10. RM, p. 61.

11. *Ibid.*

12. "Actual entities are affected by each other, but they also have what is called their 'subjective aim,' which means that there is an end in view of their activities. This 'subjective aim' is not necessarily conscious or purposeful, although it may be at higher levels. Thus an organism determines its own end, its ultimate definiteness, although influenced by eternal objects and other actual entities. At this higher level is freedom, 'which is the whole

point of moral responsibility.' " (From my *The American Spirit in Theology*, p. 150; see PR. p. 390.)

13. SMW, p. 192.

14. We think of God as dipolar. "We can imagine abstract forms, or potentialities waiting to be born, or even a primordial reality that structures what would otherwise be chaos. Without some kind of direction, limitation or persuasion, life would be like a river that has no banks, a flood with no dike to control it. With no aims or goals in mind, life would go on in a chaotic sort of way, if at all, but there would be no goal.

"If we think of God as a creative order, we are joining together two basic ideas: the ordering and the creative aspects of God. When Whitehead spoke of the 'primordial' nature or aspects of God, he had in mind the immanent process which is at work in our midst, which we experience, and which is the persuasive love of the Galilean vision. It is God's grace, God's free gift of self, God's consequent nature." (From *This We Can Believe*, pp. 63-4.)

15. PR, p. 522.

16. PR, p. 525.

17. PR, p. 526; cf. pp. 373-4.

18. PR, p. 532.

19. RM, p. 155.

20. RM, p. 156.

21. SMW, p. 192.

22. RM, p. 96.

23. RM, p. 97.

24. RM, p. 95.

25. RM, p. 100.

26. Charles Hartshorne, *The Divine Relativity* (New Haven: Yale University Press, 1948), p. 138.

27. RM, p. 143.

28. Alfred North Whitehead, *Aims of Education* (New York: Macmillan, 1929), p. 37. Hereafter cited AE.

29. RM, p. 144.

30. Alfred North Whitehead, *Adventures of Ideas* (New York: Macmillan, 1933), pp. 108-9. Hereafter cited AI.

31. "When an actual entity has ceased to exist and therefore lacks living immediacy, it has attained 'objective immortality,' so that it does not now exist for itself but for other occasions. It is no longer actual but is to be used for future acts of experience. It is nonexistent and yet a fact for the future." (From my *The American Spirit in Theology*, p. 151; see AI, pp. 248, 305). "Death is the last page of the last chapter of the book of one's life, as birth is the first page of the first chapter. Without a first page there is no book. But given a first page there is, so far, a book. The question of death then is, How rich and how complete is the book to be?" (From Charles Hartshorne, *The Logic of Perfection* [Open Court, 1962], pp. 250-1.) "For this book to have value, there must be a reader, and for some generations after we die our book can be read by our successors. But in time they will cease to be. Even now, they will be unable to grasp the whole book. But, according to Hartshorne, God reads our book everlastingly. God omits nothing and adds nothing. So there is an important way in which we continue to live in God's memory."

(From my *This We Can Believe*, p. 136.) This is what we mean by objective immortality.

32. AI, p. 266.
33. AE, p. 40.
34. Cf. PR, p. 513.
35. *Essays in Science and Philosophy* (New York: Philosophical Library, 1947), p. 117.
36. AE, p. 37.
37. PR, p. 532.
38. Daniel Day Williams, *God's Grace and Man's Hope* (New York: Harper & Row, 1949), p. 59.
39. SMW, p. 192.
40. Cf. Randolph C. Miller, "Process Theology and Religious Education," *Anglican Theological Review*, July 1975, 271-88; R. C. Miller, "Whitehead and Religious Education," *Religious Education*, May-June 1973, 315-22; R. C. Miller "Theology and the Future of Religious Education," *Religious Education*, Jan-Feb 1977, 46-60.

Suggesting Readings

Brown, Delwin; James, Ralph; and Reeves, Gene, eds. *Process Philosophy and Christian Thought*. Indianapolis: Bobbs-Merrill Co., 1971.

Cobb, John B., Jr. *A Christian Natural Theology*. Philadelphia: Westminister Press, 1965.

Durka, Gloria, and Smith, Joanmarie. *Modeling God*. New York: Paulist Press, 1976.

Griffin, David R. *God, Power and Evil*. Philadelphia: Westminster Press, 1976.

Hamilton, Peter N. *The Living God and the Modern World*. Philadelphia: United Church Press, 1967.

Hartshorne, Charles. *The Divine Relativity*. New Haven: Yale University Press, 1948.

Lee, Bernard. *The Becoming of the Church*. New York: Paulist Press, 1974.

Meland, Bernard E. *Modern Man's Worship*. New York: Harper & Row, 1934.

Miller, Randolph C. "Continuity and Contrast in the Future of Religious Education." *The Religious Education We Need*. Edited by James Michael Lee. Mishawaka, IN: Religious Education Press, 1977.

Miller, Randolph C. "Process Theology and Religious Education." *Anglican Theological Review*, July 1975, pp. 271-88.

Miller, Randolph C. *This We Can Believe*. New York: Hawthorn, 1976.

Underhill, Evelyn. *Worship*. New York: Harper & Row, 1937.

Westerhoff, John H., III. "The Liturgical Imperative of Religious Education." *The Religious Education We Need*. Edited by James Michael Lee. Mishawaka, IN: Religious Education Press, 1977.

Whitehead, Alfred North. *Adventures of Ideas*. New York: Macmillan, 1933.

Whitehead, Alfred North. *Aims of Education*. New York: Macmillan, 1929.

Whitehead, Alfred North. *Process and Reality*. New York: Macmillan, 1929.

Whitehead, Alfred North. *Religion in the Making*. New York: Macmillan, 1926.

Whitehead, Alfred North. *Science and the Modern World*. New York: Macmillan, 1925; Mentor edition, 1948.

Williams, Daniel Day. *The Spirit and Forms of Love*. New York: Harper & Row, 1968.

9.
Liturgical Suggestions for Celebrating the Para-Feasts of the Lord of All Distributions, the Holy Probability, Blessed Student, and the Memory of Kurt Gödel

John H. Peatling

The rather unique title of this piece sets the tone for a novel wedding of the cognitive and affective. John Peatling, a researcher in religious development, locates the most recent findings on the crisis of midlife as a homily in a liturgy that celebrates scholarly inquiry.

Few aspects of religious life are as persistant as the liturgical. Yet few things so persistent are also so amenable to the influence of time and place. While many religious groups have found new and contemporary ways of celebrating old and unchanging verities in recent years, only within the sphere of right lobe religion is it possible to imagine celebrating empirical research. However, that observation is itself obviously time-and-place bound. Therefore, the following is almost certainly a vision, glimpsed in a clouded mirror, of some other time and some other place. in all likelihood, it is a distorted vision of a time and place in the not yet we call the future; a time and place when the radical implications of the Johannine Prologue will be commonly accepted and, so, the study of accessible reality will be honored as a fundamentally religious task. Until that time and place, then, visions should not be mistaken for present realities, although that is not to say they are inherently false; within the sequence of time, they are merely anticipations.

A SALUTATION OR INITIAL GREETING

Celebrant: May the One who has designed and formed, founded and created all that is, be your guide and your goal!

Response: And may that One be your guide and goal, too.

AN APPROPRIATE PRAYER

Lord of all the distributions that are, whose will is worked out in strange and remarkable ways as you effect your intent through what we see as probabilities, keep us honest and, well, faithful to both our ideals and our need for truth; that we may trace out the ways of reality and, so, fool no one, may we clearly label and separate our facts from our interpretations; since in honesty we come to know both things that are new and our own ignorance, preserve us, O Lord, from confusing the one with the other.

READINGS OR REMINDERS

+ One, two or three of the following passages may be read as reminders of the challenging n-dimensional conceptual space encountered by those who undertake to trace out the ways of reality via research.

+ In between each Reminder it is appropriate if a song expressive of human wonder, awe, or delight before Beauty, Truth, or Design be sung.

A. "Look yonder," said my Guide. "Behold yon miserable creature. That Point is a Being like ourselves, but confined to the non-dimensional Gulf. He is himself his own World, his own Universe; of any other than himself he can form no conception; he knows not Length, nor Breadth, nor Height, for he has had no experience of them; he has no cognizance even of the number Two; nor has he a thought of Plurality; for he is himself his One and All, being really Nothing. Yet mark his perfect self-contentment, and hence learn this lesson: that to be self-contented is to be vile and ignorant, and that to aspire is better than to be blindly and impotently happy." (Section 20, *Flatland*, c. 1884)

B. "In 1931 Kurt Gödel . . . established definitively that the formalist program cannot be executed . . . In other words, since Gödel we know that the axiomatic method has certain inherent limitations, though these limits can be 'shifted' by shifting systems. . . . The hierarchy that was thus introduced into the realm of logic and mathematics soon gave rise to an idea of 'construction, . . . (that) . . . is incompatible with any simplistic theory of mind or intellectual activity.

"Gödel showed that the construction of a demonstrably consistent, relatively rich theory requires not simply an 'analysis' of its 'presuppositions,' but the construction of the next 'higher' theory! . . . Now, 'simplicity' becomes a sign of weakness and the 'fastening' of any story in the edifice of human knowledge calls for the construction of the next higher story. In short, rather than envisaging human knowledge as a pyramid or building of some sort, we should think of it as a spiral the radius of whose turns increases as the spiral rises.

"The basic epistemological alternatives are predestination or some sort of constructivism. . . . But God himself has, since Gödel's theorem, ceased to be motionless. He is the living God, more so than heretofore, because he is unceasingly constructing ever 'stronger' systems."

(Selections from J. Piaget, *Structuralism*, c. 1968)

C. "Statistical procedure and experimental design are only two different aspects of the same whole, and that whole comprises all the logical requirements of the complete process of adding to natural knowledge by experimentation. . . . Experimental observations are only experience carefully planned in advance, and designed to form a secure basis of new knowledge; that is, they are systematically related to the body of knowledge already acquired, and the results are deliberately observed, and put on record accurately. . . . The liberation of the human intellect must, however, remain incomplete so long as it is free only to work out the consequences of a prescribed body of dogmatic data, and is denied the access to unsuspected truths, which only direct observation can give."

(Selections from R. A. Fisher, *The Design of Experiments*, 7th Ed., c. 1960)

D. "The psychologist, for all his apartness, is governed by the same constraints that shape the behavior of those whom he studies. He too searches widely and metaphorically for his hunches. . . . If he is not fearful of these products of his own subjectivity, he will go so far as to tame the metaphors that have produced the hunches, tame them in the sense of shifting them from the left hand to the right hand by rendering them into notions that can be tested. It is my impression from observing myself and my colleagues that the forging of metaphoric hunch into testable hypothesis goes on all the time. [Therefore,] I find myself a little out of patience with the alleged split

between "the two cultures," for the two are not simply external ways
of life, one pursued by humanists, the other by scientists. They are
ways of living with one's own experience."
    (Selections from J. S. Bruner, *On Knowing. Essays for the Left
Hand*, c. 1962)
E. Philip Morrison—Cornell's head
    Of the department of nuclear physics—
    Talks about what he calls
    "Left-hand" and "right-hand" sciences.
    Right-hand science deals in all the proven
    Scientific formulas and experiments.
    Left-hand science deals in
    All of the as yet *unknown* or *unproven*—
    That is: With all it is going to take
    Intellectually, intuitively, speculatively, imaginatively
    And even mystically
    By inspired persistence
    To open up the as yet unknown.
    The great scientists were great
    Because they were the ones
    Who dealt successfully with the unknown.
    All the "greats" were left-hand scientists.
    (R. Buckminster Fuller, "How Little I Know," c. 1966)
F. Novelty, synergy and the possible presence
    Of unknown additional principles
    Call for both deliberation
    And recognition of the inherent
    Fallibility of wisdom itself,
    Which fallibility hazard
    Wisdom appreciates
    As nonwisdom does not.
    (R. B. Fuller, "A Definition of Evolution," c. 1976)
G. "In short, philosophy, due to its reflective method, raises problems, but does not solve them, because reflection does not by itself
involve methods of verification. . . . It is of little importance whether
we restrict the term 'philosophy' only to that of philosophers, or also
include that of scientists who 'reflect,' and whether we restrict the
term 'science' to scientists alone or include the great philosophers
who have known how to experiment and to make deductions; all this
is unimportant. What is important is the trilogy reflection X deduction X experiment, the first term representing the heuristic function
and the other two cognitive verification, which is alone constitutive
of 'truth.'

"But there remain problems that science cannot solve either temporarily or in some cases can only solve on a provisional basis, which no doubt will remain final. These problems can be of vital importance. . . . They therefore require equally 'provisional' solutions. . . .

"To want to consider them as modes of knowledge is a constantly recurring illusion of some philosophers. But in interpreting them as a wisdom (or, since the solutions are numerous and irreducible, as 'wisdoms'), and as wisdom as rational and as basic to 'knowledge' as one would wish, the agreement between knowledge and *praxis* will no longer be disturbed."

(J. Piaget, *Insights and Illusions of Philosophy*, c. 1965)

A DISCOURSE OR REPORT OR APPROPRIATE HOMILY

+ Following the reading of one or more of the Reminders, it is most appropriate if the Celebrant, or an Assistant, reads or delivers a short Discourse or makes a Report of research (underway or recently completed).

+ Such a Discourse or Report may, if desired, be introduced by the following Statement of Intent, to which the indicated response is appropriate.

Celebrant: Let these words be just and kind.
Response: And may you live in quiet fellowship with the Eternal
(After Moffatt's translation of Micah 6:8)

+ The following Report is offered only as an example; other original statements summarizing research, or suggesting implications of research analyses, are appropriate and may be used at the discretion of the one who presides at or is responsible for the celebration.

FIVE CRIES FROM MID-LIFE: A PARADIGM FOR RESEARCH

Beginning in late 1974 I started to report on the responses of children and adolescents to a simple, fairy tale-like moral puzzle.[1] In 1975 and 1976 I also began to report on the responses of a select sample of adults to that same moral puzzle.[2] As a result of those reports, articles appeared during 1976 and 1977 in the journals *Religious Education*,[3] *Character Potential: A Record of Research*,[4] and the *Vocational Guidance Quarterly*.[5] The reports began as detailed albeit simple empirical reports of responses by children and adolescents in grades 4-12, However, when the analyses began to include post-adolescents, the reports increasingly became concerned with the exploration of possible ways of understanding what appeared to be theoretically unexpected, if not downright inexplicable, responses from the select sample of adults.

Whereas I began within a thoroughly Piagetian conceptual context, I came increasingly to recognize that the data challenged the normal "developmental" model. By March, the response from the adults suggested a progression that went backwards.[6] In April I compared adult responses to other test results with responses by the same adults to the moral puzzle, reported "a growing disparity between levels of thinking and judging," and suggested that it seemed useful to call upon the theories of Robert J. Havighurst,[7] Donald E. Super,[8] and Erik H. Erikson,[9] as well as those of Barbel Inhelder and Jean Piaget,[10] if one was to "understand" the data.[11] In November it seemed that the observed disparity between thinking and judging during much of the period of adulthood might enable a new and useful "realism" in educational work with adults.[12] In the same month, I published the article, "A Sense of Justice: Moral Judgment in Children, Adolescents & Adults," in which it was suggested that it would be useful to invoke Gödel's theorem and, as a result, attempt to identify a *macro*-process within which "developmental" sequence might exist as a *micro*-process.[13] While acknowledging the speculative nature of the proposal, the article concluded by affirming:

> For the moment, then, it may be more appropriate to consider the development of moral judgments as a peculiarly complex example of personal/psychological "energy": both wave and quantum appear useful and necessary models of a life-span *macro*-process of moral judgment "development."[14]

In March of 1977 a panel at the Dallas meeting of the American Personnel and Guidance Association continued the consideration of the relationship between Career, Mid-Life, and the Crises peculiar to that portion of adulthood, a consideration which had been initiated the previous April in Chicago. While building upon the analyses of adult responses completed and reported earlier, I sought to move beyond description of a puzzling phenomenon to a provisional interpretation of the data in terms that could have meaning for an audience of counselors of adults during the years of Mid-Life. I chose to cast that interpretation into the form of what I called *Five Cries From Mid-Life*.

The presentation of the Five Cries theme was set within the context of a recognition that a growing disparity between attained (or achievable) levels of cognitive operation and patterns of response to a moral puzzle might explain an adult's growing Sense of Absurdity. For example, it was noted that the word absurd can be defined by two other words: ridiculous and unreasonable. Then, noting that both of the defining words presume one's own standard of what is "reasonable," it seemed that level of cognitive operation *should* be an important contributing factor in any adult's sense of what was either ridiculous or unreasonable. Since the previous analyses suggested an *increasing* level of cognitive operation during the years between 20 and 55, it was posited that adults were quite likely to repeatedly come into new understandings of what it meant to be reasonable. Thus, as an adult's understanding of what it means to be "reasonable" changes or "grows," it seems quite probable that an adult's understanding of what is simply so *un*reasonable as to be ridiculous would also change. An analysis of this data suggested a series of what I call "speculations" about Mid-Life, its Crises, and a Mid-Lifer's Sense of Absurdity. Those speculations are organized into Five Cries.

A. The First Cry: THE BASTARDS WON AGAIN!

During Mid-Life many adults have the often wrenching experience of discovering that Sometimes the Good Guys Lose. Although the example of the anti-hero might well have suggested as much, many adults have not really believed that it would happen to them. Of course, for this experience to have its full impact, one must see oneself as reasonable, insightful and, on the whole, quite knowledgeable. In addition, one must clearly recognize that something of value has been "lost" to the present power of ignorance, blindness, or simple *un*reasonableness.

This sort of experience probably is common to laborers and managers, and it is likely that during Mid-Life it assumes a peculiar poignancy. That poignancy comes from an adult's "new" powers of cognitive operation, for far too often Mid-Lifers clearly recognize that the liveliest option open to them is what a Piagetian might call Accommodation, rather than Assimilation. For the adult to issue this First Cry, the unlikelihood of assimilation must be sharply felt, along with the resigned recognition that one's own Crisis concerns how one may accommodate to the "loss." Probably the Cry also owes something to the possibility that in earlier years successes had been either more frequent or, if not, the patent absurdity of losing out to ignorance or to the unreasonable was not so clearly perceived.

B. *The Second Cry: MY GOD, THEY'RE IN COLLEGE!*

At some period during the Mid-Life years adults with offspring suddenly realize that the postal system is now delivering notices of parents' weekends. In all likelihood, well before that sometimes shocking recognition, adults have agonized over the all too pragmatic problem of paying for their offspring's continuing post-secondary education. But with those messages about parents' weekends there comes, perhaps as never before, a clear understanding that Time Does Fly (regardless of how "impossible" it may seem!). Along with that recognition there is a fair chance that Mid-Life adults will also recognize that, for all of those interesting earlier years of childhood and adolescence, it is now their turn to Pay the Academic Piper.

Unless the Mid-Life adult has been sufficiently foresighted, these twin recognitions bring an adult face to face with what often seems like a financial "burden." The clarity with which Time is perceived to be an inexorable flow does nothing to help one bear that burden. Moreover, this encounter may well be one's best and strongest clue that the Mid-Life adult is just that and, so, no longer an eager Young Adult. The emotions probably do not "feel" any older, but the possibility of "new" levels of cognitive operation may well suggest that what one knows to be so is more than a little unreasonable, ridiculous, absurd. At the heart of this Second Cry there is likely to be adults' almost overwhelming sense that neither TIME nor COST should exact SO MUCH from them.

C. *The Third Cry: THANK GOD, WE'RE ALONE!*

Increasingly, as one's offspring couple (if not marry), Mid-Lifers find themselves in either of two different situations, each of which often seems to involve more than a modicum of absurdity. *First*, with offspring off to college, or trade school, or work, adults in Mid-Life find that the house is "empty." Suddenly, adults realize that their offspring are living *their* lives somewhere else, with some "others," and the adult is here with another adult, just the two of them.[15] In the midst of Mid-Life, adults find themselves couples again. *Second*, many Mid-Lifers experience a slow, inexorable recognition that while they "love" their offspring, there is a distinct sense of "relief" when the offspring return to school, or apartment, or wherever "else" it is that they *now* live an ever larger portion of their life. Mid-Lifers encounter the paradox of Loving 'em, But . . . being *glad* when the visit is over!

Both experiences challenge the Mid-Life adult's "new" powers of thinking. Indeed, even with those new powers of cognitive operation, the Mid-Life adult may experience *both* a sense of absurdity *and* an acute sense of guilt. On the one hand, it seems impossible that one's offspring are living somewhere else. On the other, our "missing" them can seem all too marred by our evident "relief" when they return to their own life. In fact, the guilt some adults feel may be one of the more poignant examples of absurdity in Mid-Life. If so, then this Third Cry takes on a different tone—almost as different as that variation of the Cry that expresses the absurdity of discovering that two adults seem to have "lost" their most powerful common reason for being a couple, the offspring. That variant, of course, is *not* "thankful" and, so, becomes the despair-tinged Cry: GOD, WE'RE ALONE![16]

D. *The Fourth Cry: DAMN, WILL IT EVER LET UP?*

At some time during the period of Mid-Life, an adult's "new" and growing ability to think at an "advanced" level of Piagetian formal operations will probably lead to the recognition of two things. *First*, simple honesty (coupled with a growing objectivity toward oneself) tends to lead persons to acknowledge that they simply are Frazzling Faster Than Before. Brute strength may be waning, or one's emotions "let go" more easily, or the heretofore normal working day leaves one noticeably more "exhausted." In a word, Mid-Life involves the seemingly absurd recognition that one is *not* the young thing one once was. In fact, it may even be possible to recognize a certain absurdity in pretending to be but 29, when 45 is the fact, and one feels it! Those Mid-Lifers who recognize that sort of thing about themselves may also find that the unchanging pace of work, or even of social life, begins to assume an absurdity all its own, especially if one feels not so subtly impelled into acting "as if" it were not true. *That* a Mid-Life adult knows for a certainty is ridiculous!

Second, at some moment during the 40's many adults begin to realize that Mid-Life is *exactly* where they are. Half of one's career is behind, and no more than half is still ahead. With a "new" appreciation, such Mid-Lifers begin to read about the Social Security system, or "check" on their pension plan, or even start to consider that their own retirement is no longer unthinkable. If persons reach this point fortunate enough to be doing something they like to do, they may "settle in" for what is (now!) the not-so-long haul. But if persons reach this point and look at their work and know it is just too frazzling, too pressurized, those Mid-Lifers may begin to entertain the idea of "changing" before they are either fired or, perhaps, fall over with a heart attack!

This Fourth Cry quite obviously arises out of personal frustration. But that frustration may, in turn, be the result of growing and changing understandings of what it means to be reasonable and, so, of what it is to be faced by the *un*reasonable, the ridiculous, the absurd. Mid-Lifers who issue this Cry, then, are likely to be persons whose level of thinking is continuing to grow. Their Cry is a sign of potential strength, not merely an indicator of weakness (let alone of premature senility)!

E. *The Fifth Cry: I KNOW I CAN DO IT, BUT I DON'T WANT TO!*

Many adults in Mid-Life reach a point where they take their own wants seriously. They know (often quite objectively!) what they CAN do. Their evaluation of their abilities to manage, direct, supervise, or create is often quite accurate. They recognize equally well just how good they are at lifting, hauling, stacking, or organizing. But for some Mid-Lifers that accuracy about themselves becomes less and less important, for they begin to think of "other" things they would LIKE to do. Suddenly CAN do and LIKE to do become distinctly different things; for many adults their previous assumption that the two were synonymous becomes less than reasonable, more and more ridiculous, increasingly absurd.

Although not all Mid-Lifers issue this Fifth Cry or, even if they do, find themselves prepared to act upon it, many do and some are. When that happens, an adult may look squarely at an "advancement" and (probably in all honesty) simply say *I Know I Can Do It, But I Don't Want To!* The "advancement" is turned down. When such intriguing behavior accompanies this Cry, it probably is a sign that those "new" cognitive abilities have enabled persons to recognize that there is an element of absurdity involved in "merely" continuing to do what they know very well they CAN do, and do very well indeed. Such a "new"level of thinking may, in fact, lead to the "discovery" that one's own experience has both a *reality* and a considerable personal *value*. In addition, some Mid-Life adults discover that what really "challenges" them is the opportunity to work with the new and the not yet tried![17]

When adults in Mid-Life recognize any such thing, or discover that "challenge" is important to them and, so, a thing of personal value, some older patterns of judgment are seen to be patently absurd. Thus, these Mid-Lifers are more than likely to say, BUT I DON'T WANT TO! They mean it. Perhaps for almost the first time in many years that expression has meaning. They both KNOW and they VALUE their own *experience*, and their known *competency*. As Mid-

Lifers they are prepared, often to *cooperate*, but are increasingly dissatisfied with merely being *controlled*. This Fifth Cry, then, can be a Mid-Lifer's "offer" just as much as it can be an act of "refusal": the only condition being that humanity be recognized, accepted, and accommodated.

A FIVE CRY PARADIGM: SHIFTING FROM THE LEFT HAND TO THE RIGHT
HAND

The inherently speculative nature of these Five Cries must not be overlooked. I have written elsewhere:

No one should misunderstand what I have said. I do NOT claim that empirical data from my select sample of adults says those persons were issuing one or another of these FIVE CRIES FROM MID-LIFE. What that data does clearly indicate is a growing disparity between achieved "levels" of cognitive operation and moral judgment. I have used that indication as a basis for the relatively "positive" inference that adults grow into "new" levels of thinking and, so, come progressively to find hitherto "acceptable" albeit controlling experiences to be "infected" with simple absurdity.[18]

Clearly one would misunderstand these sentences if they were read without the recognition that the Five Cries *per se* are specifically labeled as" . . . (a) relatively 'positive' inference. . . . " The Cries, then, can best be understood as an exercise in what, some time ago, Bruner might have called Left Hand thinking. However, just as Bruner reminded his readers that such metaphorical thought is *often* (if *not* always!) the source of scientific hunches, or ideas on the way toward becoming testable hypotheses, these Five Cries require a translation if the Right Hand is to research what the Left Hand has identified.[19]

While I have not completed the process of translation in my March, 1977 paper, there does seem to be an intriguing start in a lengthy final Note. Given the original audience—professional counselors, many of whom were working with adults in Mid-Life and in Mid-Career—the invitation to use the Five Cries as a paradigm for the gathering of data (an action which would permit initial, gross estimates of incidence and, so, the discerning of any examples of ordered change) was probably all that could be done within the constraints of a panel presentation. However, at this later date it is evident that the Five Cry paradigm presumes (for complete generality) a married adult in Mid-Life with offspring. The applicability of the paradigm to unmarried adults, or to married adults without offspring, is therefore somewhat limited. *For example*, while the first, fourth, and fifth Cries are quite general to Mid-Life, the second and the third Cries seem (at first) to be sharply limited to Mid-Lifers with offspring. While not completely satisfactory, it probably is possible that single adults or married adults without offspring may "issue" something similar to the second and third Cries as they (a) recognize How Time Does Fly (See the Second Cry), or (b) recognize, perhaps in terms of nieces and nephews, the paradox that one may Love 'Em, But . . . (See the Third Cry).

Even so, it is now possible to *extend* the initial paradigm and, thereby, envision a process of simple but fundamentally scientific exploratory research. The left handed insight can be tamed sufficiently so that the right hand can operate. Moreover, if one's expectations are carefully restrained, there is no reason why *any* person with repeated access to human beings can not participate in what, to appropriate a phrase of R. Buckminster Fuller, could legitimately be described as Left-hand science.[20]

The 1977 Note identified two sub-Cries within each of the major Five Cries From Mid-Life. These "minimal" sub-divisions, therefore, offer a remarkably simple but rich paradigm for creating what R. A. Risher called " . . . experience carefully planned in advance," that is, a set of experimental observations ". . . designed to form a secure basis of new knowledge. . . ."[21] Consider, then, the simple two-fold hierarchy created by those original Five Cries and their pairs of sub-Cries:

1. *THE BASTARDS WON AGAIN!* . . . . Cry #1.
   a. Sometimes the Good Guys Lose . . . . Cry #1.a.
   b. Accommodation Over Assimilation . . . . Cry #1.b.
2. *MY GOD, THEY'RE IN COLLEGE!* . . . . Cry #2.
   a. How Time Does Fly . . . . Cry #2.a.
   b. Paying the Academic Piper . . . . Cry #2.b.
3. *THANK GOD, WE'RE ALONE!* . . . . Cry #3.
   a. Couples Again . . . . Cry #3.a.
   b. Love 'Em, But . . . . Cry #3.b.
4. *DAMN, WILL IT EVER LET UP?* . . . . Cry #4.
   a. Frazzling Faster Than Before . . . . Cry #4.a.
   b. Settle In or Change? . . . . Cry 4.b.
5. *I KNOW I CAN DO IT, BUT I DON'T WANT TO!* . . . Cry #5.
   a. Looking Out of the Rut . . . . Cry #5.a.
   b. My Experience Counts . . . . Cry #5.b.

If one can imagine that one human can know "enough" about another human to decide whether that "other" *does* or *does not* issue one or another of the Five Cries, something very like Fisher's "experience carefully planned in advance" can be imagined without much trouble. Essentially, all one must be able to do vis-à-vis another human being is, upon the basis of one's knowledge of *that* person, decide that he DOES or DOES NOT issue one or another of the Five Cries. If, in addition, one can decide that one (specifically) issues one or another of the ten sub-Cries, the Fisherian "new knowledge" will be *vastly* increased.

For example, if one adopts a simple albeit thoroughly arbitrary convention that the plus sign (+) indicates that a person *does* issue a particular Cry, and that the minus sign (−) indicates that a person *does not* issue that same Cry, one can easily identify *all* of the logically possible combinations of decisions regarding an individual vis-à-vis the set of the Five Cries From Mid-Life. In fact, were one prepared to make *ten* rather than *five* such decisions, and symbolize those decisions in the same dichotomous manner, one could do the same thing. However, since the total number of logically possible combinations equals (a) the number of possible states or decisions vis-à-vis another, which in this case is 2, raised to (b) a *power* equivalent to the number of samples or questions or, in this instance, Cries (or sub-Cries) From Mid-Life, which in this case would be either 5 or 10, the mathematics are quite straightforward. That is, if one deals with the Five Cries, there are exactly 32 possible combinations of decisions vis-à-vis another person. But if one were to deal with the ten sub-Cries, there would be 1024 possible combinations of decisions. It is this exponential increase that justifies the observation that the sheer amount of Fisherian "new knowledge" would be vastly increased by making (if possible) ten instead of five decisions about another person.

For purposes of illustration, it probably is best to stay with the smaller number. Especially if one is at all intrigued with the possibility of doing some actual data gathering and, so, contributing to the fund of natural knowledge about that important period of human living referred to as Mid-Life. In fact, since it is just that possibility which is most intriguing about the paradigm of the Five Cries, pragmatics dictate such a restriction.

The restricted but exhaustive set of 32 logically *possible* combinations can be listed by appropriating from symbolic logic the device of a truth table. In such a truth table there would be 5 columns, each of which would represent one of the Five Cries, and 32 rows, each of which would represent a five-fold *logically* possible combination of dichotomous decisions vis-à-vis another person's issuing each of the Five Cries From Mid-Life. Naturally, since the combinations are only logically possible, observation and decision regarding *any* select group of persons will probably *not* involve examples of all of the possible combinations. However, as the number of persons in any such select group increases, the *confidence* with which one can *infer* individual or group *intention* will increase. As that confidence increases, so will the likelihood that one's observations are a useful-to-important contribution to "new knowledge" about Mid-Life, as discerned through the paradigm of the Five Cries.

The 1977 initial Note on the Five Cries paradigm suggested that the 20 years from age 35 through age 54 would be the place to begin gathering such data. The suggestion was based upon a prior pattern analysis of adult responses to a moral puzzle and, for the purposes of one's own research into Mid-Life, I suggested sub-dividing the span into *four* 5-year groupings: 35-39 years, 40-44 years, 45-49 years, and 50-54 years. If that were done, I concluded that signs of ordered change across the four age levels would probably be evident in a changing percentage of an age level grouping issuing one or another of the Cries (or sub-Cries). Now it is possible to extend that earlier observation by noting that such ordered change across those four age level groupings might well be seen in a shifting percentage of each grouping judged to issue a *particular* 5-fold (or 10-fold) combination of Cries (or sub-Cries). If one were willing to make such a "fine" discrimination, which obviously would depend upon the record one could and would make a series of decisions vis-a-vis another, the potential for genuinely helpful counsel should increase.

In fact, what has happened is that something closely akin to a full cycle of the theory production process has been outlined. I began with a simple empirical description. My data led me to search for a way of making that data's results "reasonable," which led me into the realm of theory itself. There I identified a way to achieve the goal of reasonableness, even if it was not a way I had initially anticipated. That discovery, in turn, led me to develop an "interpretation" of the data (*via* inference) that took the form of the Five Cries From Mid-Life. What has just been done is to bring that paradigm back toward the level of simple empirical research. While the pathway may have seemed long and even tortuous, the result is a way to continue empirical research and, so, further check, develop and (if necessary) emend the theory that in Mid-Life there are *at least* five Cries.

In addition, one other thing has happened. Beyond the description of another's research, including his speculations upon its meaning, each of us has been invited to use a research-based paradigm to do our *own* research into Mid-Life. A way of recording decisions has been given, and the range of possible combinations has been identified. What we have, therefore, is a chance to contribute something to the fund of "new knowledge" available to humankind. *That*, if we have the ability to recognize it for what it is, should be a cause for celebrating the possibilities of tracing out the reality we encounter. If we will, we can do it. The Left Hand of metaphor can be tamed for the Right Hand of research into a fascinating, only partially studied 20 year segment of the human life cycle.

+ At the end of a Discourse or Report it is appropriate to conclude with an Ascription and response, such as that which follows.

Celebrant:	May the Source of truth, and the Designer of that which is, Accept these words, Correct any falsehood, and Clarify any confusion; to our continued benefit and the triumph of truth.
Response:	Let it be so!

A Directed Meditation or Litany

+ It is appropriate that an Assistant, where available, bid the partipants' meditation. The biddings may be especially constructed for the occasion, or may be in the form provided below, so long as the themes of gratitude, wonder, and humility are expressed.

+ A period of Silence should follow each bidding. Such period of silence may be terminated by an appropriate interchange, such as that provided in the Directed Meditation or Litany below.

Introduction A: IN GRATITUDE LET US CONSIDER OUR DEBT TO:

Bidding A1:	All those in ages past who have built natural knowledge through experimentation (especially N. N.); (Silence for Meditation) Bidder: For what we have received; Response: We are thankful.
Bidding A2:	All those who have given us insight (especially N. N.); (Silence for Meditation)

	Bidder: For what we have received; Response: We are thankful.
Bidding A3:	All those whose theories have directed our search (especially N. N.); (Silence for Meditation) Bidder: For what we have received; Response: We are thankful.
Bidding A4:	All those whose probing questions have kept us aware of our ignorance (especially N. N.); (Silence for Meditation) Bidder: For what we have received; Response: We are thankful.
Bidding A5:	All those whose belief has supported us in our work (especially N. N.); (Silence for Meditation) Bidder: For what we have received; Response: We are thankful.
Bidding A6:	All those who, by their own work, have given us the tools we use (especially N. N.); (Silence for Meditation) Bidder: For what we have received; Response: We are thankful.
Introduction B:	IN WONDER LET US CONTEMPLATE THE AS YET UNKNOWN; (Silence for Meditation or Contemplation) Bidder: For all we have yet to learn; Response: We are thankful.
Introduction C:	IN HUMILITY LET US SEEK INSIGHT FOR THE CHALLENGES THAT ARE OURS; (Silence for Meditation or Seeking) Bidder: For what we can do now; Response: We are thankful.

+ At this point, participants may appropriately add other biddings.
+ The Celebrant may conclude the Directed Meditation or Litany with an Appropriate Prayer, such as the following:

Celebrant:	Founder, Designer, and Creator of all that is, may our gratitude remain lively, our wonder fresh, and our humility unfeigned; for your ways are remarkable, and in their discerning we find meaning and truth.
Response:	It is so!

+ Following the conclusion of the Directed Meditation or Litany it is appropriate if a song expressive of human wonder, awe, or delight before Beauty, Truth, or Design be sung by the participants, all standing. At the end of such a song, all remain standing for the Exchange of Greetings and the Conclusion of the Celebration.

AN EXCHANGE OF GREETINGS

Celebrant: The joy of work well done be your reward;
Response: And yours, too.

+ Following the Exchange of Greetings between the Celebrant and the participants, participants may appropriately exchange the greeting with one another, using this or some similar form to express collegiality.
+ When the participants have completed their exchange of greetings, the Celebrant may conclude the celebration in the following or some similar manner.

A CONCLUDING CEREMONY

Assistant: Let us all attend!
Celebrant: This day we have remembered and paused to celebrate the Para-Feast of (here the Para-Feast is mentioned by title);
Response: That is so.
Celebrant: We have considered our debt to many, without whom our tracing out of Design, or our discovery of truth, would be difficult, if not impossible;
Response: That is so.
Celebrant: We have paused in wonder before the as yet unknown, and sought for the necessary insight to meet those challenges that are ours;
Response: That is so.
Celebrant: We have greeted one another as colleagues in the high pursuit of truth;
Response: That is so.
Celebrant: Therefore, may the One whose design we encounter, whose creation we study, and who is our goal and guide strengthen and preserve us, now and always.
Response: Let it be so!
Assistant: Our celebration is concluded!

+ A song may be sung at this time, as the Celebrant and any Assistants retire in some appropriately orderly manner, as they choose.

Notes

1. John H. Peatling, *Truth Telling and Peer Protection: A Report* (Schenectady, N.Y.: The Author, 1974). Originally delivered as a paper at the 1974 Annual Meeting of the Association of Professors and Researchers in Religious Education, Washington, D.C., on October 26, 1974.

2. John H. Peatling, *A Piagetian Perspective on the Development of an Aspect of the Sense of Justice* (Schenectady, N.Y.: The Author,1975). Originally delivered as a paper at the 1975 Convention of the Religious Research Association, Milwaukee, Wisconsin, on October 24, 1975.

John H. Peatling, *Signs of Structure and Signs of Dissonance: Adult Response to a Piagetian Moral Puzzle* (Schenectady, N.Y.: The Author, 1976). Originally delivered to a meeting of psychologists from Baptist colleges in North Carolina, Meredith College, Raleigh, North Carolina, on March 6, 1976.

3. John H. Peatling, "Research on Adult Moral Development: Where Is It?" in *Religious Education*, 72 (1977), 212-224.

4. John H. Peatling, "A Sense of Justice: Moral Judgment in Children, Adolescents and Adults," in *Character Potential: A Record of Research*, 8 (1976), 25-34.

5. John H. Peatling, "Careers and a Sense of Justice in Mid-Life," in *Vocational Guidance Quarterly*.

6. See Table 8, Three Theoretical Models of Possible Developmental Sequences for Aspects of a Sense of Justice, in *Signs of Structure and Signs of Dissonance: Adult Responses to a Piagetian Moral Puzzle* (Item 2, above), p. 48.

7. See Robert J. Havighurst, *Human Development and Education* (New York: Longmans, Green and Company, 1953), esp. pp. 259-267.

8. See Donald E. Super, *The Psychology of Careers* (New York: Harper and Row, 1957).

9. See Erik H. Erikson, *Childhood and Society* (New York: W.W. Norton & Company, Inc., 1950/1963), esp. pp. 273-274 in 1963 ed.

10. See Barbel Inhelder and Jean Piaget, *The Growth of Logical Thinking From Childhood to Adolescence* (New York: Basic Books, Inc., 1958), esp. pp. 343-346.

11. The references to Havighurst, Super, Erikson, Inhelder and Piaget were used by the author in a paper, "Continuing Development of a Sense of Justice in Life," which was read at the 1976 Convention of the American Personnel and Guidance Association, Chicago, Illinois, on April 13, 1976. This paper has been published as Item 5, above.

12. This suggestion was originally made in a paper read at the Conference on Adult Religious Education jointly sponsored by the Religious Education Association and the Religious Education Section of the Adult Education Association, New York City, N.Y., on November 22, 1976. This paper has been published as Item 3, above.

13. See Item 4, above.

14. *Ibid.*, p. 32.

15. Obviously when a Mid-Life adult with offspring encounters this leaving-home phenomenon depends upon when in their own life cycle offspring were born. Equally obviously, if death, divorce, or separation has taken place (without remarriage) the experience will be noticeably different. This description presumes that the experience of many adults during Mid-Life occurs within the context of a still existing marriage; when an adult reaches Mid-Life in some other context, experience and Cry will differ.

16. The identification of this despair-tinged variant form of the Third Cry is due to the pastoral experience of the Rev. Richard E. Barrett, Rector of Calvary Episcopal Church, Burnt Hills, New York, who read an early form of the author's paper on Five Cries From Mid-Life.

17. While this Mid-Life discovery that an opportunity to work on the new and the not yet tried is a "challenge" that is enjoyable is, in some ways, similar to ideas expressed by some late adolescents, the author tends to think that there is more substance and depth to the Mid-Lifer's discovery, and (probably) less ideological basis than is true of younger human beings. However, this is no more than an hypothesis.

18. John H. Peatling, "Five Cries From Mid-Life." (A paper read at the 1977 Convention of the American Personnel and Guidance Association, Dallas, Texas, on March 8, 1977), pp. 5-6.

19. See Reading or Reminder *D*, p. 123. Also see Jerome S. Bruner, *On Knowing. Essays for the Left Hand* (New York: Atheneum, 1965), pp. 4-5.

20. See Reading or Reminder *E*, p. 124. Also see R. Buckminister Fuller, "How Little I Know," in his book entitled *And It Came To Pass—Not To Stay* (New York: Macmillan Publishing Company, Inc., 1976), esp. p. 48.

21. See Reading or Reminder *C*, p. 123. Also see Ronald A. Fisher, *The Design of Experiments*, 7th Edition (New York: Hafner Publishing Company, 1960), p. 8.

22. The Five Cries From Mid-Life paradigm, however useful it may be as a way of thinking about Mid-Life, or however helpful it may be as a way of structuring observations of Mid-Lifers, certainly is *not* an *exhaustive* analysis of the human experience during the years we now call Mid-Life. Therefore, it is possible that there may be one or more "other" Cries that can be identified. The author recognizes the possibility, and he hopes readers will also.

Suggested Readings

Abbott, Edwin A. *Flatland. A Romance of Many Dimensions*. (New York: Dover Publications, Inc., 1952). Sixth Edition, Revised.

Bruner, Jerome S. *On Knowing. Essays for the Left Hand*. (New York: Atheneum, 1965). Originally published by Harvard University Press, 1962.

Fuller, R. Buckminister. *And It Came To Pass—Not To Stay*. (New York: Macmillan Publishing Company, Inc., 1976).

Piaget, Jean. *Insights and Illusions of Philosophy*. (New York: The New American Library, Inc., 1971). Meridian Book #M235.

Piaget, Jean. *Structuralism*. (New York: Basic Books, Inc., 1970).

Peatling, John H. "A Sense of Justice: Moral Judgment in Children, Adolescents and Adults," in *Character Potential: A Record of Research*, 8 (1976), 25-34.

Peatling, John H. "Cognitive Development: Stages in the Development of Abstract Religious Thinking Across the Human Life Span," in *Character Potential: A Record of Research*, in press.

Peatling, John H. "On Beyond Goldman: Religious Thinking and the 1970s," in *Learning for Living*, 16 (1977), 99-108.

Strommen, Merton P., Milo L. Brekke, Ralph C. Underwager, and Arthur L. Johnson, *A Study of Generations*. (Minneapolis, Minn.: Augsburg Publishing House, 1972).

10.
A Model for Aesthetic Education

Maria Harris

*A religious educator, not an artist by profession, Maria Harris
describes her concrete experience in offering a course in aesthetic
education. It will be obvious to the reader that the model she
describes can be implemented on any level.*

The music makes me sing, in my searching
For answers to the big questions. I wonder
How the sparkle of mountains
Relates to candlelight. And opera
Seems a frivolity of celebration.
Where am I going?

To class and we dance and with puppets
We haggle over yarn and
Who performs first.

But back to opera and that big question:
Significance!
Who knows where the time goes,
Until the time is up

And I still can't get my kite flying.

Somehow the significance lasted despite
The paint I dripped, the tangled string
The significance of Frustration;
Acceptance for okay-ness?

In a festival of doing—Striving
For together. Laughter
In the glow of afternoon—wanting to Be there
As elves climbing Christmas
With trees of holly, candy, candles.
Children dancing before night
To the significance . . . Vitality: of
Singing (and all the world's a chorus),
Of meticulous macrame
Concern for detail and watching where the children go.

It makes our sense.

I dance in my humanity,
The clown sang so today,
For then the world's insanity
Skips briskly from our way.

People ask, "What happened in class today?"
"Everything, oh everything" and I hold up evidence in
Silk-screened perception.
"Creative self" I say, in giggles.
"Created self" I know how today happened.
                      —Diane Lockwood

For the past several years, first at Fordham, and more recently at Andover Newton Theological School, I have put my name next to a course description which reads:

"THE AESTHETIC AND RELIGIOUS EDUCATION. Exploring the arts in religious education and the aesthetic as a quality of religious education. Participation in artistic activity; emphasis on non-discursive learning."

With as few as four students, and as many as thirty, I have explored the relationships between religion, education, and the aesthetic, sometimes in highly structured and verbally significant ways, sometimes in spontaneous and serendipitous play, but almost always in experiences that have enlarged vision and deepened insight. This article is an attempt to share some of the excitement that has been part of that ongoing adventure. I will begin with the underlying philosophy of the course, move on to a description of its design, and conclude with some of the results that have occurred. In doing this, I hope to present to readers a model of aesthetic education which they might consider as a possibility in their own religious education practice. I want to emphasize that the model is presented by one who is not an artist by profession, but, like most of her readers, a religious educator.

POINTS OF DEPARTURE

Theoretically, the starting point for this course is the notion that religious education is a field where the religious intersects with education, and that the aesthetic is a dimension of both. If Suzanne Langer is correct that art is the creation of perceptible form expressive of human feeling, then both religion and education are particularly appropriate vehicles for such expression. Religion, with its ties to creativity and feeling, has always been the vehicle through which peoples have expressed their relationship to the divine. Education, with its focus on the intentional reconstruction of experience, has relied strongly on the creation of *conceptual* form, but is in need of the *perceptible* form more proper to art. Thus, the field can only be enhanced by inclusion of the aesthetic.

Another starting point has to do with the notion of what constitutes the mature adult. What I would take to be the over-reliance on psychology in our century has obscured the fact that integrity as the goal of psycho-social development, universalizing faith as the goal of faith development, formal operational thought as the goal of cognitive development and postconventional judgment as the goal of moral development are each only interpretations of maturity. To these must certainly be added a description of the end point of aesthetic development, what Howard Gardner refers to as "full participation in the artistic process."[1] In saying this, I do not want to negate the findings of the developmental theorists. I do, however, wish to go on record as noting that in religious education, we have not generally studied aesthetic or artistic development as much or as carefully as we have those just mentioned, and that we are in danger of assuming that we now understand the nature of adulthood. In addition, the aesthetic, with its natural avoidance of any one answer as *the* solution and its susceptibility to multiple interpretations, is a corrective to any such assumption.

Speaking for inclusion of the aesthetic is also a speaking for a special kind of healing needed by religious education. Just as there is a possible over-reliance on psychology, there is a possible danger in all educational circles of separating such persons as artists and poets from others who come to be referred to as scientists and thinkers. As

John Dewey has noted, "Only the psychology that has separated things which in reality belong together holds that scientists and philosophers think while poets and painters follow their feelings."[2] Actually, Dewey goes on to say, in *both* there is "emotionalized thinking and feelings whose substance consists of appreciated meanings or ideas."[3] Religious education as a field needs not only to be wary of making this separation, but also to be active in seeking to remedy the situation of separation when it is apparent.

Finally, the philosophy of the course is based on a set of assumptions about adult students in theology and/or religious education. Some students are *afraid* of the artistic. Far too many recall one or both of two terrible childhood incidents: the experience of gustily and lustily participating in a class chorus only to hear a teacher whisper gently, "Don't sing, dear", or the equally devastating moment of holding up a drawing in first or second grade with the hope that it will be displayed, only to be told to return it to one's folder, and try again. Nevertheless, such students, as adults, are sensitive to the truth of whose fault those early experiences were, and are eager to overcome the fear and try out powers that have been held in abeyance for years.

Then there are students who are especially sensitive to the aesthetic, who need artistic expression as much as they need food, and who are aware of this. They come, many of them, from having been fine arts, or drama, or dance majors in college, or from being avocationally and vocationally, musicians, weavers, poets. They see the course as an opportunity to integrate and pull together disparate elements within themselves and in their lives, as well as an opportunity to plan procedures for their own work with others.

Most of the students, however, even if they do not articulate it, come because they have a desire for space. There is a personal, religious and educational need for a spot, a place in the curriculum where they can integrate what they are learning. My own mentor in the aesthetic, Dr. Mary Tully, once said of her work with students in a similar course at Union Theological Seminary,

> I'm assuming that my job is to help students, through art, to make some sense of the content they're already getting, or have had. My experience has been that most of these young people have had so much input that has not been digested that it's really a form of indigestion. And they need an area—and I think art is marvelous for this—where they can in secret, without somebody bothering them, integrate some of this material.[4]

My own conviction is the same, borne out in the last decade with other students. Though I would not for a moment advocate the aesthetic as the *only* course in a theological or religious education curriculum, I would fight for it as an essential course, precisely because of this integrating, holistic, and digesting quality. It provides an oasis where people can, in stillness, let their understanding, their intellect, and their feeling come together without pressure, but with support from within the institution where they are learning.

THE DESIGN

The design of the course has varied somewhat through the years, although one basic assumption has always operated: that is, that participation in art forms at some point is essential to understanding the aesthetic. Some years, this participation has been minimal, and discussion has been predominant. Other years, discussion has been almost non-existent, and participation has been central. The best approach, on paper, is a blend of the two, not always achievable as smoothly as I, or the students, would wish. However, the original purpose and description are generally presented something like this: "The purpose of this course is to provide understanding of, participation in, and expression through various art forms. Class members will be required, either individually or as a group, to choose an artistic form, research it, and develop a process which will engage the other class members in this form. At various times, class members will act as creators, performers, audience members, and critics. Actual attendance at class sessions is expected, since these form a key part of the course, and are its focal point. Class members with expertise in various forms may be called on as resource persons in these forms, but are encouraged to choose for presentation an area with which they are not familiar. It is strongly recommended that all class members keep a journal to record their impressions for themselves as the semester progresses."[5]

Through the years, I have shared the teacher role with students in the choice and the presentation of "artistic forms," a phrase which we have corporately agreed can cover a wide variety of possibilities. We have engaged in dance, song, sculpting, and silkscreening; in puppetry, choreography, poetry, and creative dramatics; in kite-flying, fairytales, frottage, and food. ("What does kite-flying have to do with ministry?" one women was asked. She replied, "Everything." And then went on to tell them about religious contributions of this course—about how the awareness of self, of others, of God is needed and how the openness to all the talents around is needed. Another student, Diane Lockwood, put it differently.

And I still can't get my kite flying.

Somehow the significance lasted despite
The paint I dropped, the tangled string
The significance of Frustration;
Acceptance for okay-ness.

Acceptance. Understanding of what it is to fail.
And of what it is to soar.)

These artistic forms, new to us when we present them, are then presented either by me, or by class members so choosing, so that we are enabled to take the four artistic roles.[6] The one rule for all presentations is that they be designed in such a way that the class members are engaged in the form; although there is time for initial demonstration and giving of background, description, and directions, the objective is involvement. When someone is "on" for the day (sometimes two are "on"; hence the "haggle over who performs first") she or he is engaged in the act of being a creator. When she or he demonstrates or presents, the role taken is that of performer, with the rest of the class as audience members. But, when the class begins to take part, each member becomes a performer. Finally, each person is requested to act as critic by assessing the class presentation *following* one's own: the point here is that once one has designed and presented, he or she is in a better position to critique.

I would be less than candid if I did not note the considerable risk such involvement in the artistic roles entails. One student, reflecting on his experience at the end of the course, put it thus:

I am more comfortable in the safe modes of academic endeavor, among the papers and the exams—it is a hard thing to be creatively dramatic. It brings tears to the eyes sometimes, and feelings of tightness and embarrassment at unaccustomed actions in sight of others. What are *they* going to think? Worse yet, what am I going to think of myself when I realize that all these unexplored possibilities are in me dormant? And that is just one of the forms we explored. Each one brought its own peculiar terrors along with its joys. I guess I realized again how far we drive the child in us under cover, and how hard it is to trust the flow that pulses in and through us.[7]

Besides engagement with the four artistic roles, I have discovered through the years that the course tends to be anchored around three conceptual poles: word, world, and wisdoms. Word is an appropriate starting point because of the heavily verbal nature of all education, particularly the teaching act. (I should note, at least in passing, that some years I have presented an entire two hour class in silence, however, which is itself a provocative artistic form.) I often begin by sharing Langer's distinction between discursive and presentational form as the starting point for word, which is her way of analyzing verbal symbolism.[8] Discursiveness is what Langer calls the temporal nature of verbal symbolism which requires us to string out our ideas even though their objects are related all at once. For her, discursivenss compels us to treat serially what happens simultaneously. The issue this raises is whether what is knowable is confined to the requirements of discursive projections. If it is, what can be known can also be said. If it is not, then there are innumerable possibilities of meaning beyond the limits of discursive language.

It is, of course the latter position which Langer adopts. While affirming the necessity of language for human exchange, she points out that its characteristics necessarily limit it. She distinguishes this limiting, discursive kind of symbolism from a second kind, which she refers to as *presentational* symbolism. This latter symbolism is one where a simultaneous, integral presentation is made all at once, integrally as distinct from the serial quality of discourse. The significance of this understanding for religious education is twofold. In the first place, word can be understood as both discursive and presentational, and the aesthetic form of words—in poetry, drama, literature, fairytale—studied as educational vehicles. Religiously, however, especially in the Christian religious tradition, the Word is central—the word is not only that which humans speak, through which they communicate, in which they dwell. It is the metaphor for the divine: the Word which becomes flesh.

World is the second focus of the course. The understanding for world here is of the earth, the stuff of which the world is made. The aesthetic is the human way of establishing relationship with this world-stuff: clay, paint, water, color, line, point, sound, and body. John Killinger once commented that our education has tended to make us de-corpitated persons, cut off from our bodies. That may also be true of religion. In our everlastingly talkative ecclesial circles, the bodiliness we must call on in order to shape and mold clay, to dilute and mix color, to harmonize and project sound, and to freely and ecstatically dance is often minimized. A course such as ours has always had a heavy emphasis on world and our relationship to it, and this is manifested not only in the times we remain indoors and design form together, but in the yearly experience (which, I reflect now for the first time, *has* been a yearly experience) of going outside the classroom, to sketch, to do rubbings, to find a sound, to fill a silence.

(The process required that I go outdoors, perceive something in nature thoroughly enough to get some relationship with it, and then, through the disciplined structure of a poem, express what I had encountered. The "something in nature" turned out to be the strong bark of an oak tree, which I attempted then to express in the following:

Fibre
Rough-layered,
Stretches, routes, contains,
Tough, enduring shell of life.
Bark.

It may not be great poetry; on the other hand, I surely know more about the subject than I would through many other processes, and not only more *about* it, but know *it*, in itself. When I was with the bark, it gave itself to me, and through the poem, possibly to others.)

WISDOMS

The third and final element of the course has been its wisdoms. In other terminology, these might be called learnings, results, conclusions, but I prefer the notion of wisdoms, because of the richness of that word and its multi-layered meaning. To begin with, it does mean learning, as well as the "understanding of what is true, right, or lasting". But playing with it a bit one comes to the Middle English *wisedom* and then to the Old English root *weid*. And weid is *to see*; as the Germanic *witan* is *to look after* and *guard* (cherish?) and the old German *wissago* is *a seer* or *prophet*; as the Greek *weid-os* is a *form* or *shape*, an *idyll*; as the Old Irish *white* is *clearly visible*. What is it that one sees after a course like this? What takes form, takes shape? What becomes clearly visible?

Four wisdoms stand out. The first is foolishness, demonstrated of late in presentations of fairytale, puppetry, and more recently, clowning. Spending an entire semester on the aesthetic is a reminder that not all knowledge is for use, and, in our culture, that is undoubtedly foolishness to many. The aesthetic is a reminder that the more-than-rational exists, and that it nurtures and feeds the human spirit if we let it. But there is also the foolishness in this course of making a fool of oneself in the sense of trying something in front of others where we do not come off as experts. For such activity, one of the guiding aphorisms of the course is a caution Corita Kent uses with her art students: "There is no win, no fail, just make."[9] So, together, we agree to be fools in class, putting on the baggy pants and outlandish costumes of the clown, holding up mirrors for one another as we change our features to make bulbous noses, purple eyelashes, and oversize mouths, imitating slapstick gestures and purposeless phrases. And gaining, in the attempt, the wisdom of our own finiteness, our limitedness, our foolishness in a symbolism simpler than discourse.

> I dance in my humanity
> The clown sang so today,
> For then the world's insanity
> Skips briskly from our way.

A second wisdom is our own creativity, given possibility by the absence of pressure to win, and the shared commitment to make which tends to grow as the course continues. "I noticed," observed one doctoral student, "that as our class became engaged in the process of this course, there developed a sense of community. We took risks in each other's presence and with each other's support. We became resources to one another as we encouraged and critiqued our performance." That climate, that environment is essential if the conditions for creativity are to exist: the *detachment* that is willingness to accept any outcome; the *passion* that can be expressed in an unthreatening atmosphere; the *immediacy* of involvement in a process, with the *deferral* of satisfaction almost always present in a two-hour segment; the *letting the art work*, art object, art process *take over*, or the letting of the internal drama unfold so that one can *let the material be* what it must be; the relinquishing of the urge to control and to be in charge. And in doing so, coming to a new seeing, a new understanding of oneself. "I gave myself and parts of me that were new to me to this class. My participation in the various classes was not outstanding but it was outstanding to me. Me—who seldom did anything creative (other than having children); me—dancing around the room (at my age!); me—making a puppet (not a good one, but I made it); me—weaving and on and on; me!! And especially me! having the courage (no, guts!) to teach a class with a new friend."

A third wisdom is a sense of wholeness. Most times, students in theology or religious education work with words, and with books. Although I go to great length in the class to point out that dealing with the aesthetic, the artistic, the non-discursive is NOT a denigration of the world of discourse and rationality, but a complementing of it, the sense of wholeness does seem to come through more easily by encountering the material universe, and working in the intuitive, the imaginative, and the perceptual modes more proper to art. I also try not to name the wisdoms for students as the course draws to a close, though I must admit to hoping that such wholeness will occur. For this reason, I cherish the end of semester response of the woman who wrote, "The course helped me to be integrated; it gave me an opportunity to use and develop my intuitive side while the rest of my courses demanded the activity of my analytical side. Religiously, this is significant for me because I believe in a holistic view of life, that work and play, joy and sorrow, day and night are all important parts of life, all equally important. I try not to divide the secular and the sacred; I try to live as if my life is a sacrament. The integration of the aesthetic and the intellectual is part of the synthesis I keep trying to incorporate in myself."

Finally, there is the wisdom of worship. Although the course is not a course on or about worship, it steals into the curriculum each year. At times, someone chooses to conduct a class on prayer, or liturgical celebration during the course; more often, there appears to be an appropriateness in choosing the form of worship as a closing. Most memorable to me was the last class of this past year, where the artistic form chosen was food, and where together, as a class, having been together for thirteen weeks, we made bread, butter, salad, and sweets in the course of the two hour session and then sat down to a shared meal, notable for bread, for wine, for community, and for the grace before and throughout the meal which was an acknowledgment of our dependence upon the divine for those fruits of the earth, and for one another.

In *Lives of a Cell*, Lewis Thomas suggests that if we decide to send a time capsule out into extra-terrestrial space, we ought to begin any tape recording placed aboard with Bach. He points out, correctly I think, that we will most certainly not be faulted if we begin by putting forward our very best; the less pleasant details of our existence can come later.

I have a little of that feeling as I conclude this essay. In describing a course that is now almost a decade old, I have shared the best moments, and those experiences and insights which have proven most satisfying and most enriching, for me and for the students. I have done so in the belief that what is done in a course like this is enormously important, and with the hope that others will try something similar. I am not an artist by training; I am a teacher, a religious educator, and I am convinced that what I have done, others can do, and do better. My essay is a challenge and an invitation to make that attempt, and an affirmation that to do so is to enter a world of words and wisdoms yet to be named.

Can you see? Can you see?
It makes sense
To try
To try Vitality,
Than to wallow
In obscurity and miss
The may-flowers hiding.

—Diane Lockwood

Notes

1. Howard Gardner, *The Arts and Human Development* (New York: John Wiley and Sons, 1973).
2. John Dewey, *Art as Experience* (New York: Capricorn Books, 1934), p. 73.
3. *Ibid*.
4. In an interview with me December 9, 1970.
5. There are required readings for the course too, usually at least four or five books, which vary except for Dewey's *Art as Experience*, which is always required. I have come to believe this is a very important element in the course, helping students to name and to conceptualize what they are experiencing.
6. The formulation is Gardner's, *op. cit.* See my review in *Andover Newton Quarterly*, 16 (March, 1976), pp. 284-286.
7. This, and other student comments quoted throughout, are from final papers I request from each student. Usually, I ask them to respond to three questions: a) Their contribution to the course; b) The contribution of the course to them; c) What the relationship between the aesthetic and religious education is.
8. S. Langer, *Philosophy in a New Kay*, 3rd edition (Cambridge: Harvard University Press, 1969). First published 1942. Note especially chapter 4, "Discursive Forms and Presentational Forms," pp. 79-102.
9. The phrase, although simple, appears to have a powerful effect on students in helping them through initial fears. In time, they come to believe that it is true, at least in this situation.

Additional Resources

Crossan, John Dominic. *Raid on the Articulate*. New York: Harper and Row, 1976.
Harris, Maria. "Religious Education and the Aesthetic," in *Andover Newton Quarterly*, 17 (1976), 125-132. See also *The D.R.E. Book*, New York: Paulist, 1976, esp, pp. 121-124, 168-172.
Koch, Kenneth. *Wishes, Lies and Dreams*. New York: Vintage, 1970.
Robertson, Seonaid. *Rosegarden and Labyrinth: A Study in Art Education*. London: Routledge and Kegan Paul, 1963.

11.
Teaching Within Revelation

Gabriel Moran

Gabriel Moran compares liberal and conservative notions of revelation. He demonstrates that in spite of a current anxiety to return to static verbalizations of doctrine, revelation is essentially an aesthetic category, more concerned with the how *than the* what *of religious education.*

A peculiar thing has been happening to the word revelation in Christian theology: it has been disappearing. Anyone who wishes to verify this claim needs only to look at the index or text of most theology books in recent years. As a general rule, the more liberal the theology is, the less the word revelation is used.

In conservative circles, Carl Henry is publishing a series of volumes on the authority of revelation.[1] Further to the right, Sun Myung Moon and others use the word revelation more aggressively than ever. In contrast, the word revelation is almost completely absent in theology described as middle of the road or liberal. I should think that this fact would invite comment from all sides. Surely the near disappearance of such a central category must have some significance for the Christian churches and religious study.

I indicated above that the word revelation had *almost* disappeared in liberal Christian theology. That fact is perhaps more troublesome than if the word were entirely absent. Absence might indicate that the word is no longer necessary or that it had been replaced by a more useful word. Instead, Christian theology still assumes that there is a Christian revelation but one looks in vain for an exposition of the meaning and coherence of the concept.

The literature of religious education in the churches does not show the same embarrassment with the word revelation. In fact, the word revelation has probably become more prominent in recent years, especially in Roman Catholic writing. How does one explain this contrast? Is religious education literature simply a step behind theological writing? Or is religious education groping toward a new meaning which is beyond the view of Christian theology?

I am not certain that the second response is an accurate one. But on the hope that religious education may be already discovering a wider and deeper meaning for the word revelation, this essay will try to contribute to the exploration. My central proposal is that revelation is better approached as an "aesthetic" rather than a "scientific" category. What I will oppose is the use of the word revelation as a scientific or pseudo-scientific category. It is this scientific meaning of revelation in Christian theology that has become indefensible, a fact that is implicitly admitted by theology's embarrassed silence.

The term aesthetic may not be fully adequate to my intention. However, it does convey some alternative way of feeling, knowing, and behaving. Three characteristics of the aesthetic can be offered as a preliminary basis for the word's meaning. 1) Aesthetic activity pertains to concrete materials and does not abstract to a level of general ideas. The universal can be approached only through its embodiment in particular events, people, and things. 2) Aesthetic knowing is neither rational nor irrational; it is reason and more than reason. 3) The aesthetic dimension is a concern for wholeness; truth is primarily sought not in statements about the world but in the relation of human organism and environment.

If the word revelation is useful as an aesthetic category it would indicate the *how* of religious education as much or more than the *what* of religious education. The word revelation would then encompass a style of teaching, a way of using books, film, music, etc., a communal form of institution and many other facets of education that are often neglected. In this context, religious education is not the teaching of a "content" first processed by Christian theology. The content of religious education would no longer be under the control of theology; as *educational* content the material can come from a great variety of sources that help to clarify a religious life.

In advocating an aesthetic meaning of revelation I am acutely aware of the sloppiness and irrationality that can easily substitute for the scientific. I sympathize with these sentiments of James Hillman:

> The movement from one side of the brain to the other, from tedious daily life in the supermarket to supra-consciousness, from trash to transcendence, the "altered state of consciousness"

approach—to put it all in a nutshell—denies the historical ego. It is an approach going back to Saul, who became Paul, conversion into the opposite, knocked off one's ass in a flash.[2]

Whether Hillman is unfair to St. Paul may be debatable but certainly the problem he is describing has never been more apparent than it is today. The splits of rationalism/irrationalism or historical ego/mystical absorption are accompanied by "conversions" which do nothing to heal the splits.

There are two main defenses against being caught in these inhuman splits and false conversions: 1) Learn something about the history of the terms one is using. 2) Develop an educational setting adequate to the exploration of these human mysteries. If religious education is to make fruitful use of the word revelation then it has to know some of the historical meaning of the word. The "retrieval" of meaning can begin within one's own Christian history though if pursued far enough it will lead to meaning beyond that history. I shall first sketch some of that history and then offer some conclusions for religious study and some educational implications.

HISTORICAL CONSIDERATIONS

In the earliest period of Christian history the word revelation was used to cap the entire process by which the problem of the human condition was resolved. The humans had been looking for a way out, a resolution to human affairs. The people who were called Christians announced that they had the answer. God had taken a personal interest and intervened on behalf of the race. Within the Christian scheme Israel had been the preparation and Jesus the risen Lord was the culmination. In one of the patristic images, Jesus "recapitulated" the process, becoming a summary of past history and a foreshadowing of the future.

Isolated texts of St. Paul may make him sound like a twentieth century kook but the whole Pauline corpus fits into some thought out pattern for the human race. Such an ambitious viewpoint was not without its riddles and paradoxes. The "Christian view" led immediately into disagreement, debate, and church disarray. The last book of the bible, named Revelation, was for centuries considered unintelligible but it reemerged as a key to prophetic interpretation in the Protestant Reformation.

When the word revelation was used in the early church, it did not refer to something contained in the bible or the biblical text itself. Rather, revelation was one of several words (e.g. dispensation, economy, salvation) that could refer to the entire divine plan of things. The word revelation emphasized the element of *knowing*. The Christians claimed to know the way to God (or God's way to us) because they possessed a key to interpreting the universe.

The line-up of the competitors appeared to be: *Philosophy and (pagan) religion vs. (the) (Christian) revelation* There wasn't a *Christian* revelation as opposed to other revelations. There was simply a revelation of God which took precedence over all the human attempts of philosophy and religion. Almost immediately, as the Christian claims encountered education and classical learning some realignment began to occur. The reinterpretation of Christian claims has continued to this day. But whereas the church has made political, social, and other kinds of adjustment, the claim of possessing the revelation of God has never been adequately addressed.

The middle ages saw the emergence of reason not as an equal partner with revelation but as a negotiator. Reason, particularly as represented by pagan philosophy, was not an enemy of revelation. Human rationality was a reflection of that divine reason which illuminates the universe. The human ability to reason, it was thought, is limited by reasons being located in a bodily creature. Furthermore, human reason is distorted by the existence of sin. Revelation adds to and corrects the knowledge of human beings.

In the work of Thomas Aquinas the interplay of reason and revelation is complex and careful. Aquinas wished to give every credit possible to reason, incorporating into his "Christian philosophy" the body of classical learning as he knew it. Reason could not be undercut or substituted for but it did find fulfillment in (the) (Christian) revelation. Neither reason nor revelation referred primarily to processes inside of the human head. Reason and revelation were ways of being in the world and of human participation in a divine pattern.

The period after the Renaissance, Reformation, and Scientific Revolution represents a decisive change in the Christian use of the word revelation. The main field of interest became interiorized with the participants in the discussion being reason and faith. The word revelation was still used, functioning now as the object of faith. That object was now in some dispute. For centuries the Protestant-Catholic conflict was formulated as "scripture alone" vs. "scripture and tradition" as the place of revelation. That difference was a minor one compared to the fundamental agreement between Protestant and Catholic, viz., that revelation is an object located somewhere.

To cope with the era in which the churches found themselves, Christian theology conceived of itself as a science in the modern sense of the word. Theology could use the same stringent controls of reasoning as the other sciences but it could outdo them in one respect: its premises were absolutely certain because they came directly from God. As befits a science, theology proper did not have to examine revelation because revelation was a premise and premises are assumed in science. The pre-theological defense of the concept of revelation was largely an examination of the credibility of the bible (and for Catholics, tradition as a source of truths).

Looking back on the period of modern Christian theology, one can see a missed step in the assumptions about revelation. The theologian assumed that the method of modern science was the game to be played. That assumption entailed the existence of data (the given object) to be reasoned from. "The Christian revelation" now functioned as "the given" for the science of theology. Arguments about *where* that revelation was located and *who* was final interpreter obscured the more important development, viz., the assumption that there was a thing called "the Christian revelation."

If the premise could be assumed, then the science of Christianity was impregnably strong. A divine science provided total security and absolute certitude. Charles Finney, one of the most influential preachers in nineteenth century United States, could say: "I had read nothing on the subject except my Bible and what I had there found. . . . I had interpreted as I would have understood the same or like passages in a law book."[3] By the 1950's the scientific model had shifted from law to psychology but the guarantee of certainty was the same. In one of the best selling books of that decade Norman Vincent Peale presented Christianity as having "the characteristics of a science in that it is based upon a book which contains a system of techniques and formulas designed for the understanding and treatment of human nature."[4]

The continuance of this science for "the understanding and treatment of human nature" rested upon the accommodation which Christian churches had made in the seventeenth and eighteenth centuries. Since there were two sources of knowledge, faith and reason, there were bound to be conflicts. Neither church spokesmen nor scientists in the early modern period wished to incite open warfare. In the English speaking world John Locke provided the acceptable solution in his influential essay, *The Reasonableness of Christianity*. One should note not only the first but the last word of the title. "Christianity," a word connoting a self-enclosed system of ideas was largely an invention of the eighteenth century and, of course, "Christinaity" was, if anything, "reasonable."

John Locke may seem far away but it is his accommodation that we are still using. Some of Locke's statements on the need for reason may sound similar to those of Thomas Aquinas but the intervening five centuries had transformed the word "reason." In Locke's world the two poles were not reason/revelation but reason/faith. Revelation entered the picture only as the "proposition" to which faith assented. From that starting point, revelation could only go in one direction, namely, in subordination to reason. "Faith," writes Locke, "is the assent to any proposition not . . . made by the deductions of reason, but upon the credit of the proposer, as coming from God, in some extraordinary way of communication. This way of discovering truths to men, we call *revelation*."[5] Locke allows that revelation may be followed when it speaks on matters on which reason has nothing to say or when it deals with matters on which reason yields only probabilities. When reason conflicts with a supposed truth of revelation, it is reason that must be followed.

The Lockean solution seemed a "reasonable" one—which indeed it was. The catch was the shifting meaning of the word reason and the uses to which reason might be put. Anyone who did not go along with the accommodation of "Christianity" and modern science was pushed to the fringe of social acceptability. The legacy of the eighteenth century to the centuries that have followed is the choice between a cool, liberal, reasonable religion and a hot, reactionary, irrational religious life.

Reasonable gentlemen like Ben Franklin could never understand all the fuss about religion. If people wanted some religion let them have it so long as we all remain civil and rational. People who knew that there was something wrong with this choice but who could not restate the issue became increasingly shrill. By the beginning of the twentieth century, Billy Sunday was screaming across the land: "Thousands of college graduates are going as fast as they can straight to hell. If I had a million dollars I'd give $999,999 to the church and $1 to education. . . . When the word of God says one thing and scholarship says another, scholarship can go to hell."[6]

We look back condescendingly to Billy Sunday and his era but it is not clear that our era has progressed to another plane of understanding. For much of the twentieth century it seemed that Locke's reasonable solution was carrying the day. Reasonable religion was protected because it was useful and innocuous. Unreasonable religion was allowed because it was soon to disappear. There were signs as far back as World War I that this edifice was built on shifting sands. But it is in the last few decades that massive breaks have appeared in the structure. Faith/reason on the subjective side and science/reasonable Christianity as the objects are now threatened by chaotic upheavals.

THEORETICAL CONCLUSIONS

It would be nice if as conclusion to the above problem I could state the *right* answer. But I think that neither I nor anyone else at this juncture of human, religious, and Christian history can supply the answer. When a problem is this deeply immersed in historical complexity, any words one might choose for an answer are already part of the problem. What one can do is propose radical surgery on one or two key terms that might offer a new route of exploration.

Christian theology cannot handle the issue by putting band-aids on the word revelation but neither can theology avoid the question. The premise of Christian theology is in question and for this problem theology is not the judge. The body of Christian theology needs to be placed in an educational setting where the arbiter is neither the "norms" of theology nor the reason of eighteenth century enlightenment. The educational judge is human experience conceived of as broadly and as deeply as human beings are capable.

1) My first conclusion is negative in form but ultimately positive in effect: The Christian churches do not possess an object that can be called "the Christian revelation." Centuries of defending the proposition that there does exist such an object have trickled down to embarrassment on the left and irrationality on the right. Liberal Christian theologians ought to feel some relief at this admission though they also need to recognize that the effect is revolutionary in religious studies. The word revelation cannot be left to die quietly; its history needs to be studied. Possibly the word revelation has a future which is radically different from the one which modern theology assumed since the age of John Locke.

Some people get very angry at the suggestion to eliminate "the Christian revelation." I hope it is clear at this point that my argument is with the *words* Christian revelation. There is no disparagement here of Christian scripture/doctrine, the person of Jesus, or the symbols of church tradition. My argument is with identifying any or all of these things with the word revelation. Ontologically and epistemologically the term "Christian revelation" is a box from which no escape has been found.

From a more positive perspective, letting go of "the Christian revelation" allows a reappropriation of early Christian history as well as a dialogue with other religions. The unwise attempt to complement "Christian revelation" with Buddhist revelation, Moslem revelation, etc., only compounds the problem. The early church was right in looking for the one and only revelation. What we can see today is that the history of Hindu, Moslem and other groups may with the Christian church be expressions or partial embodiments of that revelation.

The earliest Christian impulse was not to have the Christian revelation but to be the final revealing of God in the world. When it became evident that the world was not at its end the church had to reconceive its position. The church could still think of itself as final or decisive or culminating. But the split with Judaism and the failure of educational/institutional reform to keep pace with its missionary zeal severely limited the church. It was forced into a position of defending "the Christian revelation," which in time came to mean the truths given to the church and not available elsewhere.

The long history of "Christian revelation" is understandable but to perpetuate the inadequate language of another era is no longer defensible. One of Kierkegaard's images of faith (more attractive than some of his others) is of a man's taking his foot from the bottom of the lake to see whether he will float on the water. There is no way to explore the usefulness of the word revelation if Christian theology still presumes that the word refers to an object under the control and definition of the church. Letting go of that solid ground might lead to swimming in a new ocean of philosophical and religious possibilities.

The elimination of the term "Christian revelation" does not lessen the importance of studying Jewish and Christian history. Jewish and Christian peoples have made special contributions to world history. Perhaps every people has made a special contribution; that is mostly for them to say. The word special here does not necessarily entail a meaning of exclusivity. Jewish and Christian peoples have at their disposal more than a century of magnificent historical studies. Ironically, it was this very study of history (especially biblical history) together with further advances in science that helped to undermine the faith/reason accommodation of the eighteenth century.

2) With the upheaval of modern reason and its associates, Christian faith/revelation, a new framework is urgently needed. In this setting, the word revelation may prove valuable if its ancient Greek, early Christian, medieval Catholic, and contemporary nonreligious meanings can be tapped. That is a tall order, of course, and the odds are probably against such a retrieval of meaning. Still, almost everything is in question today and it may be an unlikely contender that

will prove adequate to the job of encompassing the unity/diversity of today.

Revelation in this context is not a noun/object but an umbrella word for the total relational pattern. It is what I have called an aesthetic category. It would be a word not under the control of the Christian church but one in which the Christian church could participate. It is not immediately a religious word though it can obviously incorporate religious meaning. The word revelation does not imply any splits (cognitive/affective, active/passive, human/nonhuman) but it does connote elements of surprise and spontaneity. In short, it is not reducible to reason but neither is it irrational.

The word revelation is alive in contemporary writing outside of church circles. But if the word is not simply to feed irrational tendencies in a world threatening to go mad, then it needs moorings of philosophical and religious history. Revelation is not primarily what occurs in the human mind (or human emotions) but what the human being participates in. This point would surely be intelligible to Plato, John the Evangelist, Aquinas, or Luther. But we have to restate the point for our age. The task of a teacher is to relate the questions, issues, and movements of today to the profound insights of earlier ages.

EDUCATIONAL IMPLICATIONS

1) Religious education may be defined as the attempt to keep education open to the undreamt possibilities of the human race. There is nothing vague or general about this description of religious education; the job is specific, urgent, and practical. The puzzle within this definition is *how* to do it. If possibilities have not even been dreamt, how can one keep open to them? The beginning of an answer to that question is found in this statement of G.K. Chesterton: "There is a thought that stops thought and that's the only thought that ought to be stopped." Instead of saying "Be open," Chesterton calls attention to the particular closures of the mind which must be opposed. My only argument with Chesterton's statement is that though thought is not directly available language is. That is, there are words which close off reality and those words need systematic resistance.

Speech that is sexist or anti-ecological obstructs the exploration of reality and the receptivity of the human being. For example, modern Christian theology consistently spoke of "man and God" or "man and nature." The language of contemporary religious education has to be "men, women, children, and others." The meaning of the religious and divine can only be found by examining the total interplay of men/women, adult/child, human/nonhuman. The gradual purification of sexism, racism, ageism, etc., is not a peripheral issue for religious education; it is what makes religious education possible at all. A "scientific" meaning of revelation presumed there was a body of knowledge that God had given to man. An "aesthetic" meaning of revelation is an invitation to discover the divine in the present experience of humans and nonhumans.

2) Religious education is a combination of silence and paradoxical speech. Speech originates and ends in silence; the crucial question is whether the final silence is empty or full. If one uses only modern reason and discursive speech then the system completes itself at some boundary and there is nothing more to be said. However, if words function as choreography for the human body in relation to artistic materials, then silence emerges in the middle of life. Silence is also an inner moment of all education.

The basis of religious education is bodily and social ritual. In the face of both life and death, nonverbal gestures provide the essential stability for the human person. An education that is religious preserves important rituals that are salvageable from the past. Although the modern west is obsessed with the future, religious education ought to be a reminder that when it comes to the basic human gestures of living and dying there are no wholly new answers. Religious education needs to deal with modern rationality neither by denying it nor by submitting to it. Religious education has to challenge modern reason to find its bodily and social roots in symbols, community, and bodily environment.

Within a context of community and ritual, the religious use of speech is a subverting of speech. That is, speech bends back upon itself leaving us speechless in the middle of a community. The parables and sayings of Jesus are not, as the eighteenth and nineteenth centuries supposed, a rational system of moral truths. Instead, they are extraordinary paradoxes of speech which do not fit the reason of modern times. In this respect, Christian doctrines are also enigmatic formulas whose chief function is to resist the reduction of Jewish and Christian stories to a finished system.[7]

An issue related to this question of speech and silence is the pace of schooling. Contemporary religious education requires a new coalition between school and religious organization (e.g. church). Such a coalition existed in the early period of the United States. Henry May writes of colonial education: "The inculcation of saving truth was primarily the responsibility of the churches, but schools were necessary to protect the written word, the means of revelation."[8] The deficiencies in this coalition have long been apparent. The right wing recognizes the need to read "the means of revelation," but once admitted, education seems to threaten the "saving truth." The left wing tends to let modern schooling control the religious life, though it periodically rebels against the need for school at all.

I am claiming that it was not the existence of the coalition but the form of it that needed replacement. School is and will be a main element in modern society. Religious bodies can both profit from school learning and also remind schools that they are not the whole of education. The religious body can supply experience of games, creative arts, and interaction with nonhuman beings that school will probably never be able to duplicate. The Supreme Court ruled that prayer does not belong in the public school but that is not to say that prayer is unimportant to education or that the study of religion should be excluded from the public school.

3) The Christian expression of revelation is the life of church groups. In a "scientific" meaning, the church has a revelation; in an "aesthetic" meaning the revelation has a church. The form which the church has is not derivable from "the Christian revelation." But it is that very form of institutional life which is most powerfully educative (or miseducative). To return to the question of "undreamt possibilities," the form which church could take may not yet have been imagined.

When ecclesiastical form is deduced from an object which the church itself established, then little change is possible. The form necessarily tends to be individualistic, rationalistic and bureaucratic. But if education were attentive to the very old and the very young, if education preserved and encouraged community, if education explored the entire range of symbolic and sacramental gestures, then a new institutional form might emerge. The purpose here is not to do violence to the Christian past but, on the contrary, to recover more of that past. The learning of exegetes and historians provides only the beginning of that education in what our past means within our present.

The task before religious education is breathtakingly large but it is also urgent and unavoidable. Neither reason nor faith nor both can stem the tide of what is now enveloping the human. Modern enlightenment has turned out to be a brief, illusory period in which a few humans (men) thought they were getting the world under control. The word revelation might have served as a healthy reminder of other forces but the word became encapsulated in the idea system of the time. The concept of revelation is now exploding out of all apparent control. The appropriate educational response today is an artistic approach that incorporates rational structures within itself. To teach within revelation is to acknowledge that the world goes beyond one's control. But it is also to grasp that there are artistic structurings of experience which bring the human being into dialogue with other humans and with other beings who share the earth.

Notes

1. Carl Henry, *God, Revelation and Authority*, Vol. I and II (Waco: Word, 1977).

2. James Hillman, "Peaks and Vales," in *On the Way to Self Knowledge*, ed. Jacob Needleman and Dennis Lewis (New York: Knopf, 1976), p. 128.

3. Bernard Weisberger, *They Gathered at the River* (Boston: Little, Brown and Co., 1958), p. 95.

4. Norman Vincent Peale, *The Power of Positive Thinking* (Westwood: Spire, 1956), p. 181.

5. Morton White, *Science and Sentiment in America* (New York: Oxford, 1972), p. 25.

6. Richard Hofstadter, *Anti-Intellectualism in America* (New York: Vintage, 1963), p. 122.

7. See John Crossan, *Raid on the Articulate* (New York: Harper and Row, 1976).

8. Henry May, *The Enlightenment in America* (New York: Oxford, 1976), p. 32.

Suggested Readings

Crossan, John. *The Dark Interval: Toward a Theology of Story*. Chicago: Argus, 1975.

Douglas, Mary. *Natural Symbols*. New York: Vintage, 1970.

Horkheimer, Max. *Eclipse of Reason*. New York: Seabury, 1974.

Moran, Gabriel. *The Preset Revelation*. New York: Seabury, 1972.

Turner, Victor. *The Ritual Process: Structure and Anti-Structure*. Ithaca: Cornell, 1977.

IV
AESTHETIC THEORY

12.
Right-Lobe Religion, Theology and Religious Education

Michael G. Lawler

Michael Lawler argues that religion and theology are highly symbolic in nature and are best understood not in a left-Western analysis of discrete bits and pieces, but in a right-Eastern lobe seeking out and living into total patterns of meaning. He argues further that since this is the case religious education which seeks to educate or lead out people to become human and religious according to patterns established by religious symbols and meanings, is best approached in a community context as a process of intentional enculturation, rather than in an instructional context which is suited for left-Western lobe phenomena.

PREAMBLE

Certain things are taken for granted today in discussions of the functioning of the human cerebral hemispheres. Ever since the classical investigations of Broca (1861) and Wernicke (1874), it has been hypothesized that the hemispheres of the human brain, though physiologically similar, function differently. In right handed people the left cerebral hemisphere is considered predominant in language function, the right hemisphere predominant in visuo-spatial function. And while this hypothesis arose initially from poorly controlled clinical observation, highly systematic and controlled experimentation of more recent vintage has tended both to confirm it and to progress beyond it.

As early as 1931 Jackson suggested that the real difference in left and right lobe functioning might be cognitive in nature.[1] He suggested that the left is specialized for analytic organization and the right for direct association. There is recent data to support this hypothesis. Levy, for instance, has suggested that the clear superiority of the isolated right hemisphere in the recognition of shapes and spatial constructions derives from the fact that it has a unique capacity for complex, holistic cognitive processing.[2] Bever, from his work in psycholinguistics, agrees that processing ability, and not simple verbal-non verbal distinctions, is what characterizes cerebral hemispherical dominance.[3]

The contemporary position concerning hemispherical dominance may be summarized briefly like this. The left hemisphere appears to have the capacity for treating information in discrete units. It deals with information analytically as in discursive reasoning, and sequentially as in speech. In contrast, the right hemisphere seems adapted for dealing with information holistically rather than analytically, immediately grasping whole patterns of meaning rather than discrete and sequential units.

This contemporary physiological hypothesis corresponds to the position philosophically advocated by the great Belgian *homme des lettres*, Maurice Maeterlinck. He suggested that the human brain be theoretically divided into a *Western lobe* and an *Eastern lobe*. The Western lobe is the seat of reason (*ratio*) and science (*scientia*), the Eastern lobe the seat of intuition and symbolic forms. In Western culture, deriving from and dominated by the great Greeks, the Western lobe has been so allowed to control the approach to reality that the Eastern lobe has been paralyzed. Maeterlinck issued a clarion call to reactivate the Eastern lobe.

The proposal of this brief essay is this. To accept the experimentally-supported hypothesis that first, the right and left lobes of the human brain function differently and secondly, the right-Eastern lobe dominates in holistic processes while the left-Western lobe dominates in analytic and sequential processes, and on this basis to pose the question whether religion, theology, and religious education are left-Western or right-Eastern phenomena. The answer which will be advocated and developed is that they are right-Eastern lobe phenomena and exist only as caricatures of themselves when approached in a left-Western lobe way.

RELIGION AND SYMBOL

There is no universally agreed upon single definition of the phenomenon known as religion. There are, in fact, some fifty to sixty commonly advocated definitions. And though these betray what

Wittgenstein once called "family resemblances," it is necessary to specify which definition will control the following discussion. For although definitions are not ultimate, they are aids to insight and understanding by the introduction of verbal clarity.

In this essay religion is accepted and treated within the context of social-anthropological definitions. It is, in Robert Bellah's phrase, "a set of symbols . . . (which) . . . define in broadest terms the nature of reality."[4] It is, in Clifford Geertz's more extended definition, "a system of symbols which act to establish powerful, pervasive, and long-lasting moods and motivations in men by formulating conceptions of a general order of existence and clothing these conceptions with such an aura of factuality that the moods and motivations seem uniquely realistic."[5]

The family resemblance in these definitions is in the word and the concept *symbol*. Any understanding of the definitions and of the phenomenon which they attempt to define will depend upon an understanding of the meanings of this word and this concept. It is necessary, therefore, to offer a brief discursus on symbol.

A symbol is a kind of sign; it is a species of the genus sign. Now a sign is something which points an interpreter to something other than the sign itself. So, too, is a symbol. The process of sign-ifying and the process of symbol-izing are processes in which a sign or a symbol denotes a meaning to an interpreter. This is how sign and symbol coincide. They also specifically differ, and the differences are more instructive than the generic similarity. Two differences will be considered briefly.

The first notable difference between a sign and a symbol is this: a sign declares that what it signifies is present, a symbol real-izes as present, concrete, focused, and effective what it symbolizes. Smoke is a sign of fire; a red and white striped pole is a sign of a barber's shop. But a country's flag is a symbol, not a mere sign; making love is a symbol, not a mere sign; the religious use of bread and wine is a symbol, not a mere sign. For they do not simply declare that what they signify is present. Rather they real-ize as present, concrete, focused, and effective what they symbolize: the flag the country, the making love the love between two human beings, the bread and wine the Lord whom Christians confess.

Without the flag the country is, indeed, present; without making love the shared love is, indeed, present; without bread and wine the Lord is, indeed, present. But without the symbols each is present only as abstract, diffuse, and affective. What the symbol accomplishes is to make the country, the love, the Lord present as concrete, focused, and effective, so that men and women are really drawn to respond to the symbol and what it embodies with appropriate action. It is precisely in its ability to real-ize what it symbolizes and draw people into itself that the power of the symbol, as distinct from the mere sign, lies.

There is a second difference between a mere sign and a symbol. The relationship between a mere sign and what it signifies is fixed. "A sign or signal is related to the thing to which it refers in a fixed and unique way. Any one concrete and individual sign refers to a certain individual thing." The relationship, on the other hand, between a symbol and what it symbolizes is not fixed. "A genuine human symbol is characterized not by its uniformity, but by its versatility. It is not rigid or inflexible but mobile."[6] Signs are single-meaninged, symbols are many-meaninged. Smoke means fire and nothing else; barber's pole means barber's shop and nothing else. But the Stars and Stripes means America and freedom and democracy and justice for all; making love means self-giving and other accepting, trusting and doubting, binding and freeing, pain and ecstasy, and countless other meanings; eucharistic bread and wine means Jesus and Lord, death and resurrection, woman, man and God, past and future, earthly church called out to heavenly kingdom.

The single, fixed meaning of a sign is communicated clearly and distinctly at a rational level. The many, mobile meanings of a symbol are communicated con-fusedly, that is, fused together, at a level which is both rational and intuitive. Paul Ricoeur expresses it well. Signs are perfectly transparent, symbols are opaque. "This opacity constitutes the depth of symbol, which is inexhaustible."[7]

To plumb the depth of symbolic meaning, intuition and not mere reason, warm personal commitment and not cool detached science is required. "A true symbol must be *lived into*. That is how its meaning is found."[8] Symbols are realities of the right-Eastern, rather than of the left-Western, lobe. They are best dealt with, not as the modern Western tradition has attempted to deal with them, analytically and sequentially as mediating discrete units of meaning, but rather holistically as mediating entire patterns of meaning. If this is true of symbols, it must be true also of religion which is accepted as a set of symbols. This conclusion and its implications must now be examined.

First of all, as an analogy to illumine holistic processing, consider a photograph. Like language it is composed of unit elements each of which represents respective constituents in the object. But these unit elements are not units with independent meanings. The units of light and shade which make up a photograph have no meaning in themselves. Though they faithfully represent the visual elements of the object, each unit in isolation would be simply a blotch. "They do not represent, item for item, those elements which have *names*; there is not one blotch for the nose, one for the mouth etc.; their shapes, in quite indescribable combinations, convey a total picture in which nameable features may be pointed out."[9] The information about an object conveyed by any photograph of it is infinitely more extensive than the information conveyed by a sequential language description of the object. Rembrandt's *Night Watch* conveys more information than an essay on the same topic, and the information is conveyed immediately and holistically, with no breakdown into discrete and sequential units of information.

A photograph is a quasi-symbol. Its unit elements have no meaning in themselves, but derive their representative meanings from the total reference of the photograph. So it is, too, with symbols. The meanings which they convey are conveyed con-fusedly *in toto*, and are grasped con-fusedly *in toto* in the right-Eastern lobe. That holistic pattern of meanings is degraded when an attempt is made to analytically articulate the meanings of the symbol in a series of discrete, clear, and distinct concepts in the left-Western lobe.

This is not to claim that the meanings of symbols cannot be rationally interpreted at all. It simply means that any attempt to analyze symbolic meanings translates them from the right-Eastern realm of whole patterns to the left-Western realm of discrete bits and pieces. Just as "there is no standard key for translating sculpture into painting, or drawing into ink-wash, because their equivalence rests on their common *total reference*, not on bit for bit equivalence of parts,"[10] so also there is no key for translating holistic symbolic meanings into *scientia*. The implications of this general analysis of symbols and of the nature of symbolic knowledge will now be explicated in an analysis of religious symbols.

RELIGIOUS SYMBOLS

There are three broad kinds of religious symbols. There are material realities which are religiously symbolic; there are actions which are religiously symbolic; and there are narratives which are religiously symbolic. Material religious symbols will be treated in the exemplar of the sound-symbol or language-symbol, "God"; action religious symbols in the exemplar of Christian sacraments; narrative religious symbols in the exemplar of myth.

The word, *God*, is a crucial religious symbol, in fact the root religious symbol in the Western tradition. This symbol is made part of many propositions. It is said, for instance, that "God is," that "God is creator," that "God is our Father." These propositions and countless others like them are mis-taken frequently as *scientia* about God, as scientific explication of the root symbol, *God*, and of the ultimate reality to which it points. But they are not. For this simple sounding symbol is not quite as simple as it sounds (or looks).

The word, *God*, and the propositions which employ it, are symbolic. They symbolize the Ultimate. That is, they real-ize the Ultimate as present, concrete, focused, and effective by conveying multiple meanings about the Ultimate. These meanings embodied in the symbols, however, since they are symbolic meanings, are conveyed con-fusedly and are grasped con-fusedly in the right-Eastern lobe. They are not to be thought of as rational, scientific descriptions of what the Ultimate ultimately is, and they can be translated into left-Western lobe descriptions only at the risk of losing the total reference within which they make sense and within which they communicate insight into and understanding of the Ultimate. The understanding and insight presented by these symbols can be grasped as intelligible only by right-Eastern intuition not left-Western reason, only by warm personal commitment not by cool detached *scientia*.

What this means practically is that the root symbol-word, *God* and the propositions in which it occurs are never to be thought of as literally referring to and scientifically describing some Ultimate being beyond our world and immanent to it. They do describe such a being, but only in the symbolic mode. That is, they real-ize the Ultimate as present, concrete, focused, and effective for men and women and invite those men and women to appreciative insight into the Ultimate and action according to that insight. Their function is not to convey what the Ultimate *is*, but rather what the Ultimate *is like*. The necessary further development of this statement will be reserved for a later context in which it is more fruitful.

Action religious symbols, called rituals, are to be considered in the exemplar of Christian sacraments. "I baptize you in the name of the Father and of the Son and of the Holy Spirit." These words, accompanying the pouring of water on a person, constitute the ritual of baptism, a symbolic action which, Christians confess, real-izes God in Christ as present, concrete, focused, and effective as accepting the baptized as a member of the Body of Christ. A man, or a woman, takes bread and proclaims the word, "This is my body given for you." It is the ritual of eucharist which, Christians confess, realizes God in Christ as present, concrete, focused, and effective as the one who was dead and who was raised from the dead. How are such claims to be understood?

The question is a more general question than it appears, and its analysis requires a broader canvas than that provided by theological talk about sacraments. That analysis has what might appear to be a strange starting point. One of the fathers of nuclear physics, the Dane Neils Bohr, once wrote to the equally distinguished German physicist, Werner Heisenberg, stating what they were doing when they were seeking so-called atomic structure. "When it comes to atoms, language can only be described as poetry. The poet is not nearly so concerned with describing facts as with creating images."[11]

To many that will be a startling thought: talk of atoms is not describing facts but creating images. But it is so. What lies beyond the physical world is always, and necessarily, imaginary for men and women—literally imaginary, that is dealt with in a play of concrete images. There is no other way to talk about the invisible, in science, in art, or in religion. Nor is there any other way for the invisible to disclose itself to men and women except in concrete images. That some trans-visible reality is disclosed in these images, whether of science, or art, or of religion, is strictly a matter for that crucial human decision called faith.

What then of the claim Christians make for sacraments, namely, that they real-ize God in Christ as present, concrete, focused, and effective? Sacraments are symbols. As symbols they real-ize what they symbolize, but in a way that can be grasped only by the right-Eastern lobe, not in the scientific way of the left-Western lobe. An analogy will illuminate how symbolic actions real-ize what they symbolize.

A man and a woman fall in love. The man loves the woman, and he knows he loves her. The problem is that as far as the woman is concerned the man's love for her is remote, abstract, diffuse, merely affective, until he embodies it and expresses it in some action. He says, "I love you"; he writes her a love letter; he kisses her. In these varied actions his love is real-ized, that is, made real for both him and the woman. His love which was remote is made present. His love which was abstract is made concrete. His love which was diffuse is made focused. His love which was affective is made effective, so that both he and the woman are confronted by it, enriched by it, and drawn into action in response to it.

In symbols—the words, the letter, the kisses—the man's love for the woman is real-ized precisely by being symbolized. The symbols do not merely signify his love, they also make it real. The symbols are efficacious actions; they effect what they signify. And the effect, love concretely and effectively bestowed on the woman, is wholly due to both the man's love as principal cause and his actions as instrumental causes.

This analogy yields insight into how sacramental symbols realize God in Christ. God loves his people. But as far as his people are concerned God's love is remote, abstract, diffuse until it is real-ized in some gesture. God made that gesture first of all, Christians confess, in Jesus of Nazareth. In the events of his life, death, and transformation, God's love for his people was both symbolized and realized, so that men and women were confronted by it, enriched by it, and drawn to respond to it. Jesus is the prime symbol of God's love for human kind.

Jesus, however, is now exalted to power as Lord and Christ. If he is to continue to be truly the efficacious symbol of God's love for us, he himself must be real-ized in earthly reality. He is so realized, Christians confess, in the earthly community called church which is his body. The church is now the primary earthly symbol of God-in-Christ's love for his people. The gestures which symbolize God's love, once the gestures of the earthly Christ, are now the gestures of his sacramental body, the church. In this body's actions God-in-Christ is at once symbolized and real-ized as present, concrete, focused, and effective, so that men and women are confronted by him, enriched by him, and drawn to respond to him.

Symbols real-ize what they symbolize. Sacramental symbols equally real-ize what they symbolize. Baptism is not merely the sign of vivifying grace, but is that grace real-ized as present, concrete, focused and effective in the symbol of water and words. Bread and wine do not merely symbolize Jesus, but make him present in his body, the church, as concrete, focused, and effective. The sacramental symbols of the body of Christ effect what they symbolize, and the effect—the presence of God-in-Christ, grace, Spirit, reconciliation etc.—is wholly due both to God-in-Christ as principal cause and to the sacramental symbols as instrumental causes.

There is but one caveat. As symbols, sacraments convey their many meanings con-fusedly and holistically to the right-Eastern lobe, and they are grasped there as whole patterns of meaning. A left-Western lobe analytic approach, an approach so predominant in much sacramental writing, results in the degradation of the symbols to signs and the loss of the holistic pattern of meaning within which they mediate understanding of and insight into the saving action of

God. That God in Christ is real-ized in these sacramental symbols is never demonstrated by cool, scientific analysis, but is grasped only in the warm human commitment called faith. Bohr was right, about sacraments as well as about atoms. When it comes to God and his encounter with men and women "language can be described only as poetry. The poet is not nearly so concerned with describing facts as with creating images." Symbols and sacraments are not to be understood and explained scientifically; they are to be *lived into*.

Another, and crucially important, kind of religious symbol is symbolic narrative. Such narrative is called technically myth. What myth attempts to do is to impose meaningful, and so intelligible, form upon realities that transcend human experience. Myth is presented in narrative form, but the narrative is not historical, nor are the symbols of the narrative the reality they symbolize. Both narrative and symbols are intended, not to explain the unexplainable, but to supply some understanding of and insight into reality that ultimately lies beyond full human comprehension. Such understanding and such insight, while it does not allow men and women fully to comprehend and so manipulate reality, does allow them to appreciate it and live into it. Myth is clearly a right-Eastern, not a left-Western, phenomenon. An example will clarify the above points.

For the ancient Semite, water was a primordial element to whose whim people were constantly subject. There were three layers of water encompassing the earth: water below on which the earth floated; water of the seas and rivers within the earth; and water above the earth which sometimes fell on the earth in the form of rain and snow. Always exposed to these waters the earth, and all within it, had a fragile existence. This fragility led to the creation of a mythological motif which was central in Near Eastern religions for more than a thousand years, and which left clearly discernible traces in the Jewish-Christian scriptures.

The Babylonian *Enuma Elish* represents the most complete version of this ancient motif. It begins with an account of the birth of younger gods to Tiamat, the personification of Sea, and Apsu, the personification of Sweet Water, and moves quickly to a crisis. Tiamat and Apsu are disturbed by the noisy generation, and Apsu resolves to wipe them out. They, however, know of Apsu's intentions and kill him first, an action which puts them in conflict with the widowed Tiamat. The younger gods choose Marduk as their champion and grant him supreme power over the universe. Marduk defeats Tiamat and from her corpse fashions the cosmos known to ancient men and women: the heavens and the earth, the sun, the moon and the stars, and finally man and woman. Marduk, the supreme god of the Babylonian pantheon, overcomes and controls the chaotic Tiamat-Sea.

Another Near Eastern myth with the same theme was uncovered at the ancient Canaanite city of Ugarit. The Ugaritic version depicts a great battle in which the supreme Canaanite god, Baal, "destroyed and drank Sea." Baal, the great god of Canaan, overcomes and places in control chaotic Sea. The Ugaritic document is clearly a variation on the same theme presented in the Babylonian epic.

The literature of ancient Israel has obvious continuities with these Babylonian and Canaanite myths. The priestly creation account in the first chapter of Genesis may be, indeed, a polemic against such ancient mythologies, but it betrays clear traces of the very tradition against which it polemicizes. It recounts that in the beginning "the earth was without form and void, and darkness was upon the face of *tehom.*"[12] *Tehom*, the watery abyss, the primeval deep, while it may not be identical with Tiamat and Sea, is at least a remnant of that ancient mythical personification of Sea. An even clearer remnant of the ancient battle between God and Sea is the Book of Job where it is asserted that "with his power (God) stilled Sea, with his skill he smote Rahab, with his wind he bagged Sea."[13] Yahweh, the great God of Israel, overcomes and places in control chaotic Sea.

In the Christian New Testament traces of the common theme continue. All three Synoptic gospels record Jesus' calming of the storm on the Sea of Galilee.[14] In this account the great cosmic events of the *Enuma Elish*, the Ugarit poem and the first chapter of Genesis are reduced to a natural event: a storm on the Sea of Galilee. As always the menacing Sea is overcome, and all three gospel accounts conclude with a question: "Who then is this that even wind and sea obey him?" For those who know the common theme the answer is obvious. Jesus controls the chaotic Sea. He is, at least, one in whom God's power is at work; perhaps, at most, God himself.

Such conclusions, of course, are not the obvious end-point of a scientific analysis. They are not attained in the left-Western lobe. Rather they are the result of grasping overall patterns of meaning and locating the gospel accounts within this pattern. They are, in short, right-Eastern lobe conclusions. They overwhelm and command assent, not by the force of their rational logic, but in a multiplicity of images which converge in inescapable meanings. The left-Western lobe approach to these accounts, which has been and is so dominant in popular (as distinct from scholarly) biblical interpretation, allows the inescapable meaning to escape because it sunders the pattern in which the meaning is inescapable. At the same time it does not prove, because it cannot prove. For what lies beyond the visible cannot be proved, except in the interplay of concrete images.

THEOLOGY

The foregoing has attempted to state and explain that religion is a symbolic phenomenon. Its words are symbolic, its actions are symbolic, its narratives are symbolic; that is, they real-ize as concrete, focused and effective what they symbolize. Religion communicates knowledge. But it is knowledge, not in the sense of left-Western lobe clear and distinct *scientia*, but rather of right-Eastern lobe understanding and insight and appreciation. There is, however, in religious knowledge, as in all symbolic knowledge, an inherent dynamism which calls for the interpretation of the symbols and which leads to reflection on the symbols and to the conceptual expression of the meanings contained in them. The reflection on and conceptual expression of the meanings mediated in specifically religious symbols is called *theology*. A word is necessary about theology and about what happens in the translation of religious language to theological language.

Religious language both expresses and leads to an experience, an experience of "in broadest terms the nature of reality," an experience of the Ultimate. Christian believers proclaim, for instance, "I believe in God, the Father almighty, creator of heaven and earth." When they make this proclamation they are stating both their understanding and their experience of the nature of reality. Reality is created and sustained by an almighty creator-father, and is so experienced by Christians. Is it, then, to the nature of reality or to the believer's experience that religious language refers?

There should be no doubt about it. Religious language refers first of all to the believer's experience. It expresses the way the believer *experiences* reality. However, religious language refers to the believer's experience, not as normal and everyday, but as qualified to the limit. To that extent it communicates understanding of an insight into something other than the believer's experience, namely, the ultimate nature of reality itself. There is an experience not only of an everyday father, but also of an *almighty* father. There is an experience not only of an everyday maker, but also of a *creator* (by definition one who makes from nothing). There is an experience, in the ritual of baptism, of entry not only into the everyday community called church, but also into communion with God. There is an experience, in the eucharistic meal, of symbolizing not only the body of Christ which is the church, but also the body of Christ which is the Lord.

Human experience is limited. Religious language expresses the limit of this experience and at the same time discloses, in symbol, what lies beyond this limit. Religious language, therefore, refers to an experience at the limit of human experience. It is a limit-language which refers to a limit-experience.[15] Because it does refer to a limit-experience which discloses what lies beyond the limit, it is necessarily symbolic language. For always what lies beyond the visible is dealt with only in the interplay of symbolic images. Religious language is necessarily right-Eastern lobe language, to be understood not as discrete units literally referring to respective units beyond the visible, but rather as total patterns of meaning communicating insight and understanding of these realities.

Theology reflects upon the human limit-experiences expressed in religious language and questions them. It systematically, that is, conceptually, articulates that these experiences are, first of all, human experiences and, secondly, human experiences which provide analogical bases for gaining insight into the ultimate nature of reality. It systematically cautions that the language in which these limit-experiences are expressed is human symbolic language which expresses not photographically what the beyond of human experience *is*, but analogically what it *is like*. The best theology cautions further that the *is like* implies always, and necessarily, an *is not*. God is like a father and like a creator, yet simultaneously not at all like either a father or a creator. Making Jesus in eucharist is like making love, yet simultaneously not at all like making love. The beginnings of human kind were like a garden paradise subverted by a snake's word to man and woman, yet not at all like either a garden or a paradise or a snake or a man or a woman.

What this means in simple language is, of course, that theological language is not left-Western lobe language, scientifically describing the way things were or are or will be. It does not exactly describe the way God is, or what happens in baptism or eucharist, or how men and women originated, or what will happen to them when they die. Theological language is rather right-Eastern lobe language which describes in patterns of meaning the limits of human experience and offers symbolic understanding of and insight into what may lie beyond those limits. It is appreciative language which enables us to say "so that is what Mystery *is like*," not manipulative language which enables us to say "so that is all there *is* to Mystery."

There is no new insight here, merely the reclamation of an old one, for some theologians, many religious educators, and almost all religious learners have either never heard or have forgotten what Aquinas wrote: "anything about God is completely unknown to men in this life, that is, it is unknown what God *is*."[16] Karl Rahner expressed the same idea in a lecture I heard him deliver in Rome in 1962. Commenting on 1 John 3:2, "we know that when he appears we shall be like him, for we shall see him as he is," he added simply: "and God *is* Mystery." After the most systematic and precise theological language available, be it biblical, doctrinal or ritual, there results insight into and appreciation of the limit of human experience and what lies beyond it, never *scientia* and manipulative control.

RELIGIOUS EDUCATION

The proposal of this essay was to demonstrate that religion, theology, and religious education were predominantly right-Eastern lobe phenomena. Religion and theology have been dealt with briefly, within the limits imposed by space, and their right-Eastern lobe character has been highlighted. There remains religious education.

The debate as to the precise meanings and distinctions of the terms, religious education, Christian education, catechesis, continues and remains inconclusive and unproductive. A conscious choice has been made here for the broad, and more common, term, religious education. That term must be explained.

The noun in the phrase religious education, namely, *education*, derives from the Latin root *educere*, meaning to lead out. Education, therefore, is at root a leading out, a leading out of people to become the human beings they potentially are. That leading out and that becoming, however, must be done along the lines of some meaning system. It cannot be done successfully if it is done haphazardly. The adjective in the phrase religious education, namely, *religious*, specifies the meaning system that directs the leading out and the becoming involved in religious education. It is religion. If the religious education is specifically Christian education, then the leading out and the becoming are patterned after the meaning system called Christian.

Religion, however, is a set of symbols. So, too, is Christian religion. How does one set about leading out people to become more complete persons according to a pattern mediated in a set of symbols. The telling of the answer to this crucial question for religious education is simple, the doing of it rather more complex. *One* does not do it. There is required an entire community of people who faithfully *live into* the symbols and the meanings embodied in them to lead out people successfully to the way of life demarcated by the symbols.

There is required a community of Christian faith, faithfully living into the Christian symbols and the meanings real-ized in them to educate people, especially little people called children, to a Christian way of life.

There is no new insight here either. Again there is merely an attempt to reclaim an old one. As far back as 1917, George Albert Coe invited Protestant religious educators to such an approach in his seminal *A Social Theory of Religious Education*. Contemporarily, among Protestant educators, John H. Westerhoff III continues and expands Coe's tradition. His early phrase, "intentional religious socialization," and its later surrogate, "intentional enculturation," have supplied the almost programmatic label for this approach.[17]

Within the Roman Catholic tradition the invitation to a community-of-faith approach to religious education was issued in a document having strong institutional authority, the *General Catechetical Directory*, published in June 1971. Its aim is to promote renewal in catechesis, but catechesis is firmly located as an "ecclesial action" (par.21), "concerned with community," and having "the functions of initiation, education and formation" (par.31). Dwelling on this section in his commentary on the *Directory*, Berard Marthaler notes that "though the *Directory* does not use the term, the educational role it attributes to the ecclesial community is a description of 'socialization'."[18]

The community-of-faith, socialization, enculturation approach to religious education has inter-denominational, and ever-spreading, roots. It is time to define this approach. For, as already noted, though definitions are not ultimate, they do make for insight and understanding by introducing conceptual clarity.

Socialization or enculturation names a process in and by which a person becomes a participating member of a society or culture. Culture refers to the totality of people, things and events that are socially symboled, and symboling is endowing concrete people, things, and events with non-concrete meaning. Enculturation, therefore, names a process in and by which a person is imbued with a set of symbols and related meanings, accepts those symbols and meanings as adequate articulations of reality, and lives into those symbols and meanings in his/her daily life. The religious enculturation approach to religious education looks on religion as a culture, as a set of symbols endowing concrete people, things, and events with non-concrete meanings, and claims that religious education names a process in and by which a person is imbued with a set of religious symbols and related meanings, accepts those symbols and meanings as adequate articulations of the ultimate nature of reality, and lives into those symbols and meanings in a community which shares the same meanings.

Religious education, therefore, is not merely a matter of instruction or schooling. It is a much more complex process in which the religious community not only accepts a set of symbols and related meanings, but also lives into them in every daily situation in which it finds itself. This idea is central to the theory of religious enculturation as a practical method of religious education: what is accepted in theory is also lived in practice. It would be useless to try to communicate in a society the meaning that dogs are for pets and not for eating if it were common in the society to serve dogs for lunch. Similarly it is useless to try to communicate in a society the religious meaning that all persons are brothers and sisters if it is common in the society to validate all kinds of inequalities between the brothers and the sisters. The intentional enculturation approach to religious education correctly emphasizes that religious education is more, much more, than mere instruction however professional. However, it also raises a problem which will be obvious when stated. But first there is another problem which must be confronted.

This essay has located religion and theology as right-Eastern lobe phenomena. That is, they yield knowledge that is not clear and distinct Cartesian *scientia*, but is rather insight and understanding. They describe not what people, things, and events *are*, but rather what they *are like*. This makes both religion and theology problematic, for vast numbers of people, religious and non-religious alike, are unable to deal with symbols. They make things easy for themselves by reducing many-meaninged symbols to single-meaninged signs. It should be clear from all that has been already said that such a reduction seriously subverts the nature of both religion and theology. For it translates them from the right-Eastern lobe, whence they are a source of powerful and liberating insight and appreciation, to the left-Western lobe where they fraudulently pose as *scientia* that gives control and manipulation. Left-Western *scientia* does, of course, offer precise and manageable ideas, but when it pretends to be religious *scientia* the price is too high because it diminishes the immensity of the Ultimate.

The community of faith must realize that when it deals with realities beyond the sensible, and it is with such realities that religion and theology deal, it cannot describe photographically what they *are* but only image in symbols what they *are like*. When it comes to educate religiously its members by enculturating them into its faith-view, it must be careful to ensure that its religious symbols and the meanings real-ized in them remain open invitations to reflect and find insight, rather than restrictive definitions of the way people, things, and events are and, therefore, always have to be.

That allowing the symbols and their meanings to remain so open is difficult cannot be denied. That it has not yet been done successfully in the various religious traditions is witnessed by the multitudes of religious folk who are so comfortable with the feeling that they know all about God and about his intentions for men and women. When the enculturation is of children, who have such well-documented problems with symbols and their meanings, the difficulty is increased.[19] But religious symbols must be allowed to retain their symbolic power, rather than being reduced to mere signs. The intentional enculturation approach to religious education insists only that this end is best achieved, not by a process of schooling and intellectual instruction, but by the religious community living into its symbols and meanings in the conscious realization that these meanings are precisely symbolic meanings that invite it to constantly reflect to discover the Ultimate that is real-ized in them.

It is here that there arises the other problem with religious enculturation that was alluded to earlier. Enculturation is for transmitting culture and, therefore, also for maintaining culture. It transmits and maintains all too easily the *status quo*. In enculturation which claims to be Christian enculturation there must be an ever-present question. Is the Christian community sure that the symbols and the meanings being transmitted and maintained are Christian symbols and meanings, rather than some cultural dilution too readily accepted and named Christian? To answer this question the Christian community of faith must engage continuously not only in intentional enculturation, but also in *critical* enculturation.

Critical enculturation intends that the first moment in the process of enculturation be a critical moment. The symbols and the meanings of the *status quo* must be critiqued, and for them to be validated as Christian symbols and meanings they must be able to stand under the glare of the gospel tradition and of the vision of the community of faith which it offers. For religious enculturation to be also Christian education the community of faith must be not only intentional enculturator, but also critical prophet. It must not only seek to live into and transmit and maintain the symbols of the *status quo*, but also continuously strive to ensure that these symbols and meanings be the word of God spoken in Christ to and in and by the community of faith today.[20]

SUMMARY

This essay has considered, however briefly, the natures of religion, theology, and religious education. It has argued that religion and theology are highly symbolic in nature and are best understood not in a left-Western analysis of discrete bits and pieces, but in a right-Eastern lobe seeking out and living into total patterns of meaning. It has argued further that since this is the case, religious education, which seeks to educate or lead out people to become human and religious according to patterns established by religious symbols and meanings, is best approached in a community context as a process of intentional enculturation, rather than in an instructional context which is suited for left-Western lobe phenomena.

The essay concludes with two invitations to the Christian community, the second of which is demanded by the first. First, an invitation to take seriously the injunction of the word of God: "My face you cannot see, for no mortal man may see me and live."[21] Secondly, an invitation to reactivate the right-Eastern lobe by and in which that hidden face may be, not indeed seen, but at least glimpsed and appreciated.

Notes

1. J.H. Jackson, *Selected Writings of John Hughlings Jackson*, 2 (London: Hodder and Stoughton, 1931).

2. J. Levy, "Possible Basis for the Evaluation of Lateral Specialization of the Human Brain," *Nature*, 224 (1969), 614-615.

3. T.G. Bever *et al.*, "Analytic Processing Elicits Right Ear Superiority in Monaurally Presented Speech," *Neuropsychologia*, 14 (1976), 175-181.

4. Robert Bellah, *Religion and Progress in Modern Asia* (New York: Harper and Row, 1965), p. 171.

5. Clifford Geertz, "Religion as a Cultural System," *Reader in Comparative Religion: An Anthropological Approach*, ed. W.A. Lessa and E.Z. Vogt (New York: Harper and Row, 1965), p. 206.

6. Ernest Cassirer, *An Essay on Man: An Introduction to a Philosophy of Human Culture* (New Haven: Yale University Press, 1944), p. 26.

7. Paul Ricoeur, *The Symbolism of Evil* (New York: Harper and Row, 1967), p. 15.

8. Theodore Roszak, *Where the Wasteland Ends: Politics and Transcendence in Postindustrial Society* (New York: Doubleday, 1974), p. 139.

184 MICHAEL G. LAWLER

9. Susanne K. Langer, *Philosophy in a New Key: A Study in the Symbolism of Reason, Rite and Art* (3rd ed.; Cambridge: Harvard University Press, 1967), pp. 94-95.

10. *Ibid.*, p. 96. Emphasis in original.

11. Quoted in J. Bronowski, *The Ascent of Man* (Boston: Little, Brown, 1973), p. 340.

12. Gen. 1:2.

13. Job 26:12-13. Rehab is one of the many titles of the sea monster in which the ancient Near East embodied the terror of the sea.

14. Mark 4:37-39; cf. Matt. 8:23-27; Luke 8:22-25.

15. These ideas have been systematically elaborated by David Tracy in his *Blessed Rage for Order: The New Pluralism in Theology* (New York: Seabury, 1975) and by Paul Ricoeuer in *Semeia: An Experimental Journal for Biblical Criticism*, 4 (1975), 107-145. Those interested in more elaborate treatment may fruitfully consult these works.

16. *Comm. in Rom.*, cap. 1, lect. 6.

17. See John H. Westerhoff III and Gwen Kennedy Neville, *Generation to Generation* (Philadelphia: United Church Press, 1974), and John H. Westerhoff III, *Will Our Children Have Faith?* (New York: Seabury, 1976).

18. Bernard Marthaler, *Catechetics in Context* (Huntingdon: Our Sunday Visitor, 1973), p. 65.

19. See Michael G. Lawler, "Symbol and Religious Education," *Religious Education*, 72 (1977), 363-372.

20. Since this essay was prepared for publication an article has appeared making in an extended way the same point made briefly in the last few paragraphs. See Thomas H. Groome, "The Critical Principle in Christian Education and the Task of Prophecy," *Religious Education*, 72 (1977), 262-272.

21. Ex. 33:20.

13.
Empirical Research and Religious Experience

Andrew D. Thompson

Andrew Thompson familarizes us with some of the latest find-ings in brain research and its pertinence to religious develop-ment. He emphasizes three parallels between the scientific and the religious: religious education and symbolic consciousness; the processes of creativity; meditation and twilight imagery.

INTRODUCTION TO CONTEMPORARY BRAIN RESEARCH

Research dealing with the human brain has delivered two prom-ises to humanity's doorstep. The first, based on the finding that the left and right hemispheres of the brain seem to have developed rela-tively distinct and specialized forms of thinking competencies, sug-gests that future generations may reap a harvest by greater integra-tion and coordination of these different potentials. The second prom-ise, based on the finding that the brain is even more complex and mysterious than known by previous scientific knowledge, suggests that each person's mind is not a puzzle to be solved reductionistically but a mystery which each person can now attempt to live to greater depths than previously realized.

The present essay addresses two questions: What are these find-ings of brain research, especially those pertaining to left-handed thinking? and, secondly, what is their significance for religious edu-cation and related forms of ministry? The finds are rooted in the complex biology of the brain, surgical technology, the psychology of consciousness and in empirical testing methodologies. For the reader unfamiliar with these concerns, an overview which highlights the main trends in research must be our starting point.

HISTORICAL BACKGROUND

We begin with the known. That the human brain has two hemispheres had been noted by Hipprocates, the father of medicine, four centuries before the birth of Christ. But it was not until the mid nineteenth century that surgeons and psychologists began to consider the meaning and interworkings of this physical duality of the brain. One of the earliest medical pioneers, A. L. Wigan,[1] claimed on what could be judged today as sketchy data, that each hemisphere was a distinct and complete organ of thought. He speculated that a separate and distinct process of thinking may be carried on in each hemisphere simultaneously.

Wigan concluded and was subsequently "supported" by other researchers' findings that some persons seemed to function completely normally even though one hemisphere had completely degenerated due to disease.[2] This train of thought was pursued by C. E. Brown-Seguard who affirmed that the "two brains" were perfectly distinct from one another.[3] In the mid 1870's, researchers found that dysphasia, the loss of the ability to use or to understand speech, seemed to stem from injury specifically to the left hemisphere.[4] Thus emerged the current wave of research which focused first on the left hemisphere, so strongly associated with speech, and then more recently on the right hemisphere, whose competencies are less easily specified. Before considering the empirical findings in greater detail, prior questions need to be raised to contextualize current findings.

CONTEMPORARY FINDINGS

It is now somewhat common knowledge that the right hemisphere receives and directs information pertaining to the left side of the body and that the left hemisphere coordinates the right side of the body. Recent research has found beyond this that each hemisphere has its relatively distinct mode of thinking, a specialization. What is yet unclear is the nature of the right lobe's specialty.

Bruner uses[5] the metaphor of a person's left and right hand cooperating in operating a screw driver for the cooperation of the right and left hemispheres in the thinking processes. Just as the left hand holds the screw while the more deft right hand operates the tool, so, says Bruner, the right lobe contextualizes the subject matter under consideration while the left lobe uses verbal and logical processes to complete the job of knowing. This suggests in effect that the right lobe specializes in generating metaphors, intuitions, images which further the human reaches of intelligence. But is there any basis for saying this?

To answer this question, we need to examine more closely current research. This more technical discussion to follow provides a basis for responding to this question and for other interdisciplinary endeavors such as how empirical research has diverse applications for religious development.

By 'empirical', in this context is meant research associated with neurological surgery pertaining to the brain. Empirically oriented readers typically want to know the basis for claiming the left hemisphere is more verbal and the right is less verbal. There are two main sources of such information: 1) observation of the effects of unilateral cerebral damage, and, 2) testing before and after brain surgery conducted for therapeutic purposes.[6]

An example of the first would be the general observations made of the differences in a person's competencies before and after the discovery that an accident, a lesion or malignancy has partially or totally destroyed a section of the brain. Typical of this type of observation would be that an individual who seems quite normal by every standard then loses speech facilities. Subsequent exploratory surgery discovers a lesion on the left hemisphere. Similarly, another normally functioning individual loses spatial coordination and subsequent surgery discovers a lesion on that person's right hemisphere. These examples are "after the fact."

An example of the more technical second source of information stems from studies which are "before the fact." Typical of this would be therapeutic brain surgery, such as cutting the connecting tissue between the two hemispheres, in order to diminish the effects of epilepsy.

The gathering of data, especially of the first less technical type has been taking place for a century. Yet, given the comparative youth of the surgical arts, the level of pre- and post-test sophistication, the newness of the field of biopsychology, all suggest that researchers' generalizations must be considered tentative. Bogen, a surgeon and recognized as one of the leading brain researchers, concluded a summary and synthesis of his research on dysgraphia and dyscopia (decreases in the ability to write words and copy drawings respectively following cerebral commissurotomy) by saying what is presently known and unknown in brain research. Basically, he says, we know more about the left, speech related hemisphere, than about the right. Structurally, the left and right hemispheres are mirror images of one another and have essentially the same metabolic rate. For human beings, speaking, reading and writing are dependent on the one side, typically the left. But what is the other side doing? Bogen believes it is doing just as much and just as important work. Researchers do not yet understand *how* the left hemisphere produces language; but of the right hemisphere Bogen claims researchers do not even know *what* it is producing. Bogen concludes that the other side of the brain, the right, is as intricately active as the side which does most of the talking. Hence that hemisphere which governs left-handed thinking and knowing seems to him to be the more fruitful area for investigation of mental activity.

Bogen's summary statement which follows gives ground for hope in fostering our innermost capabilities, as well as gives reason not to start a bandwagon defining and popularizing what is presently uncertain from a technical perspective.

"One of the most obvious and fundamental features of the cerebrum is that it is double. Various kinds of evidence, especially from hemisphereectomy, have made it clear that one hemisphere is sufficient to sustain a personality or mind. We may then conclude that the individual with two intact hemispheres has the capacity for two distinct minds. This conclusion finds its experimental proof in the research with split-brain animals whose two disconnected hemispheres can be trained to perceive, consider, and act independently. In the human, where *propositional* thought is typically lateralized to one hemisphere, the other hemisphere evidently specializes in a different mode of thought, one which may be called *appositional*."[8]

Bogen's caution, evidenced in his describing the right hemisphere in terms of what it is not, appositional, should be sufficient warning against simplification such as to claim the left is thought and the right is emotion, or male and female, and so forth. Both hemispheres think and each seems capable of emotion. Bogen footnotes approvingly the opinions of other psychologists and earlier thinkers who, based on substantive though non-surgical data, like Bogen, have posited various forms of dichotomies in human consciousness. Some of these are summarized in the following table.[9]

Theorist	Left	Right
Bruner	rational	metaphoric
Levi-Strauss	positive	mythic

Freud	secondary process	primary process
Pavlov	second signal	first signal
James	differential	existential
Pribram	digital	analogic
Young	abstract	map-like
Price	analytic	synthetic
Wilder	numerical	geometric
Head	symbolic & systematic	perceptual & non-verbal
Goldstein	abstract	concrete

Brenda Milner,[10] a British medical researcher also cautions readers not to push the left/right contrast too far. She in general agrees with the above description that the left hemisphere does seem to have a definite dominance for speech and skilled movements. However, she notes that the work of R. W. Sperry[11] indicates the right hemisphere also shows some limited verbal comprehension. Similarly, the work of Hecaen and Assal[12] indicates that although the right hemisphere has dominance in spatial processes, the left parietal lobe also has important spatial functions.

The diversity of labels researchers have given the two competencies, especially to that of the right lobe, should give the reader a hint of the complexity of the research. Like an impressionistic painting, the scene is not photographically clear. But what findings are available concerning human development and how do the two sides of the brain operate in a complementary manner? One "conclusion" comes in the form of a caveat concerning the results of over-verbalizing. Bogen has gathered limited evidence that the corpus callosum, the tissue connecting the left and right hemispheres and located several inches beneath the cortex surface, is central to interhemispheric exchanges.[13] Hence it would seem central to the integrating processes on which normal intelligence and creativity draw. This discussion of creativity in part depends on complex surgical experiments. Persons whose two hemispheres have been disconnected for therapeutic reasons, for example, experience inability to verbally describe whatever is in their left visual field. This is because their left visual field is sent exclusively to their right, non-verbal lobe. If a familiar object is placed in their left hand, typically they can not say what it is but they can point out a similar or identical object around them.[14] The cutting of the corpus callosum has divorced the knowledge of the right lobe from the verbalizing of the left lobe.

On the positive side, and extrapolating from this research, one can address the question of how interhemispheric collaboration can foster creativity. But advances here are hampered by the absence of a generally accepted definition and hence of criteria for creativity. Bogen contends that it is possible that

"certain kinds of left hemisphere activity may directly suppress certain kinds of right hemispheric action."[15]

This clearly is one form of non-cooperation. To the extent that the corpus callosum does serve this mediating function between the two lobes of the normal person, and this is not yet firmly established, then Bogen proffers that an excess of propositional thinking, the characteristic product of the left hemisphere, would have an inhibitory effect on the appositional side. Conversely, creativity then would seem to be fostered by maintaining the balanced tension between the activities of the verbal and non-verbal hemispheres.

Some evidence can be marshalled from literary critics and artists to support this claim. Bogen quotes poet and critic Steven Spender[16] who found that "The poetic imagination is harmed by absorbing more intellectual knowledge than it can digest." Writer W. Fifield, after interviewing artist Joan Miro concluded that artistic creativity is the yield of "not-think." Miro was quoted as saying "The work comes out of the unconscious, that is certain . . . If you have a preconception, any notion of where you are going, you will never get anywhere."[17] Such citations from the artistic community, although proving little, do make a bit more plausible Bruner's supposition that each person has a second resource for knowing alongside the verbal approach.

The accurate identification of this second approach however is difficult due to conflicting and piecemeal data. Psychologists Michael Corballis and Ivan Beale dispute the adequacy of Bruner's analogy between speech and manual skill. They claim the right hemisphere does not "hold" the context of the utterance while the left hemisphere "operates" upon it to produce actual speech. In their words,

" . . . the ability to speak coherently, and in context, is little impaired by surgical separation of the hemispheres (Gazzaniga, 1970) or even by total removal of the right hemisphere (Mensh, Schwartz, Matarazzo and Matarazzo 1952; Rose, 1937)."[18]

After reviewing the history of attempts to define the respective roles of the two hemispheres, Corballis and Beale offer the following pattern. The dominant or left hemisphere is the more rational, logical and analytic. The minor hemisphere is more intuitive, synthetic, holistic. Bever and Chiarello[19] claim the above distinction, which rests on a verbal/non-verbal difference, can be pushed further. A common finding among musically knowledgeable persons has been that the average person who is musically unsophisticated typically recognizes melodies better with the left ear, that is, with the right hemisphere. Bever's and Chiarello's research led them to conclude that musically sophisticated individuals show a left-hemisphere advantage; they perceive music analytically. Could it be that some persons, for whatever reasons, have different cognitive styles primarily because they have right-hemisphere dominance? Some researchers believe so.[20] One wonders as to the educational implications of these differences and the neglect of the more highly gifted appositional types. But the research to date on cognitive styles is inconclusive.

BRAIN RESEARCH AND RELIGIOUS DEVELOPMENT

How can the distance between such complex technical research and religious concerns be bridged? For some religious educators, the realm of scientific research and that of spiritual growth may seem to be not only worlds apart but antagonistic endeavors. They believe that science is a human work whereas spirituality is exclusively the gift of the Spirit. Admittedly, spiritual growth is not within our control and is a gratuitous and divine grace. But contemporary research which has clarified patterns in moral and faith development has proven to be worthy of widespread consideration and it has given considerable support to the efforts of religious educators and others concerned with moral development. Similarly the current brain research could be part of the tip of the scientific iceberg, which, as hinted in the *General Catechetical Directory*,[21] chapter seven, is capable of providing buoyancy to the efforts of various forms of spiritual ministry.

INTRODUCTION TO THE JUNGIAN FRAMEWORK

Brain research provides opportunity for an impetus to the gradual opening to and discovering of the divine. Such research provides a context and lends credibility to the less technical contributions of researchers such as Carl Jung and his depth psychology. And conversely, Jung's decades of fostering individuation, which he saw as religious maturation, suggests how religionists can utilize the findings of brain research. Hence the Jungian perspective serves as a bridge between the scientific and the religious. Religious educators such as Morton Kelsey[22] and theologians such as David Burrell[23] and Robert Doran[24] have assisted many students to cross the Jungian bridge from the conscious to the unconscious and thereby to discover the gift of divine presence within the person.

What makes it both possible and necessary to view Jungian psychology and brain research synoptically is that each has discovered and explicated similar dual processes of the human mind. Jung studied the myths of hundreds of cultures, ancient and modern. He found such consistent similarities in geographically disparate cultures that he posited each person must be born with a common psychic inheritance. That inheritance consisted in part in a tendency to perceive reality in universal patterns or in archetypes such as in basic contrasts between light and darkness, birth and death, temporal and eternal. The most fundamental contrast of Jungian psychology is that of the conscious and the unconscious. But the latter of this polarity, the unconscious, frequently has been misunderstood. Partly because of this, psychologists in the United States have dismissed Jung's theory as flirting with the mystical and with being unscientific. Even so profound a mind as Martin Buber failed to recognize the inherently communal nature of Jung's collective unconscious. Hence he mistook Jung's discussion of the therapeutic imagery of unconscious archetypes for ego-centric solipsism. Buber did not see the collective unconscious for what it is, namely deeply rooted tendencies shared in common with all mankind to perceive in specific patterns. Thus the imagery of the unconscious actually serves as a basis for communion with one's brothers and sisters.

Further clarifications are necessary to provide an interpretative context for delicately synthesizing Jungian insights, brain research and spiritual development. The Jungian unconscious, whether collective or personal, is not a place in the brain but a set of processes of which the individual is typically but faintly aware. Brain research has found, as did Jung, that individuals and to some questionable extent cultures specialize in either reason or in more intuitive modes of thinking. Jung typified the Western industrial world as more driven by or given to the rational while he saw the Eastern world as more given to the mystical.[25] Here it seems necessary to temper the tendency to reify and to absolutize east and west cultures. Similarly, brain researchers have found it is necessary to avoid stereotyping the left and right hemispheres. Findings indicate that one can not say the left hemisphere is exclusively verbal and rational while the right hemisphere is devoid of verbal skills. That there is specialization in the processes of the right and left hemispheres is clear. That in individuals there is dominance or asymmetry in competencies is fairly well established. The challenge then is clear: given that human development is fostered by maximizing one's God-given potential, clearly each person is called to utilize both the rational processes of the left and the more intuitive of the right. Carl Jung, identifying religion with fidelity to one's experiences, came to this same conclusion. He used this same left/right imagery to further the person's progress along the process of individuation, the discovery of divine presence within.

Religious educators need to exercise restraint and not give total loyalty to labels for the left and right competencies such as may be found in newspaper reports. McLuhan, for example, is quoted as saying the left hemisphere is visual while the right is acoustic. Such a colorful metaphor can then be used and misused to summarize rapidly changing cultural phenomenon. This is as dubious as trying to solve for two unknowns in a single equation. Such leaps of intuition need to be scrutinized by research and reason. McLuhan's point, that the left knows sequentially while the right knows simultaneously, leaves too little unsaid.

THREE PARALLELS BETWEEN THE SCIENTIFIC AND THE RELIGIOUS

The discussion above indicates the tension between two needs: for careful analytical explanation and for graspable synthetic imagery. Both must now be combined to address the question: of what earthly use is this brain research to religious educators?

Three areas in particular stand out as fertile ground for applying the research to various dimensions of religious education. These are symbolic consciousness, creativity and twilight imagery. Each will be addressed in turn.

SYMBOLIC CONSCIOUSNESS

The purpose of religious education, broadly understood and within a Christian context is to foster the individual believer's ability to be intimate with self, neighbors, the Lord. This in turn seems to be fostered by the ability to think symbolically and experience life symbolically.[27] In brief, such symbolic consciousness is a quality by which the person holds opposites in tension and consequently experiences life in its complexity, without being reductionistic or literal. In this view, symbols do not exist as objects in the world but as a characteristic of human consciousness. Symbolic consciousness is based on the ability to tolerate ambiguity until greater clarity is available. Integral to this quality of consciousness is a certain competence in how the person comes to understand in time. This time-competence is the ability to recognize the present experience within the broader context of the past and future. Patiently, the person brings the felt-meanings to the surface of consciousness and gives them articulation and scrutiny and further mulling over. This symbolic consciousness, with its attending competencies, seems basic to adequate interpretation of biblical, moral, sacramental and doctrinal concerns.

Religious educators who are convinced of the centrality of what is here called symbolic consciousness, have in the findings of brain research a guide to their responsibilities to their students, to themselves and to the broader Christian community. The religious educator's task, in part, is to facilitate a growth in religious understanding. To the extent that this requires logical thinking, religious educators would be nurturing the left lobe's approach to knowing. But what about the right lobe's approach to knowing? How is it nurtured?

Is the right lobe the origin of what depth psychologists such as Freud and Jung call the unconscious? To believe so would be simplistic. Carried to its popularly held extreme, this view further assumes most members of Western cultures are more rational while members of Oriental cultures are more intuitive. To the contrary, some contemporary research among Westerners indicates a widespread inability to abstract beyond the level of literal interpretation. They deal with cars, airplanes and electricity with little or no comprehension and in effect they live on the intuitive level. So for them, it is the left lobe, with its analytic, verbal and sequencing skills, which tends to be unconscious. In many areas of their lives, the right lobe, not the left, dominates. Concerning religious matters, these pseudomoderns are similar to the youngsters studied by Ronald Goldman.[28] When the British religious educator and researcher asked the youth questions such as why Moses' burning bush was not consumed by its flames, their answers were far from abstract and at best they were hung up on pseudoscientific answers. Their mixture of literal and intuitive thinking showed no sign that they understood the symbolic dimensions of the biblical narratives.

The mysterious right lobe then ought not be glibly equated with the depth dimension of the personality or with Jung's unconscious. The unconscious for the individual, whether of Eastern or Western origin, could be either the rational or the metaphoric. The ability to interpret and experience symbolically requires both competencies. Religious educators accordingly are challenged to nurture the right lobe's form of knowing by providing opened experiences, rituals, myths, the writing of poems, the mending of fences.

Jungians will recognize that in effect I am saying that this symbolic consciousness is not only central to religious education and a call to use both left and right competencies. It is another manifestation of what Jung called the "transcendent function."[29] Jung identified this as a balancing of the more rational capabilities of thinking and feeling (evaluating) with the less rational capabilities of sensing and intuiting. Individuation, the goal of fulfillment, requires the person to transcend the personal imbalance caused by the least developed of these four skills or functions. By working with the weaker competence and attending to one's dreams which surface that inferior function, the person would be better equipped and more open to recognizing and responding to the trancendent in daily experiences. The current brain research seems to substantiate both the value of this Jungian interpretation and the need for and path to symbolic consciousness.

CREATIVITY

A second area in which brain research can make a contribution to the efforts of religious educators is creativity. Rarely has a word been so stretched and suffered from lack of definition. Psychologist and educator Carl Rogers[30] assists us here by defining creativity as a sensitive openness to the world and a trust in one's ability to form new relationships with the environment.

Maslow specifies it further by describing two distinct creative processes.[31] Primary creativity consists of the imaginative divergent thinking, the unique response. Secondary creativity follows the primary and consists of grinding out the implications, critiquing the primary processes. This primary/secondary distinction seems to parallel the left/right hemisphere distinction. The more divergent and mysterious right lobe corresponds to the more intuitive or metaphoric primary processes, while the more verbal and sequential left lobe would serve to test those intuitions by logical analysis. Although Maslow does not make this connection with brain research, his description of creative persons as uniting the physical (right lobe) and abstract (left lobe) seems to be a point of tangency.

"These people can see the fresh, the raw, the concrete . . . as well as the generic, the abstract, the rubricized, the categorized and the classified . . . All these 'opposites' are in fact hierarchically-integrated, especially in healthier people, and one of the proper goals of therapy is to move from dichotomizing and splitting toward integration of seemingly irreconcilable opposites."[32]

This synthesis of two processes is consistent with Bruner's description of taming the metaphors, i.e., of shifting the hunches of the left hand to the testing of them by the right.

What have the brain researchers contributed to such existing knowledge? They have discovered some evidence that the corpus callosum, which physically connects both hemispheres, provides the basis for interhemispheric collaboration. It acts as a switching mechanism sharing information originally obtained by only one of the hemispheres. Working with monkeys, brain researcher S.R. Butler[33] found that by removing specific brain masses of the two hemispheres, the monkeys learned specific tasks quicker than unimpaired monkeys. This finding, Bogen believes, suggests that "intrahemispheric influences can interfere with interhemispheric collaboration."[34]

Direct experimentation on creativity with persons who have had therapeutic split-brain surgery is markedly absent. Such surgical experimentation is not justifiable. Therefore extrapolations concerning normal persons and their left/right collaboration is necessarily tentative. According to Bogen, the more fruitful avenue for consideration at present is in the inhibitory effect of the left on the right hemisphere.[35] Bogen cites remarks of famous scientists and artists to the effect that creativity initially stems from the non-verbal realms. In the area of art, recall, creativity is the yield of the "not-think."[36] Once the imagery or model is grasped, then secondary processes such as verbalization can come into play.[37]

In summary then, creativity, like symbolic consciousness described above, requires initially a temporary suspending of verbal and analytic abilities, an ability to generate diverse perspectives, and finally a concentrated effort to bring the gifts of the left hand to complete fruition and to other persons by means of one's own critique and that of the community.

But how does all this apply to creativity in religious education? Given that religious education has as part of its purpose fostering the person's ability to be intimate in its broadest dimensions, including social justice, then the discussion of creativity in religion can be aided by recognizing two phases. The first is the liberating of the imagination from the shackles of various forms of self-restraint. The second is the tempering and testing of the intuitions, to bend them to the needs of the community. The ramifications of such creativity within the Christian community are far-ranging. They include the individual's attempt to resolve a moral dilemma, the community's attempt to deal with constructive change, restore traditional values, democratize decision making, recognize diverse ministries and better serve the needs of the broader human community.

Concerning the learning process itself, whether the focus be religious, literary or scientific, brain research indicates that there are two paths rather than the traditional verbal path. The rational and the metaphorical, intuitional or appositional are equally valuable and equally interdependent. This invites a reconsideration not only of teaching methods as Bruner has argued, but of academia itself.

But what specifically does this mean for religious learning? There are certain obvious conclusions such as the need for more extensive use of the appositional-type students' physical movement, gesture, music or whatever will nurture the individuals' more spa tially attuned right lobe. Other contributors have explicated som ot these areas. Here I focus attention on the widespread efforts to fosrer moral development by means of moral dilemmas. Efforts such as those of Lawrence Kohlberg,[38] knowingly and properly focus on the cognitive domain, namely logical development as it pertains to justice. I maintain however that what fosters the moral development, more broadly understood, is the dynamic personal interaction among the students and teacher. Properly conducted, a major value of discussion of differences in interpreting a moral conflict, is found in the face to face confrontations, the human transactions, and not simply in the logical dissonance of the left lobe. Human transactions can function symbolically when the participants can consider the implications of the other's viewpoint. Mulling over the other's words, gestures and facial expressions is part of what above is called symbolic consciousness as well as of creativity. Thus both are means of fostering a deeper synthesis of the left and right lobe competencies and hence religious learning as well.

TWILIGHT IMAGERY AND RELIGIOUS DEVELOPMENT

Finally it seems appropriate to conclude with a correlation of how one form of meditation, that using twilight imagery, exemplifies another facet of this process of integrating left with right lobe competencies. Progoff, a psychologist who has firmly grasped the value of Carl Jung's creative imagination, trains individuals in meditative skills utilizing both the rational and non-rational gifts. Twilight imagery consists of procedures for providing the person with knowledge from "direct awareness, hunches, and inspirations"[39] from the non-rational dimensions. As the name "twilight" implies, this form of meditation is patterned after what happens to the person in that state before falling asleep. The similarity is that the meditator does not guide thought, but rather allows the imagery of the imagination to surface "on its own." The meditator attends to this imagery, be it visual, auditory such as music, bodily such as relaxation or tension. Progoff states:

"The term *imagery* refers to the fact that its main expressions are not literal in the sense of being thoughts or ideas, but that they are rather representational or symbolic."[40]

When considered in light of the hemispheric specializations, twilight imagery appears to be a product primarily of the right lobe. The procedures of twilight imagery, utilized of course at times other than bedtime, seem in effect initially to silence the constant analysis and verbalizing of the left lobe and then to attend to the intuitive depths of the person. This is in accord with the brain research of S.R. Butler who found when working with monkeys that certain physical tasks were learned more quickly when the interfering messages from the verbal hemisphere were excluded by surgically partially severing the two hemispheres. Bogen interprets this as meaning:

"certain brain functions may be independent of or even inversely related to brain mass. It also illustrates how intrahemispheric influences can interfere with interhemispheric collaboration."[41]

Twilight imagery attempts, by methodically attending to the imagery of the right lobe, to screen out the interference by the left hemisphere and allow the fruit of the right lobe to gain the light of day. Given the immense complexity and capability of the human mind, it seems likely that concentration, a form of purity of heart, is well within our reach. Singleness of purpose, not surgery *per se*, is a directional indicator toward religious development. Attending to one's images, in Progoff's method, is one step toward balancing and utilizing one's capabilities. The person records the imagery in a journal, dates the entries along with other entries descriptive of the actual outer events of his or her life. Patterns will emerge from the logs of both the inner and outer events thus allowing the meditator to feel the quality and tone of each of them, not analyzing them, allowing them to balance themselves and form a "whole message." Progoff, like Jung before him and current brain researchers, all recognize the need for and value of suspending analytical judgments and allowing a non-verbal synthesis to occur and surface in consciousness.

"What is important is that we learn to observe objectively the nature of our subjective perceptions. We *perceive inwardly* the wholeness of the situation of our lives as it is presented to us in the many aspects of its organic movement . . . we see that each moment contains its opposites inherently within itself. Growth and decay, conflict and harmony, all the opposites are part of the movement of time."[42]

This twilight imagery is true to how Jung sees the function of symbols: to unite opposites and hold them in tension. It agrees as well with specialists who have studied the meaning of creativity. Thus the three considerations herein presented as supports for furthering religious education broadly understood, symbolic consciousness, creativity and twilight imagery, all echo the call arising deep within the human brain. That call, described in terms of left and right hemisphere specialization and synthesis, invites each person to bring the intuitive and logical competencies to their fruition and respectfully integrate them in mutual cooperation.

Notes

1. *Duality of the Mind*. London: Longman, 1844, page 26.

2. D. Ferrier, *The Functions of the Brain*, 2nd edition, New York: G.P. Putnam & Sons, 1886, page 426; O'Leary, in G. Von Bonin, "Anatomical Asymmetries of the Cerebral Hemispheres" in V.B. Mountcastle, ed., *Interhemispheric Relations and Cerebral Dominance*. Baltimore: Johns Hopkins University Press, 1962.

3. *Dual Character of the Brain*. Washington, D.C.: Toner Lecture No. 2, Smithsonian Miscellaneous Collection, page 291 ff.

4. Joseph E. Bogen, "The Other Side of the Brain II: An Appositional Mind," *Bulletin of the Los Angeles Neurological Societies*, Vol. 34, No. 3 (July 1969), page 154.

5. Jerome S. Bruner, *Process of Cognitive Growth*. Worcester, Mass.: Clark University Press, 1968.

6. Bogen, "The Other Side of the Brain I: Dysgraphia and Dysopia Following Cerebral Commissurotomy," *Bulletin of the Los Angeles Neurological Societies*, Vol. 34, No. 2 (April 1969), page 73 ff.

7. Bogen, "The Other Side of the Brain II," page 105.

8. Ibid., pages 157-158.

9. Ibid., pages 158 and 150.

10. "Inter-Hemispheric Differences in the Localization of Psychological Processes in Man," *British Medical Bulletin*, Vol. 27, No. 3, 1971, pages 272-277.

11. R.W. Sperry, "Role of the Neocortical Commisures," in P.J. Vinken and G.W. Bruyn, eds., *Handbook of Clinical Neurology*, Vol. IV, Amsterdam: North Holland Publishers, 1969.

12. H. Hecaen and G. Assal, *Neuropsychologia, 8,* 289, 1970 and in P.J. Vinken, ed., *Handbook of Clinical Neurology*, Vol. IV, Amsterdam: North Holland, page 67 ff.

13. Bogen, "The Other Side of the Brain III: The Corpus Callosum and Creativity," *Bulletin of the Los Angeles Neurological Societies*, Vo. 34, No. 4 (October 1969), page 200.

14. Michael S. Gazzaniga, "The Split Brain in Man," *Scientific American*, 217, No. 2 (August 1967), pages 24-29.

15. For a more detailed explanation, cf. ibid., page 201.

16. Steven Spender, *The Imagination in the Modern World*. Washington, D.C.: U.S. Government Printing Office, 1962, page 37.

17. "Miro: An Interview in Mallorea," *Arts Magazine*, Vol. 43, 1968, page 19.

18. *The Psychology of Left and Right*. Hillsdale, N.J.: Lawrence Erlbaum Assoc., Pub., 1976, page 103.

19. T. G. Bever and R. J. Chiarello, "Cerebral Dominance in Musicians and Nonmusicians," *Science*, 1974, *185,* 537–539.

20. P. Bakan, "Hypnotizability, Laterality of Eye-Movements and Functional Brain Asymmetry," *Perceptual and Motor Skills*, 1969, *28,* 927–932; J. L. Singer and D. G. Singer, "Personality," *Annual Review of Psychology*, 1972, *23,* 375–412; H. Ehrlichman, S. L. Weiner and A. H. Baker, "Effects of Verbal and Spatial Questions on Initial Gaze Shifts," *Neuropsychologia*, 1974, *12,* 265–277.

21. Washington, D.C.: United States Catholic Conference, 1971.

22. *God, Dreams and Revelation*. Minneapolis: Augsburg Publ. House, 1968.

23. *Exercises in Religious Understanding*. Notre Dame, In.: University of Notre Dame Press, 1974.

24. *Subject and Psyche: A Study of the Foundations of Theology*. Ann Arbor: University Microfilms, 1975.

25. C.G. Jung, *Collected Works*, Volume 11, *Psychology and Religion: West and East*. Princeton: Princeton University Press, 1938.

26. *Washington Post*, May 15, 1977, H 1ff.

27. Andrew D. Thompson, "Symbolic Consciousness: A Synthetic Approach to Moral Development," *Social Thought*, Summer 1976, pages 45-59.

28. *Readiness For Religion*. New York: Seabury Press, 1970.

29. Roberto Assagioli, "Psychosynthesis: A Technique for the Use of Intuition," in Robert Ornstein, *The Nature of Human Consciousness*. San Francisco: W.H. Freeman, 1973, pages 336-342.

30. *Freedom to Learn*. Columbus, Ohio: Charles E. Merrill Pub. Co., 1969, page 270.

31. Abraham H. Maslow, *The Farther Reaches of Human Nature*. New York: Viking Press, 1971, pages 81-95.

32. *Toward A Psychology of Being*. Princton, N.J.: D. Van Nostrand Co., Inc., 1962, pages 130 and 164.

33. *Mechanisms of Sensory Integration*. Ph.D. Thesis, University of London, 1967.

34. "The Other Side of the Brain, III," page 197.

35. Ibid., page 201.

36. Ibid., page 202.

37. Ibid., page 199.

38. "The Cognitive-Developmental Approach to Moral Education," *Phi Delta Kappan*, Vol 56, No. 10, 670-677.

39. Ira Progoff, *At A Journal Workshop*. New York: Dialogue House Library, 1974, page 77.

40. Ibid., page 78.

41. "The Other Side of the Brain, III," page 197.

42. Progoff, page 84.

14.
Language and Symbols in the Human Psyche

Gerald H. Slusser

Gerald H. Slusser describes the mythic-symbolic dimension of thought and communication as the natural form for the creative imagination for dreams, visions, aesthetic endeavor and religious meditation or contemplation. Its neglect, or more correctly, its intentional disregard as an inferior form, has resulted in our alienation from the deepest centers of life in the psyche.

The witch doctor (priest, scientist, medic, politician, *et al.*) loses coercive power when his secret knowledge becomes part of the general knowledge of a people. Every advance in general human consciousness is thus marked by the desacralizing of certain ideas previously thought to belong to the gods of the external world, and hence taboo for all except those chosen few designated by the gods. Such a shift in a culture is only the outward sign of an inward change in the fundamental myth or symbol system of the culture. The basic values and assumptions of any people are bound up in its unquestioned myth system. This collective system of "obviously true" notions functions effectively to control what can be thought, believed, and to an astonishing degree, what can be experienced by a member of that culture.

One's perception of the world is not direct and straightforward, as was generally believed by the science of the 19th century, and it is not merely that the so-called secondary qualities of color, sound, taste, etc., seem to be as much in the observer as the observed. Perception, it turns out, is always a hypothetical construction, a mediated affair. *Knowing* the world requires a system of assumptions or categories not provided by the world observed. Such a set of assumptions provides not only the structure which gives shape to the knowledge, redeeming it from randomness—a mere collection of stimuli—but it makes memory and thought possible by providing names, i.e., symbols for otherwise inconceivable events or entities.

A closer look at the process of human perception shows it to be a rather complex affair in which myth, a symbol system, is the prerequisite to meaningful observation and fact. Myth, a term to be defined more clearly as this article proceeds, functions like a set of glasses for the severely myopic. Without it, the world is a blooming, buzzing, confusion, as William James said of the infant's perception. We need only add that the infant is quite unaware of this confusion because rational consciousness is also the child of myth.

Our earliest interaction with the world, either as infants or deep in the primitive zone of human development, has no significant discrimination between inner and outer. The world is one with the individual. There is no I-other separation, no discrimination of subject and object. Inner emotions are attached to outer objects in dream-like fashion and the object becomes a symbol for the emotion. This is the process of projection, the first form of knowledge. From it arose the mythic world of gods and goddesses.

The word "project" means to throw outward. Psychologically, projection means unwittingly assigning some of one's own psychic content to some person, thing, or situation outside the psyche. Projection is most common when the object or stimulus situation is quite unknown or poorly defined, i.e., when we do not have an already developed knowledge schema which includes it. In these cases the psyche attempts to "make sense" of the situation by assigning certain of its own content to the unknown. A familiar example is the Rorschach ink blots. Confronted with one of these random blots, the psyche imposes patterns from its own storehouse of images and one "sees" butterflies, trees, spiders, etc. By projection, the previously unknown is given some identification, connected with some psychic content. This process, however, is not in any sense controlled or directed by the conscious psyche, for it is quite unconscious. The selection of which content will be projected onto what stimuli is performed by an aspect of the psyche which does not appear to our conscious purview. Through the process of life, however, some of these projections are affirmed or confirmed and others negated. By this natural process of reward or reinforcement, the favorable projections are strengthened and the unfavorable ones weakened. For example, projecting our fear onto the lion, making it a fearful animal, was rewarded by avoiding the lion's clutches. At the same time, projecting that fear onto many creatures has lead to their near destruction from the earth, e.g., the greatly feared and maligned wolf, who had come to symbolize the danger that one person poses toward another, has been severely endangered as a species. Contemporary feedback from environmentalists is making us aware of the need to withdraw such a projection. In some such fashion among our most distant ancestors a body of knowledge began to develop and to be communicated, though we can only speculate about its means of development. A modern always awakens to consciousness in a world having well developed mythic schemes or modes of consciousness which constitute the patterns of perception of that culture. We are taught these patterns from earliest infancy so that we quickly come to perceive the world just as do the significant others of our environment.

These patterns of perception constitute the bounds of reality and even of sanity for the culture. In the twelfth century everyone in western civilization was expected to perceive a flat earth, with a real Heaven above and a real Hell below. Encounters with angels or demons were common, even to be expected, and the Devil himself had been known to appear. In the 20th century, people who have persistent encounters with such figures are usually considered prime candidates for an involuntary tour of the psychiatric ward or, at the least, required to spend a good many hours with the "shrink" who will help restructure one's psyche to obtain the "right" perceptions.

This shift from the twelfth to the twentieth century pattern of perception may in part be described as a withdrawal of certain projections, particularly those relating to the religious aspect of the views. Twentieth century mythology, the scientific worldview, has no real place for such concepts as Heaven and Hell or angels and demons in the outer world. Consequently they are assigned to the psyche, sometimes with the reductionist implication that they are and always were *only* the product of imagination. This rationalistic reduction comes from taking the rational-cognitive modality of consciousness to be *the* model for everything real. Even some of those most concerned to learn about the depths of the psyche, e.g., Sigmund Freud, were so bound into the nineteenth century science that they saw no value, only trouble, in the non-rational functions of the psyche. We can, however, take it as a general rule that human knowledge and consciousness increases by the withdrawal of projections. Alternatively, this process may be described as one of discrimination, the appropriate separation of inner and outer material

This does not entitle us, though, to denigrate or discount the inner material; instead, it imposes upon us a new task of evaluating such material. What is the value, place, purpose, and meaning of such concepts as Heaven with its angels and Hell with its demons? Are they simply nonsense, mistakes of the psyche, as the reductionists have argued? Or do they represent a valid way of symbolizing that is normal and necessary to the psyche and indeed refer to things which are very real, but not the real of the outer world?

Recent studies of the human brain and its activities have acquainted us with the fact that there are two sides to the brain, with two quite different modes of functioning. The left lobe functions with a process that is somewhat computer-like. It is adapted to rational processes and language, to cognitive work. The right lobe functions with a process that has a quite different pattern. It proceeds by symbolic connections or relations, a non-rational process because symbols cannot be reduced to definite fixed meanings. As was noted above, symbols come into being as a way of describing or conceptualizing the relatively unknown. Symbols are the creations of an aspect of the psyche not available to consciousness. They are always emotionally laden and relate to deep and profound processes of the psyche. As yet there is little or no data or theory for establishing the nature of the relation between the two lobes of the brain per se with these deeper processes of the psyche. The best theory suggests that the right lobe functions are related to the aspects of the psyche responsible for such things as projections, dreams, and unconscious phenomena. The left lobe functions are then connected with more conscious and cognitive aspects of the psyche.

However true or false this division of labor in the brain may turn out to be, it is similar in pattern to the polarities observable in human language systems. The two poles of language may be represented by the terms myth and fact. Myth in the popular usage has come to mean something which is not truly factual—to which one is tempted to reply, of course! It was never intended to speak about mere fact. The popular use of this word "myth" is mostly a result of the reductionist meaning given to such concepts as angels and demons. If these are construed as scientific factual entities of the outer world, they are not true. But as we shall see more clearly, this is simply a case of misplaced reference, as with every projection.

The mythic pole of language is its metaphorical, religious, and poetic usage. To this pole belong the most profound insights and the deepest values of humanity. From the aspect of the psyche which functions symbolically come not only our hopes, fears, and dreams, but our creativity. The creative insights of the human race, whether of religious and philosophical or scientific and practical nature, first appear in symbolic poetic form. Often they appear as dreams or visions. Moses was guided by his vision to become a political-religious leader and revolutionary freedom fighter. He was also given, in a mountain-top religious experience, a supreme view of desired human morality which has stood the test of 3000 years of human history. Descartes was granted a dream-vision which unlocked the secret of analytical geometry to his conscious mind. Isaac Newton was given the breakthrough into his theories about the universe in a dream-vision. In each case, a remarkable and unpredictable new way of "viewing" or conceptualizing the world appears, introduced to consciousness by that other and relatively unknown aspect of the psyche. Once the world is viewed in the new way, it becomes very difficult to go back. The old is now less complete, less satisfying; it leaves too many unanswered questions.

In the field of science these new ways of construing experience are often called paradigms. One or more such paradigms form the foundation on which the remainder of the particular scientific structure rests. Paradigms are, in this respect, like myths. They belong to the language form found at the symbolic end of the language continuum. It is from this realm that knowledge structure begins.

The opposite pole of language to the mythic-symbolic is the factual-rational. The language structure of this pole is discursive and logical. The terms used are expected to be universal and clearly defined, leaving no place or cause for either mystery or confusion. The ideal is prose constructed like a mathematical formula, having one and only one meaning. It is customary to think that all scientific knowledge can and should be constructed in this unambiguous form. The virtue of this form is also its vice. To the degree that such a form is attainable (and even in mathematics it is not fully attainable), it is sterile, stating only the known with no possibility for further exploration.

The symbolic pole is quite the contrary. The symbol has no clearly defined meaning because it refers to an entity or process that is only partially, perhaps only slightly, known. The symbol captures something of the essence of the human experience of this unknown and thus suggests there is more to be explored. As Dr. Paul Tillich noted, a symbol participates in the reality which it represents, i.e., it has the property of making present (re-presenting) that reality to *some* degree for those for whom the symbol is living. Thus, quite unlike discursive language which has no dynamic mystery, the mythic-symbolic is a heuristic, living treasury. Every living, vital symbol has more to reveal than it has yet made manifest. One thinks of the saint meditating on the cross of Christ; what new truth is yet there waiting the right opportunity?

It is possible to construct a scale of language forms showing the placement of each major type between the mythic-symbolic and the factual-rational. Beginning at the mythic pole, there would be found clustered near it fantasy, dreams, poetry, myth, religious traditions, and holy writ, folk tales and scientific paradigms. Pure math like scientific paradigms probably also belongs to the mythic-symbolic. It is pure abstraction. These are all products of that deep and mysterious aspect of the psyche that has been associated with the right lobe of the brain. Products constructed in any of these forms spring unbidden and uncontrolled from the depth of the psyche into consciousness. This deep source which bubbles forth like a spring has been mostly neglected during the past few centuries because our attention has been focussed so obsessively on the cognitive aspects of the psyche, on the left lobe activity, i.e., on the factual-rational pole of language.

Adjacent to this first group of forms, one would likely place novels, drama, legend, and science fiction. These all spring mainly from the generative source of symbols in the psyche, but are shaped also by material taken from the factual-rational, i.e., they are made to conform in some measure to the dominant paradigm of the day and the ideas derived from it, e.g., the various sciences. Science fiction and fantasy appear to be the literary forms nearest to pure myth that is being written in our culture. The work of C. S. Lewis, Robert Heinlein, Arthur Clarke, Ray Bradbury, J. R. R. Tolkien, and Frank Herbert, to name only a few, demonstrates this literature and its power most significantly. Hence, one might agree that this form belongs, along with poetry and religious mythology, to the pole position. The variables of this placement may be visualized by comparing Clarke's *2001 Space Odyssey* with Tolkien's *Ring Trilogy*. Clarke has placed a mythic drama in a world created by extending our present scientific beliefs. Clarke's major characters are much like ourselves. They think in patterns similar to our own, their mode of behavior is not in the least alien, and they speak the language of the contemporary world. The plot is mythic. By contrast, however, Tolkien has given us a mysterious fantasy world, and his Hobbits belong there, not to our customary scientific world, nor are his characters modeled upon our typical views of human beings. They are even given their own language, Elvish, in which to communicate. Both the plot and the setting are mythic.

Legend is a clearer illustration of the mixed nature of this group of language forms. The sagas of heroes and heroines have long been recognized as having their roots in fantasy. Only within the past century, though, have we recognized their debt to events of history. Archaelogical work has shown in many cases, the most notable being Troy, that the places, events and persons of legend are grounded in factual-rational memories. At the same time, it is clearly a mistake to fail to notice the mythic-symbolic character of these tales. They do not merely report the observed and/or observable, but combine it, or transform it through fantasy, the mythic-symbolic. An important element, due to the nature and meaning of the mythic-symbolic, is visible just here. Why do authors find it either desirable or necessary to add so much from their own or other's fantasies? Why not just give the facts? In answer to this question, it is, first of all, necessary to note that the mythic-symbolic language form probably long antedates the factual-rational as a literary form. Certainly, legend preceded history by many centuries. History, as *we* conceive it, is a form that only developed to its fullness in the nineteenth century, and then, as we shall note below in the further discussion of the form, only by accepting as true a somewhat false notion, viz., that everything real can be adequately and accurately rendered in factual-rational language.

Legend makers, like myth makers, have always been passionately and instinctively concerned with meaning. Their inspiration has been a symbolic insight into the character they are trying to portray, into the inner drama which makes one's life partake of the life of the gods. This inspiration comes in what may be called a mythic view of historical events. Myth is the language and natural form of religious insight. Under inspiration (working out of the right lobe of the brain?), the author sees the events illuminated from within with symbols redolent of religious implications. The author is no longer limited to factual-rational knowledge; something transcendent has been revealed. The event/person is now seen as actually having had mythic-symbolic form. In this fashion, mere event, mere history, is clothed with symbols which link it to those infinite wellsprings of human meaning in the psyche.

The mythic-symbolic is the language of religion and meaning, it links time to eternity; it founds value as well as scientific paradigms or world-views. The events of history, to be meaningful, must be clothed with the language symbols of myth. Religious tradition, like legend, belongs close to the mythic-symbolic pole. Holy writ, whether Christian or of another world religion, encompasses virtually the full gamut of language forms, but myth overshadows all the rest. The Genesis creation and garden stories may be considered pure myth, inspired stories which reveal the ultimate meaning of life. So also is the apocalypse of St. John. *Closer* to the other pole, the factual-rational, are some of the accounts of the kings of Israel, but even these are at least equally concerned with meaning. David is not merely a leader of Israel. Kings are usually mythic figures, and David is a religious hero whose struggles with the powers of evil within and without are the mythic structures of his story.

The next group of language forms is often thought of as being truly factual-rational. News reports, biography, and history are often accepted as neutral, theoretical, and assumption-free writings, whose virtue is objectivity. Whether or not any author, scientist, or reporter is free of bias is to be doubted, but that one is free of assumptions and theories is clearly false. Assumptions about the factual nature of our world and ourselves are essential before any conscious meaning can be assigned to experience. Experience, apart from assumptions, is unstructured, meaningless, empty, and form-less, and thus only the blooming, buzzing confusion of infancy. (It is beyond the scope of this paper to deal with animal perception. Briefly, however, animals are born with a set of instincts which serve as a symbolic repertoire equivalent to myth in orienting power. The infant chick, fresh from the egg, will scurry under its mother's wing at a mere glimpse of a hawk or hawk-like silhouette. The freshly hatched sea turtle immediately scrambles *toward* the sea and swims away to safety. Who is to say that human myth-symbols are not our form of instincts, God-given guides to our destiny?) We generally pass so rapidly from experience to interpretation that we do not observe the intermediate steps necessary to meaning.

A brief description of the human perceptive process is instruc-tive. First, assuming we are dealing with an external stimulus, some nerve endings are stimulated. Take the very simple experience of feeling a surface with a fingertip. Depending on the temperature and nature of the surface and the nature of the touching, various combi-nations of nerve endings of the fingertip will "fire", i.e. generate and release a tiny burst of electrical energy to the nerve. This is the first step of a coding process and it is fully involuntary. Here the mechan-ical stimulus of the touch and the surface temperature are trans-formed into the electrical code of the nervous system and transmitted to the brain. In the brain a second series of operations takes place. The incoming code is compared with stored patterns already in the brain. These stored patterns represent not just previous experience, but experience which has been given symbolic or factual identification. If the incoming pattern matches a stored pattern, it is then given the proper symbolic or factual name and *voilà*, it is "understood," it has meaning. We observe a particular pattern of light, shadow, and color. The coded information flashes to the brain; the code is analyzed; it matches another stored in the brain; so we call the source of this light and shadow a chair.

The historian or biographer or newspaper reporter must so analyze hundreds or thousands of patterns, give identification, look for more complex patterns or relations, etc. etc. It is thus more accurate to speak of the work of these people as an art rather than a science, but then even science is only the methodical practice of a more or less well established and defined art. The paradigms of the science provide this definition. The art or science remains stable only until its established paradigms are exhausted and new ones appear. The historian's task may then be spoken of as an art of imagination: the creation of a story which appears to explain the existence of the artifacts which have come to the historian's attention and to do so within the confines of the reigning paradigms, i.e., the collectively authorized, stored patterns of the science of history.

Kenneth Boulding, in his work *The Image*, suggests that these stored patterns fall into two basic sets, those of fact and those of value. Images of fact serve to orient us in our world both physical and social. We orient ourselves by a far different set of images than did our ancestors of the twelfth century. Our universe, though mostly still thought in three dimensional pictures with bits of matter scurrying about in otherwise empty space, has been somewhat affected by the twelfth century views of relativistic physics. We think of our universe as infinite, though that term means little more than unimaginably vast to most. We know that there is no matter per se, no solid bits of substance which make up this mind-boggling vastness in which we find ourselves, only patterns of dancing energy, whatever that is. But we find it too hard to think of the world that way, so our images of fact about the physical world are still mostly Newtonian, even though we know them to be in error in some respects.

Every bit of incoming information is filtered through this image-matrix, this myth-paradigm system; it is there evaluated, given meaning, according to the stored system. There is in our storehouse a pattern relating to religion, economics, politics, sociology, philosophy, and psychology, to mention only a few. These may be old or new, conscious or unconscious, useful or misleading, but they determine what our incoming information will be allowed to tell us about nature, person, God, society, or whatever.

These sets of images, as Boulding terms them, clearly include or are comprised of myths, models, and paradigms. Myth is the closest to the symbolic pole of language, along with vision and dream. Unlike visions and dreams, myths are not purely spontaneous. They have their origin in spontaneous processes of the psyche, but they are shaped by one or more mythmakers within a community setting, i.e., the community participates in the shaping of the story so long as it lives in a plastic state in oral tradition. Myths include ethical and cosmological implications which can then be formulated as models for understanding the universe and for human behavior. Myths also provide the foundation for religious models and theological models. Paradigms represent a more conscious process of formulation within a religious or scientific tradition. Barbour defines paradigm as a tradition (in science, a research tradition) transmitted through historical exemplars.

Incoming patterns which can be matched, more or less, to those of the stored set pose no problem; they are identified and a response can be made. Not infrequently, however, data refuses to fit, no matter how we try. If the data is not insistent, it is usually classified as error, or "noise," mere "static" in the system somewhere. This has been the major way of dealing with dreams and visions for the past two centuries. "Static" may be called mistake, lie, superstition, fantasy, or nonsense. All these are wastebasket categories, ways of disposing of information that does not fit the reigning patterns of myth, model, or paradigm.

A clear demarcation between these three concepts is difficult because they have related functions and are often mixed in our psychic processes. Myth, as used here, is a broader term, more inclusive, and is applied to any symbolic scheme which serves as the foundation for meaning and purpose in human life. Thus myth usually includes cosmological and other "scientific" imagery or assumptions, e.g., the three story world-view extending historically from the Bible to the early modern period in the West. Paradigm is usually the term applied to the founding or orienting assumptions of a science, e.g., physics, psychology, theology, etc. Loosely speaking then, myth is more cultural, more oriented to religion, values, and meaning in the existential sense, whereas paradigm is that set of assumptions mediated through historical examples and underlying a particular science.

When the major myths of a culture, its mythology, begins to show signs of age and weakness, the culture itself also suffers. Tension, disturbances in the body politic, crime, and dissatisfaction increase rapidly. There is usually a ringing call on the part of the conservative and reactionary elements for a return to the old values, i.e., they attempt to shore up the old myth with its models and paradigms. This response only delays a cure, for recovery can only come as one of the blessings of a new myth-paradigm system.

Just here is where society and religion meet their most difficult problems, for both have well nigh irrevocable commitments to the *status quo*, i.e., the reigning myth-paradigm system. Society, religion, and science, in fact all the ordered life of mankind, seem to possess a basically conservative nature. This conservative trend has also been termed the inertia of the psyche. Change is, however, as essential as stability. The universe simply will not stand still and there is deep within the human soul a drive for creative novelty. It is from that creative depth that a new myth emerges, that new paradigms spring. But those who are still under the sway of the old, regard any new system which may be coming to birth in the right lobe as heresy or nonsense.

In particular, change is always resisted by those who have not made peace with the deep creative aspects of the psyche, the Myth-Makers within. Our own Western culture has been highly resistant to any change in its basic symbol-system, because it has committed itself so fully to a rational view of reality. Our myth-system might be labeled "rationalistic humanism." Its roots are found as the beginnings of modern science in Francis Bacon, Isaac Newton, John Locke, and René Descartes. The epitome of the movement was reached with Auguste Comte who formulated a point of view called positivism. Comte said that all real knowledge consists of observations of sensory phenomena and the classification of the data therefrom according to the categories of causality, coexistence, and resemblance. He believed this process led to theory-free facts. Comte believed that all real knowledge is limited to what can be observed by the five senses, or inferred from such observations by rigorous logical deduction. In terms of the language continuum described above, Comte believed that the factual-rational pole could be cut away from the symbolic pole.

Comte had little or no understanding of the nature of human perception; modern psychology was not even born yet. Nor did he have an inkling of the different functions of the two lobes of the brain and their interrelationship in the knowing process. Still less did he know of the deeper psyche. Positivism, however, despite its ignorance of human nature and its lack of philosophical rigor, captured the day and came to dominate the mind of the public and of the scientific community for over a century. It still has strong defenders, but a far broader empiricism has been rapidly sweeping to the fore during the past quarter century, so that even the hard-nosed positivist has been forced to modify his claims.

Because it did permeate the culture so thoroughly, the rationalistic-humanistic positivism influenced all aspects of thought in Western civilization, even religion. Step by step, symbolic materials belonging to the realm of mythic tradition were justified and rendered meaningful by interpreting them as history, e.g., as God's mighty acts. Because the Biblical myth-maker's art very often began with an historical event which was seen clothed in mythic garb as noted above, the result of an historical interpretation usually contained partial truth, but was often total disaster. The latter is exemplified by the monstrosities of the literalist-fundamentalist who still seeks for the remnants of the ark of Noah, who insists that the waters of the Red Sea literally parted upon Moses' command, etc. etc. The literalist of Biblical interpretation has fully accepted, though usually quite unwittingly, the positivist myth-paradigm about reality, i.e., that anything real is perceivable by the senses, or once was. Thus to be really real, the Biblical material must describe historical-observable events. For the book of Jonah to be religiously meaningful the fundamentalist argues, Jonah must have been a living man, along with the great fish that swallowed him, and the gourd tree, whose demise led him to be angry with God, and at last to engage in dialogue.

There are other forms of Biblical positivism which are less obvious, but still based on similar misunderstandings of human perception, knowledge and the art of myth-making. (Dietrich Bonhoeffer, in his maturity, referred to the work of his former teacher Karl Barth as Biblical positivism and, we may note, the movement known as Biblical theology suffers somewhat from the same fallacy.) It is bad enough that the positivistic assumptions, applied unwittingly in theology and Biblical study, distort much of the material, but worse yet, this approach passes by much of the great truth of scripture and tradition by treating as historical that which is mythic, thereby reducing transcendent symbols to mere fact.

Now we must note that there are not only two poles to the language continuum, but that the languages of the two poles are best designed to refer to two poles of experience, the experience of the inner or psychic world on the one hand, and the experience of the outer or physical world on the other. The major reference of myth is the inner world of the psyche. This inner world is not divorced from the outer world of the physical but is, so to speak, the inside of it. Human consciousness is, as it were, a screen upon which the realities of the inner and outer world, or rather certain of their interactions, are projected. The concern of the inner or deep psyche, the dream and myth-making aspect of ourselves, is not usually to speak about the outer world as such. Dreams, visions, and myth are stories the deep psyche tells about itself in the light of its own structure and destiny or goal. The world religions have always proclaimed that this ultimate goal cannot be found within the confines of the material or external world of rational fact, because it belongs to the realm of the psyche, i.e., the realm traditionally called spiritual. The proper reference of mythic accounts is not whatever bit of history may have precipitated or been used in their manifestation; their reference is to the pilgrimage of the psyche itself, its spiritual task and destiny. Myths tell us about the inner world, the realm of religion proper, of faith, hope, and love, heaven and hell, angels and demons, God and the idols. Here we must be clear: the psyche is not limited to the confines of the body, not tied to the realms of space and time as is the body. The inward dimension has its own contact with infinity just as does the outer. The locating of these various mythic references within the psychic domain does not mean that, metaphysically speaking, they are *merely* part of the psyche. It is rather that we now can be sure that the manifestation of the Transcendent is found within the locus of the psyche. The experience of the Transcendent is inner rather than outer; the psyche is the agent for the manifestation of Transcendence. With this understanding, the religious terms that were cast into the discard under the aegis of Rationalism or Positivism can be seen to be quite meaningful; their reference is now seen to be the psyche and its affairs, not external events per se.

It is beyond the scope of this paper to discuss the nature of the psyche and its pilgrimage as revealed in the myths, but reference must be made to the very important pioneering work of Carl G. Jung, the Swiss psychologist. Jung was always skeptical about the exclusive claims of Positivism because he had such profound respect for the symbolic products of the psyche. He was never comfortable with the cavalier dismissal or reductionist treatment of dreams, visions, fantasies, or religious experience and dogma. Jung demonstrated with empirical and logical rigor the reality of the psyche and developed the key to understanding its symbolic mode of working. His work in particular marks the beginning of the recovery of the neglected half of the language continuum and the overcoming of the alienation of modern culture from the deep psyche, which produces and uses mythic-symbolic language. Many, many others have made valuable contributions, but only Jung has offered a comprehensive and empirically based theory of the human psyche and its languages. His work also has laid the groundwork for overcoming the unfortunate and unnecessary split between science and religion. This essay is an application and extension of Jung's discoveries about the psyche, with the added data now available regarding right and left lobe functions.

It should be clear from the preceding discussion, that we can no longer responsibly neglect the symbolic-mythic dimension, the right lobe functions, the story the psyche tells about itself in the myths. The ever growing perils of the Twentieth Century are teaching us (with deathly consequences, if we do not learn rapidly) that we have grossly over-estimated the power and accuracy of human reason, the factual-rational cut away from the mythic-symbolic, the left lobe of the brain severed from the right.

The Christian religion, at least, and probably non-mystical Judaism and non-mystical Islam, has been as detrimentally affected by this misguided severance as have the other aspects of culture. The tragic result has been the impoverishment, to the vanishing point, of religious experience, with the consequent decline in meaning and morals. (As Jean-Paul Sartre has written, where there is no God, everything is permitted.) Small wonder that the Churches find their social pronouncements ignored and resented; there is no foundation of religious faith to build upon, no transcendent God whose ethics permeate the universe as irresistibly as natural "laws." Only a full appreciation for the processes of the right lobe, the mythic-symbolic, fruitfully related to the factual-rational, will serve to lead us out of this cul-de-sac.

Who are some of the bridge-builders working on this crucial relationship? Space permits only a hint, but there are a considerable number at work within and without the institutions of religion, with varying degrees of consciousness and clarity. As a group, the analytical psychologists (mostly, these are Jungian analysts) have a phenomenal grasp of the mythic-symbolic and the skills to explore the psyche as it works in symbols. Many scientific investigators are at work in the field of brain research and there are exotic explorations, like those of John Lilly, M.D. and Carlos Castenada, endeavoring to understand not only the brain, but the mind and the psyche. Mircea Eliade and Joseph Campbell, although with differing approaches and goals, have mined the field of mythology and world religion with rich results. Theologians like the Niebuhrs, Paul Tillich, and the Process theologians, have become sensitive to the need to incorporate the symbolic domain in their work, but seem not to have discovered the key which Jung has made available. Although these various sources disagree in some respects all have, at least in part, transcended the too narrow confines which grew out of the cultural commitment to the factual-rational as the *one* valid way of knowledge.

The field of Religious Education has been as seriously affected by the cultural bias as any other. The most commonly apprehended description of the task of Christian Education is the teaching of the Bible, doctrine, church history, and liturgy, as content with some application to life. The content is taken to belong to the factual-rational pole, whether given the flavor of Liberalism, Biblical positivism, or Fundamentalism. Little, if any, attention is given to the mythic-symbolic dimension. This analysis should not be taken to mean that everything done is totally wrong or that no worthwhile education takes place. It does, however, mean that all our previous theory and practice needs thorough reworking and reformulating; a new beginning must be made. As a number of modern Christian theologians have discovered upon their encounter with the World Religions, it is not a minor revision that is needed, but a total recasting. The discovery of a new paradigm is like that always; you can't go home again.

The new paradigm under which we must now learn how to think and work, transcends the old dichotomies of mythic-symbolic versus factual-rational, of subjective versus objective, of spiritual versus material, or imaginative-intuitive versus logical-cognitive, of religion versus science. The brain's two lobes, our twin sources of knowledge, can and must now be allowed to function coordinately. Dream-visions, mystical religious insights, fantasies, etc., are views from and about the inner world of the psyche primarily. When elaborated into a mythology by the processes of culture, as happened in the World Religious traditions, they describe the pilgrimage of the psyche—its goal of spiritual development as well as the pitfalls and perils of the journey. But dream-visions and imaginative leaps are also our cues for new paradigms, ways of construing external and internal experience. They provide the basic symbols of every paradigm. Friedrich Kekule's theory of the benzine ring, from which modern organic chemistry sprang forth, began as a dream-vision of a snake curled about with its tail in its mouth, an ancient religious symbol for the wholeness of primordial reality. This kind of flash of imagination, a gift from the deep psyche, is always needed to start the work of the left brain, the cognitive-rational thinking consciousness. As Sir Herbert Read has noted, "The image has always preceded the idea in human history. The Greeks drew their notions of beauty, harmony and balance from Greek sculpture, not the other way around." The artist is unusually sensitive to the symbols of the pysche and not infrequently "leads" the culture into new mythic symbols, the foundation of new paradigms. Without the input from the right lobe, the deep psyche, output from the left lobe becomes increasingly sterile and amoral, doomed to self-destruction, but able to take the whole world with it.

SUMMARY AND CONCLUSION

The psyche seems to have provided us with two major language and thought forms, each adapted to a specific task of the psyche. During the pre-historic and early historical periods of human existence, the major language used was symbolic or mythic. During this period, religion was the dominant form of cultural organization. Western Civilization has throughout its history, but most especially during the modern period since the Renaissance, been dominated by discursive, or rational cognitive language, the language of the left brain lobe. We know this language formally as the way of scientific thought, but it also is the most usual way of thinking and speaking in our civilization, including even the realms of religion and morals for which it is quite unsuited.

In the modern period symbolic language and thought, the language form of the right brain lobe, the form found in world mythology, has been seriously neglected. This way of thought and communication is the natural form for the creative imagination, for dreams, visions, aesthetic endeavor, and religious meditation or contemplation. Its neglect, or more correctly, its intentional disregard as an inferior form, has resulted in our alienation from the deepest centers of life in the psyche. Unlike discursive language and thought, whose goal is the prediction and control of events in the external world, mythic thought is presentational; it conveys meaning, purpose, implication, delight, wonder, and ecstasy.

We very much need to reacquaint ourselves with the nature and forms of symbolic language and thought without, however, neglecting the use of discursive thought. The two forms require each other, just as unconsciousness, the creative fount of the psyche, needs consciousness to perceive its wonders and make appropriate evaluations of them.

Suggested Readings

Barbour, Ian. *Myths, Models and Paradigms: A Comparative Study in Science and Religion*. New York: Harper, 1974.

Campbell, Joseph. *The Hero with a Thousand Faces*. Princeton: Princeton University Press, 1949.

Campbell, Joseph, ed. *The Portable Jung*. New York: Viking, 1971.

Castaneda, Carlos. *Journey to Ixtlan: The Lessons of Don Juan*. New York: Simon and Schuster, 1972.

Jung, Carl G. "Two Kinds of Thinking." *Collected Works*. Vol. V. Princeton: Princeton University Press, 1967.

Jung, Carl G. *Man and His Symbols*. Garden City: Doubleday and Co., 1964.

15.
Creativity in and beyond Human Development

James E. Loder

Focusing on the case studies of Freud and Erikson, James Loder contributes to expanding scholarship in stage theory by describing the levels of the creativity process. He asserts that the creativity by which persons are developed and by which they create and compose their world, not only transcends them, but is finally explicable only in terms of God's revelation of himself as Holy Spirit.

The two-fold purpose of this study is (1.) to explore the heuristic power of the creative process as model for the reinterpretation of human development and (2.) to illustrate the hypothesis that in relation to the hierarchical structures of human development, this process is primary in that it precedes, transcends, and "produces" those structures.

Creativity is commonly spoken of as taking place in four stages: preparation, incubation, inspiration, verification. Without developing an argument but merely working descriptively, I want to expand and reinterpret this sequence into an initial stage plus five subsequent steps, and to set it up as a model for looking at human development. The result will be instructive for how one might relate the dynamics of human development to a theology of God's Spirit.

The initial stage in the context of which the creative process begins to move is one of dynamic equilibrium. Since the process as we will discuss it pertains to a range of psychic strata, dynamic equilibrium as the initial stage may pertain to the psyche as a whole or any number of psychic sub-systems (i.e., ego development or part-processes such as language or intelligence) depending upon what is to be created.

The first step in the creative process itself is a disturbance of the equilibrium, a baffled struggle or conflict which is supported by a context of rapport. That is, when a conflict becomes overwhelming it can become so disruptive to the psyche that no creative movement can be made, and anxiety runs rampant. Conflict then needs a context of rapport if the creative process is to follow. However, the psyche moves to resolve conflict the way in which nature moves to fill a vacuum, so the presence of conflict in rapport is, automatically, motivation potentially leading to a creative resolution.

The second step is the interlude during which time the conflict is moved even if ever so briefly out of focused conscious attention. The scanning of possibilities is, then, done under the surface of consciousness in dreaming, day dreaming, fantasy, and playful hypothesizing often not directly subject to recall except as one interrupts one's dreams, daydreams, or fantasies. During this step it may seem as if the conflict or problem had been forgotten; one might say it had been put "out of mind."

The third step is decisive since this is the moment of insight in which two or more hitherto unrelated schemes or frames of reference come together to create a wholly new outlook. Arthur Koestler called this "bisociation" linking it to humor (e.g., "A sadist is someone who is kind to a masochist" bisociates the notion of kindness with sado-masochistic behavior), to scientific discovery (Archimedes' bisociates the displacement of water in the Syracuse baths with measurement of the specific gravity of gold),[1] and a variety of other sorts of insight. The insight that works creatively integrates the disarray or confusing elements of the conflict in such a way as to resolve the conflict not by repression, elimination, or habitual response, but by coming up with a new point of view.

The fourth step is the release of energy that was bound up in the conflict, i.e., bound by each of the disparate elements of the conflictual situation. When these elements come together in the insight, energy is released just as when a chemical reaction takes place creating a more stable molecule at the expense of energy loss. The insight involves a complex transformation of energy some of which works to stabilize and vivify the insight, the rest of which is "given off" in the Eureka effect.

The fifth step is the summary and interpretation. That is, the insight must now be put back into relation with the original conflict to establish the continuity between the aspects of the insight and the disparate factors of the conflict to see whether, in fact, the resolution is what it feels like. Then the whole process must be put into the public sphere to test whether the continuity established has congruence with the context in which the conflict appeared.

This is the essence of the model, but certain variations and one invariant must be articulated before we investigate its relevance to human development. First, *the invariant* is that once the sequence has been entered, the psyche or psychic subsystem to which it pertains is restless until it reaches a completion of the sequence. In this respect the conflict acts like an unfinished task and the whole sequence like a gestalt seeking closure. Having said this, though, certain variations as to where one entered the system can be described.

One may consciously enter the sequence at either step one, three, or five. If he/she enters at step one, the sequence follows as described. If at step three, then one has the not uncommon experience of having an intuition of thoroughly convincing proportions, but of which one does not yet know the significance. This is like having an answer and going in search of the question. Although this may sound like playing with terms, it is actually very familiar, for instance, to graduate students who know they have answers if they can only find the questions they are prepared to answer. Again, it is a common occurrence in relation to religious conversion that the magnitude of the insight so exceeds the conflict as originally perceived that one knows that he/she has solutions to questions he/she has not yet been able to ask.

Another major variation on this aspect of the model is that one may have the sort of insight that proves to be not a resolution to the conflict as first conceived but proves that the original conflict was erroneously constructed. This sort of negative insight occurs frequently in the course of psychotherapy when the insight reveals that what one thought was his/her problem is not the case. It is, let's say, the man's relation to his mother rather than to his wife. This comes as a relief and one then works back through the sequence revising the conflict stage and moving forward toward interpretation again. It occurs also in scientific research when one discovers that the problem as formulated is not the "right" problem and may indeed be insoluble as stated.

Finally one may enter at the fifth stage, the stage of interpretation as when the conclusion to a discovery provokes a curiosity and eventually a working back to the conflict that generated that provocative conclusion. Some such process as this is what Ian Ramsey argued was the case with religious language. Namely, its very logical "oddity" was provocative, and when seen as such, disclosure language calls one back into the process that generated that language in the first place. This, in fact, is the most hopeful assumption we make when we teach stressing cognitive formulations, namely that the student will be provoked to discover what process gave rise to them, what are they the conclusion of?

This then is the five-step model plus the initial context for the process. It should be repeated that regardless of where the process is entered its gestaltist character remains intact, and the psyche, then, moves forward and backward until the sequence is complete.

TRANSPOSITIONS OF THE PATTERN IN HUMAN DEVELOPMENT

In relating the creativity model to human development, the most obvious sort of connection to make is with the stage-transition process. Perhaps the most careful integration of psychoanalytic and structuralist views on this process has been done by Peter Wolff.[2] The integration is worked out only for the sensory motor period, but the model of transition follows essentially the same steps set forth above for the creativity model.

Wolff uses Heinz Werner's model of orthogenesis (ortho-straight and genesis-development) as the basic sequential gestalt, arguing that this makes the bridge between structuralism and psychoanalysis, between cognitive development and "ego" development.[3] We are arguing that it is also the biological base of the creative process. The three basic phases of orthogenesis are (1.) a state of relative globality, (2.) increasing differentiation and articulation, (3.) hierarchic integration yielding greater operational complexity. This sequence placed alongside the creativity model quickly discloses the baffled struggle as the conscious effort to deal with increasing differentiation. Interlude and scanning is tantamount to articulation of the parts of the potential integration. Hierarchic integration describes an emergent synthesis which is the functional analogue to insight in creativity. Increased operational complexity corresponds to interpretation and verification.

The action of orthogenesis includes the principle that the organism tends to develop in a straight line, i.e., unfold the sequence, assimilating the environment to an unfolding and progressively complex series of equilibria. This assimilation may be seen as a synthetic process that interweaves two antithetical organismic tendencies: (1.) to maintain continuity in order to conserve integrity and (2.) to elaborate discontinuity in order to develop. The creativity model is the same synthesis with one major difference; it is under the direction of conscious intentionality. Therefore, it is moved forward less by genetic forces and more by choice, passionate interest, care, and concerned effort. Development unfolds rather automatically but creativity—even though it follows essentially the same sequence—is a matter of choice and investment of oneself in the sequences of the model; creativity may be seen, then, as the stage-transition process of development transposed to the level of conscious intentionality. Such transposition does not imply mutual exclusion because creative efforts may interact with the more fundamental or primitive forces that urge increased development upon a person, just as advances in development enhance one's creative potential.

The same sort of observation could be made for E. Erikson. Coles[4] has remarked that it is not generally appreciated how Hegelian Erikson's stage sequences are.[5] By this he intends, I think, not only the way in which each resolution to a developing ego struggle (i.e., favorable balance of trust and mistrust) combines opposites in a synthesis, but also the sequence by which one moves developmentally, say, from the shocking differentiation and disequilibrium of birth (Leboyer to the contrary notwithstanding) to the articulation of part-process potentials (e.g., reaching, grasping, taking-in, etc.) to the relatively stable equilibrium of basic trust. The way in which personal developmental history informs the future of the person would suggest that it is not merely the conclusion, but the process with its conclusion that accounts for "hope," the character strength or virtue which accrues to a person at this stage. Hope endures not only because this acquired trust is solid ground on which to build, but also because each new state of disequilibrium can be met with the anticipation of an emergent synthesis yielding increased complexity structurally, heightened perception, and functional or operational competence in relation to the environment. Having gone through the process once when one's whole existence seems at stake is thoroughly promising for confronting the next upheaval in "ego" equilibrium, but of course the opposite in turn is proportionately discouraging and burdened with hopelessness.

By using the same patterned process for describing stage transition dynamics, structuralists such as Piaget and Kohlberg have much the same notion about how developmental dynamics unfold. What we have noted is that the process of orthogenesis used to describe these dynamics follows a pattern which is parallel to the creative process. The following case lifts the power of these dynamics into view and makes this parallel more explicit.

The classic case in the study of human development from the psychoanalytic perspective is Freud's account of "Little Hans." The salient features of the case are that a three year old boy, Hans, is caught masturbating and is threatened with castration by his mother. He is told that a certain doctor will do it, and it happens that Little Hans' father is also a doctor. From the period age three to five, the mother gives birth to a daughter and Little Hans develops overwhelming phobic reactions. The father begins to write to Freud for advice, and eventually the father, with the help of advice through the mail from Freud, is able to help Hans formulate his problem in terms reminiscent of the Oedipus drama. When the problem is adequately formulated, Little Hans has two fantasies, one in which he is visited by a plumber and supplied with male sexual equipment as great or greater than his father's, and a second in which he is married to his mother and they have children while the father is at the same time married to the grandmother. After these fantasies appear, Little Hans announced that his "nonsense" was gone.

What Freud saw in this case was the foundations of childhood sexuality and the Oedipal situation in particular. What I would propose through a reinterpretation of this case is that what appears here is as much a contribution to the dynamics of healing and development as it is a piece of evidence that children at this age have sexual feelings and Oedipal-type struggles.

The essence of the healing process operative in this case can be described as resolution to an arrested state of development. In the *normal* course of things Little Hans would have come to surrender his sexual longings for his mother, repress them through an identification with the father, and enter into a period of latency. The Oedipal struggle, however, reappears in middle adolescence. Up to that time the repressed Oedipal resolution that takes place around age five has been gathering force in the unconscious and erupts with the added energy of "the return of the repressed." If the early resolution has been relatively uncomplicated, the adolescent can yield to the incest taboo and redirect his (the male is the paradigm in this scheme) sexual desires toward members of the opposite sex outside his original family. In Hans' case the trauma inflicted by the mother's threat could have disrupted subsequent development, but through the therapeutic process the little boy was led into a reworking of the developmental struggle, and his psyche produced a remarkable resolution. We know that it worked from the fact that when little Hans grew up and reached the age of 19, he met and spoke with Freud in person for the first time. Freud's follow-up indicated that Hans, a normal young man, remembered almost nothing of the sequence surrounding his development from age three to five. That one should not recall the early Oedipal struggle and its resolution is as it should be. Thus, we can conclude that the therapy effectively reconstructed the developmental process.

If now we look at the dynamics of that therapeutic process it is evident that the critical turning points of the process, and by implication the developmental process, followed the creativity model. Summarily, the conflict was first felt but not articulated or "owned" by Hans until the conversations between the boy, his father, and Dr. Freud (by letter) began. (1.) The first critical turning point occurred when, after the rapport between the father and his son had been built up, the conflict could be articulated by the father (under Freud's instruction) to the boy, and Hans could readily accept it as adequate expression of his feeling. The conflict as articulated was not pressed or confronted, merely borne. (2.) An interlude followed during which time Hans slept—and presumably the scanning work of dreaming did its work. (3.) On the following day he was visited by two remarkable fantasies which embodied resolutions to the specific conflicts of the situation and to the Oedipal conflict generally. That is, in fantasy number one, threatened with loss of penis, the plumber supplies him with an extra large one; in fantasy two, threatened by the overpowering father and loss of his love, little Hans replaces him and identifies with him; threatened implicitly by retaliation from the father, Hans' second fantasy marries off his father to the grandmother in a double Oedipal triumph; threatened with loss of the mother's love and her making him impotent, he now possesses her in marriage and they have children; threatened at first by the rival sibling, Hans now is the proud producer of children, so new arrivals complement rather than threaten him. The power of imagery to work out resolutions to opposites in conflict is here functioning with dramatic effectiveness. However, the net result of these resolutions is that a positive identification with the father was effected and apparently the positive affection for the mother was restored, though the sexual aspect was repressed and successfully redirected. (4.) Following the occurrence of the fantasies and his playing them out, Little Hans announced "my nonsense is gone." This announced the release of tension generated first by the situational conflicts but present at a deeper level due to the failure to come to a satisfactory solution to the Oedipal stage of development. (5.) The continuity between fantasy and conflict was interpreted to him at the time and the resolution was verified by a relatively normal subsequent development indicating that Hans was not bound in any maladaptive way to his developmental past.

Certain conclusions may be drawn from this. *First*, there is here further evidence that the developmental process raised to the level of awareness transposes into the creativity model. *Second*, the therapeutic process then may be seen as a variation on the creativity model in which the therapist supplies the intentionality which is disfunctional in the patient and works toward the facilitation of that very process in the patient as if the two were one. Speaking generally, some such dyadic arrangement is probably necessary in any situation when the process is supposed to work cooperatively rather than individually. *Third*, the fantasies, however bizarre or removed from the realm of actuality they seemed, were effective in restoring actual ego functioning at the appropriate level of development. The significance of this is very far reaching, but notice that in this case the distinction between bizarre images that erupted as symptoms (phobic fantasies) and those which worked a resolution lies in the difference between their respective structural compositions. Not only do the healing fantasies resolve surface conflicts, but they also bring forward the basic structure of the Oedipus complex, treating it as resolved. Since coming up with some positive resolution to the Oedipal structure is a necessary step in the structural development of the ego, it must be concluded that the dynamics of creativity have the power to call forth and reconstruct latent or arrested ego structures—even if that be done through bizarre phenomenon. *Fourth*, as we will indicate later in the argument, this process is a far better psychic analogue for the interpretation of religious experience than obsessional neurosis— the analogue Freud preferred. This is not to say that some religious experience does not follow the neurotic pattern. Surely Freud has been immensely helpful in analyzing and interpreting religious pathology.[6] The problem is that Freud did not recognize in the dynamics of this case and in the healing process generally (e.g., the same sequence could be demonstrated for the working through of a transference) that what little Hans went through dynamically was an excellent psychic analogue for the dynamics of positive religious experience. The implications of this conclusion will become clearer as we progress.

Generally the basic assertion being made is that the dynamics of this process are in some distinctive ways in control of the structures of awareness and of the ego itself. The interplay between structures and process is here being given a reversal of the usual emphasis. Namely, instead of conceiving of structure as the basic controlling factor and this process simply subsisting in the developmental matrix serving a fixed schedule of structural emergence, this view argues that the process is able to be exercised in a variety of ways to call forth structural resources from the substrata of the psyche in order to meet a great variety of conflictual situations whether governed by or embedded in the developmental sequence or matrix, or not.

Restoration of an arrested state of development is only one of the possible variations in the structure/process relationship. As indicated redevelopment would most likely be performed in the context of therapy and deal with the personal unconscious. However, at a deeper psychic level, the process may cover a wider scope and involve much more of the life span than restoration of a developmental structure within the period specified for its emergence. The most well known case which may be used critically to illustrate this increased reach of the creative process is Erikson's study of *Young Man Luther*.

The rather striking thing about Erikson's treatment of Luther's case is that even though he has a prestructured view of development from which he works it was necessary for him to construct the special pattern of "homo religiosus" to account in developmental terms for the range and depth of Luther's struggle with identity, ideology, and the spirit of his time. This pattern, though very clearly embedded in a historical context, has a definite but extraordinary developmental description.

The decisive, precipitating period for "homo religiosus" is adolescence, though the roots of this pattern extend backward into earlier stages and forward to the end of the life span. Adolescence is prolonged because the characteristic loneliness and overwhelming sense of proximate death that marks especially middle adolescence becomes an overwhelming reality bringing the sense of nothingness into irrevocable and persistent immediacy.

The normal identity solution allows the process of socialization and expectation of future rewards to suppress this awareness while one learns to affirm himself/herself in the rather narrow scope of his/her own identity. Luther accepts just this sort of solution for the period of time that he spends preparing to be a lawyer following his father's expectations. Eventually, however, this solution is not sufficient to cope with the magnitude of his sense of nothingness, so a solution as big as all life, history, and the cosmos had to be found.

This existential need for an "allness" adequate to transform the threat of nothingness, not only greatly prolongs adolescence in the "homo religiosus," but also requires a religious solution. Whether or not one comes up with a solution that fits any current or socially recognized religion, such a solution would be for that person a gift from beyond him/herself, provide order to the person in relation to the whole of being, and be not only that which countered the nothingness but that which ultimately affirmed life in the face of it. In Luther's case the religious solution was sought during a developmental moratorium in an Augustinian monastery in Erfurt.

The roots of the prolonged identity crisis in Erikson's scheme, of course, extend back into the first phase of the Oedipal period. Not strictly following the Freudian position, but centering around the basic triad—mother, father, and son—Erikson considers the unfinished business of psychic development in this period to be the source of the prolonged adolescence. Primarily due to the early intense love-hate ambivalence young Martin held toward his father, subsequent socialization into the father's world became problematic and eventually explosive. However, the conflict was not only this but also Martin's personal intensity and his latent longing to continue the subjective satisfactions of nurturing and the personally enriching life he received from his mother, first at her breast but later in their rich and satisfying conversation.

Clearly any resolution to the conflict would have to reflect the triadic shape of these primary object relations, and that resolution must also deal with the pervasive sense of nothingness that prevails when such a resolution is not at hand and its absence is continually being confronted as "anfechtung" or temptation to disprove the graciousness of God with one's very existence. Working out the solution to how a gracious God may be discovered for oneself is the story of Martin's early life, the climax of which comes with the "revelation in the tower" (1512). The first integrated theological interpretation of the resolution begins to emerge when he reaches 30, and culminates in the nailing of his famous 95 theses on the church door at Wittenburg (1517). Thus, at the age of 32, Martin had reached a resolution to his prolonged identity crisis, a resolution he was to live with, for better or for worse, the rest of his life.

The positive side of the solution as Erikson sees it may be schematically summarized in this way. The resolution in relation to the father comes in what looks like a splitting of the ambivalence. In the tower, Luther was convinced that the just God does not condemn but instead justifies. However, that resolution depends upon Luther's having been identified with Christ. That is, Luther's identification with Christ makes him the acceptable and beloved son of the just and justifying father. The negative side of the ambivalence when it is projected is directed at the pope and the devil who are by virtue of Martin's identification with Christ alien to him. The mother is the biblical matrix (mater) from whom Luther continues to derive nurture and which gives shape to his words and world. At last he is both the justified son and his mother's child.[7]

The question, then, is what happened to his overwhelming sense of nothingness? Erikson treats Luther as emerging from a pathological episode, saying that the ego in such an emergent state tends to reinterpret itself in terms of extreme opposing totalisms blending them into balanced, tensive wholes. Thus for Luther, human nature came to be seen as totally sinful and totally just, both damned and blessed. In this way the ego transforms and incorporates the rigidly negative conscience and enables negativity to take part in the future creativity of the ego. To the ego of the "homo religiosus," the negative conscience is a constant threat and will overwhelm the ego with a sense of its own death whenever the ego loses battles of mastery with it or with the world from which it derives. For this reason Erikson says that in the special case of "homo religiosus," the last stage of human development (integrity versus despair) in which the integrated person "affirms life itself in the face of death itself," is a crisis met in the early 30's and repeated with every new developmental period. In effect, its power of nothingness confronted as intensely as Luther did it in early adolescence engenders a developmental leap to the end of the life cycle, and enables one to work out in a fundamental way the solution to that final crisis while still in one's early 30's. The developmental crises of the intervening years still have to be met, but they are confronted in the strength of the religious solution formulated at the end of the prolonged adolescence.[8]

Now the general conclusions to be drawn from reexamination of this case study are: (1.) in the special case of "homo religiosus" there is a religious solution to identity and ideology which represents resolution to an enduring conflict which resides at the very center of ego development; (2.) this resolution represents a double leap in development: *backward* to the earliest triadic encounter of the ego, and perhaps further, to the face-to-face encounter between mother and child, and *forward* to the conclusion of the life span and the inherent capacity to affirm life with integrity in face of one's own death. (3.) In Luther's case, it is evident that the five-stage creative process was operative as the persistent and pervasive pattern reaching over the whole range of his life span. Brief notations indicating this are: (a.) the triadic *conflict* in opposition to the proximate death of nothingness; (b.) the prolonged monastic *moratorium* on adolescent resolution; (c.) the surprising *emergent resolution* in which the triad—Bible,

God, and living Christ—provide an incorporated symbolic resolution capable of controlling and/or integrating the fourth factor, nothingness, into a basic holistic sense of himself; (d.) the first great *release* follows the revelation in the tower (in which all of (c.) is implicit and condensed); (e.) the *expression* of the resolution begins to take shape as Luther's theology begins to crystallize at about age 30 and reaches its first expressive culmination with the 95 theses. I believe it could be argued that at various times Luther's psyche sought to repeat this process in his subsequent life since it has become for him paradigmatic of how Christian theologians are made.

On the critical side, it should be noted that Erikson's richly sensitive study is carefully governed by a schematic design—the stages of human development. However, his basic model for dealing with Luther's aberrations from the usual sequence is the pathology of neurosis and psychosis. Luther simply succeeded in making his pathology and that of his time, synonymous; as he worked through to personal "normalcy" as determined by the stages, he brought his part of the Protestant reformation with him. Although Erikson is much more sensitive to religious reality than Freud, he still has the same problem in dealing with religious behavior that departs from normalcy as determined by the stage sequence analysis. The alternative viewpoint I am suggesting here for religious consciousness states that the dynamics of the creative process constituted the primary reality; this process has a power and pattern of its own and, if Erikson's position is as we have outlined, it can move not only backward in development to bring forward unresolved structural patterns (as also in the case of Little Hans) but it can reach forward to the end of life, pulling the extreme limits of both the past and the future into a decisive, life sustaining religious solution.

The importance of insisting on the *primacy* of the process is that it provides a way of dealing with two fundamental problems in Erikson's analysis of Luther. The first is the question of the locus of truth in the Eriksonian interpretation of Luther's life, claims, and theology versus what Luther himself considered the locus of truth to be. When the truth is radically relocated from God's revelation in Christ to conformity to a developmental pattern designed to establish optimal normal conditions, then of course Luther's ideology must be considered at some major points pathological because it led him into extreme actions and circumstances running contradictory to the kind of survival and satisfaction by which the so-called healthy adaptive ego is governed. This leads to the sort of theological and historical distortion which so plagues religious psychohistory as an emerging discipline, and from all viewpoints sympathetic to Luther—to say nothing of Luther's self-understanding—into a severe reductionism incapable of grasping the central motivational matter, Luther's theological understanding of himself. So the first problem is how can Erikson's admittedly valuable analytical understanding of Luther avoid a distorting relocation of the truth question, and so avoid a reductionistic, hence distorted, view of Luther's self-understanding?

This leads directly into the second major problem in Erikson's treatment: namely, the substance of Luther's theological ideology has not been taken seriously at the critical point of Luther's supposed identification with Christ. Erikson's statement of it is just the opposite of Luther's great persistent claim that Jesus Christ was always to be understood as an "alien righteousness." We may correctly interpret this as ego alien, and not the sort of ego identification that would work to resolve the matter as Erikson suggests. Thus it would seem that the reductionistic tendency expressed in the first criticism leads to the crucial error of the second.

If we ask what contribution to this situation is made by the heuristic power of the creativity model, it would be first to restate the contribution of Erikson's analysis in terms of its unearthing the profoundly creative movement that Luther's intense moratorium produced in him and in his times. However, instead of thinking of Luther's extraordinary dynamics here in terms of pathology—a position one must take if the stage sequence remains set and normative—think of the patterned dynamics as normative and the stages as crucial points of reference and/or structural potentials in a vast reservoir of possibilities for ordering life which is available to the psyche. Then the dynamics and that which they produce out of the range of possibilities within the matrix comprised by the person and his situation is the reality to be affirmed; that is, the dynamic force of this creative process is to be climbed into and ridden through to its conclusion. This, I submit, is much closer to Luther's self-understanding, but instead of calling it a pathology or a developmental process or even a creativity model, he called it "Spiritus Creator," the Holy Spirit of God. Thus if one shifts the latent value emphasis or preference from structure to dynamics and from stages to the process by which they come into being, and by which the whole psyche is ordered, then the analytical work remains intact but its significance is shifted back into greater conformity to Luther's self-understanding. Luther's understanding of life in the Spirit then may be enhanced for us by the analysis, but not thrown into a radically different truth frame.

This has the positive effect of permitting a resolution to the second problem with Erikson's analysis, how is ego maturity related to alien righteousness? The error occurs because by Erikson's predilection for structure, Luther's solution has to be accounted for in terms of ego structure and its expansion. However, if the shift in valuation suggested above pertains, then another possibility presents itself. Namely, that the ego may itself be transformed by the process such that it necessarily feels passive before the unfolding of these dynamics and at the same time is greatly empowered for self assertion in so far as assertion is in conformity with that unfolding dynamic. In essence, the ego, sensing its self being recreated, is freed for creativity in a new way, i.e., according to the direction of its own transformation.

The self-conscious relationship to Jesus Christ under such circumstances is not the identification figure introjected as a maneuver for psyche defense but the one to whom the ego is "paradoxically bisociated." Paradoxical bisociation means that there is simultaneously a continuity and a discontinuity between the factors involved in the bisociation, and both are distinct such that their distinction is an internal condition of their association. It is, if you like, an antithesis-in-synthesis, and so very different from an identification in which antithesis engenders a breakdown of the synthesis or unity between the two factors. In Luther's case, the radical difference between Christ and the ego by which the ego recognized itself as totally sinful was dialectically the very ground for the affirmation of the ego in relation to Christ. Christ is not God if the relation is initiated and sustained by the ego as Erikson suggests; any relation initiated by the ego is bound to and reaps the results of its own corruption. However, Christ is not man if the ego is totally crushed by his opposition; his very incarnational accommodation to human nature affirms in the ego the power to assert itself in response to the purifying initiative of God in Christ.

Moreover, it is clear in this perspective that Christ deals with radical nothingness; it is not manageable by the expanded and potentially inflated ego. Moreover, he deals with it by negating the ego's chronic tendency to deny or contain it. This double negation, i.e., negation of the ego's negation of that which is undeniably present and overwhelming to it (i.e., nothingness) frees the ego for its positive response to the presence of Christ. By Luther's perspective only Christ can confront the nothingness so as to "fire one into the world with a velocity not his own."

It is precisely this paradoxical bisociation between the ego and

Christ which in Luther's view is the creative work of God's Spirit. Though there is a decisive period of "justification" such as we have described based on Erikson's analysis, the on-going process of repeatedly renewing the paradox, i.e., bringing Christ out of the remoteness of history into the present moment in ever new and renewed aspects is a "vivification" created continually for the ego by "Spiritus Creator." Thus, the creative dynamics operative in human development may be seen from a theological standpoint as a human figure for the person-creating, person-revealing work of God's Spirit. In this view, the dynamics of creativity find their ultimate ground and explanation in the dynamics of revelation. By an analogy of the Spirit, then, we preserve and interpret the value of Erikson's analysis in light of Luther's vision of the truth in Christ.

In conclusion we may distinguish five strata of human existence on which the model of the creative process may be seen as conjointly operative. Seeing this stratification however requires a consistent viewpoint, so it should be clear that this concluding compound model is constructed relative to the ego, though it might be possible to view the same phenomena in other ways, i.e., from the standpoint of God's revelation in Christ or from within the process itself.

The *first* is at the level of the stage transition process where the development of the part processes of ego functioning (e.g., language and intelligence) unfold according to a sequence which parallels the creativity model. Here Piaget is the key figure.

The *second* is at the level of the ego's own development particularly as the unity of the personality emerges through object relations in a socio-cultural context. Here the major figure is Erikson.

The *third* level has to do with raising the creative process to the level of intentional behavior so that creative thinking can take place under the initiative of the ego. It is at this level that all the classical studies of creativity are made and from which this study has extracted the five-step model.

The *fourth* level uses the creative process intentionally in order to reconstruct cases of arrested development. Thus this level makes primary use of the personal unconscious for the sake of redevelopment of the ego. Here the primary figure is Freud.

The *fifth* level has to do with the power of this process to transcend the seemingly "necessary" structural sequence of ego development over the life span, and, by reaching both backward to its origins and forward to its conclusion in death, create a transformation of the ego in relation to a transcendent reality. Such a transformation will necessarily be experienced as religious. The key notion here is Erikson's view of "homo religiosus" in Luther as reinterpreted by the creativity model extracted at level three.

A *sixth* level might be inferred from what we have said so far, but describing this requires a shift in perspective from a naturalistic ego stance to the position of God's self-revelation. Namely, there is a level at which the process may be said to subsist in God's nature as the Holy Spirit. This gives the transcendent movement of level 5, experienced by the ego as transformation, its ultimate definition. That is, we find the ultimate basis for our assertion that the creativity by which persons are developed and by which they create and compose their world not only transcends them, but is finally explicable only in terms of God's revelation of himself as Holy Spirit.

Notes

1. Arthur Koestler, *The Act of Creation* (N.Y.: Dell Publishing Co., Inc., 1964).
2. This study was Piaget's recommendation (personal conversation) for integration of his developmental structuralism with psychoanalytic theory. "The Development Psychologies of Jean Piaget and Psychoanalysis" in *Psychological Issues* monograph 5, Volume II, No. 1 (N.Y.: International Universities Press, Inc., 1960).
3. *Ibid.*, p. 29
4. Robert Coles, *Erik H. Erikson: The Growth of His Work* (Boston: Little, Brown and Co., 1970), p. 136.
5. Piaget has commented on his own stage transition processes to the effect that although Aristotelian logic is the structural outcome of the development of intelligence, Hegel's logic accounts for the process better (personal conversation).
6. James Loder, *Religious Pathology and Christian Faith* (Philadelphia: Westminister Press, 1966).
7. Erik Erikson, *Young Man Luther* (N.Y.: Norton, 1958), esp. 201-213.
8. This obviously bears resemblance to Carl Jung's thought on transformation of the ego through "individuation," a process begun in one's early 30's culminating in a balance of opposites not entirely unlike what Erikson describes. See Jung's *Psyche and Symbol* (N.Y.: Doubleday Anchor, 1958), esp. Part I, "Aion."

Suggested Readings

Erickson, Erik. *Young Man Luther.* New York: Norton, 1962.
Freud, S. *Creativity and the Unconscious.* New York: Harper, 1958.
Jung, C. G. *Psyche and Symbol.* New York: Doubleday Anchor, 1958.

Koestler, Arthur. *The Act of Creation*. New York: Dell Publishing Co.,
    Inc., 1964.
Lonergan, Bernard. *Insight*. New York: Philosophical Library, 1970.
Prenter, Regin. *Spiritus Creator*. Philadelphia: Muhlenberg Press,
    1953.
Rugg, Harold. *Imagination*. New York: Harper, 1963.
Vernon, P.E. *Creativity*. Baltimore: Penguin Books, Inc., 1970.